Since memory is composed of the past, present, and future, I would like to first dedicate this book in honor of my parents, Max and Ann Felberbaum, who during their lifetime provided me with a wonderful childhood filled with love and devotion. They will always be in my heart and memory.

To my wife, Jeanie, who has been my love, my best friend, and my true inspiration to write this book. This work is the culmination of the joy she has brought to my life all these years. My love for her is infinite.

To my son, Bob, and my daughter, Nancy, whom I love with all my heart and who have always been supportive of my ideas.

To my grandchildren, Catherine and Morgan: I love you very much. You are the memory of the future.

CONTENTS

ACKNOWLEDGMENTS

Thanks to Lynn Sonberg of Lynn Sonberg Book Associates, a wise, very perceptive, and highly knowledgeable book producer who has managed this great experience to completion. Thanks also to Roger Cooper, who has been and will be a major part of the marketing process. They're a great team to work with. I'm extremely grateful to my editor at Rodale, Leah Flickinger, for her energy, clarity, enthusiasm—and patience—in the editing of my manuscript. A salute to Jeremy Katz at Rodale for his insight and foresight in recognizing a great idea when he sees one! Rachel Kranz, a warm, very talented wordsmith and human being, transformed my thoughts, ideas, and emotions into this highly readable and important work. She has made the experience of creating this book an absolute joy.

Michael Freedman, a very good friend and business associate, convinced me to write this book and introduced me to the perfect people to get it done. The late, great Dr. Bruno Furst was my mentor and teacher. He introduced me to the memory development field and changed my life forever. Tony Buzan, a close friend, made me appreciate the unlimited power of the human brain. Thanks, Tony! Dr. Scott Parry, a longtime friend and business associate, taught me the true process of training and development. Thanks for the foreword, too, Scott!

I'm grateful to Alan Alda, a great actor and delightful person to know; thanks, Alan, for the chance to film two PBS specials on memory with you.

My son, Bob, provided just the right touch by creating the graphics and also offered insightful feedback. My daughter, Nancy, gave me some highly innovative suggestions about what to include. I'm grateful to you both. My brother, Harvey, provided me with the wonderful story about meeting Joe DiMaggio. Thanks, bro! My closest friends, Jerry and Diane Uslaner, have always shared their enthusiastic support for my ideas and have made my life more interesting and enjoyable. Lou Ellenport, a wonderful and witty person and another of my closest friends, has been pushing me to write this book for the past 10 years. Thanks, Uncle Louie! Thanks always to my mother-in-law, Belle Vogel, who has given me wisdom and an appreciation for life. I'm ever grateful to Richard Rothman, attorney-at-law, for all his excellent advice and for our great friendship since childhood. Thanks to Jay Maisel, one of the truly great photographers of our time, for his generosity, suggestions, and friendship.

Finally, thanks to my many clients, students, and business associates, with admiration for the success they have achieved in memory performance. You all make me very proud.

FOREWORD

I first met Frank 35 years ago in Geneva, Switzerland. We were both working for Investors Overseas Services (IOS), he as sales training manager and I as a consultant. IOS had become world famous as a giant financial conglomerate with representatives spread across the globe.

As I sat in the back of the conference training room watching Frank go around the large, U-shaped configuration of tables and chairs, asking each of 100 participants from around the world to stand and introduce themselves by stating their names and countries of origin, I thought, "Why is he wasting all this precious time?" (I had taught countless instructors in my train-the-trainer workshops to dispense with introductions if the group has more than 16 participants.)

Frank then launched into the dos and don'ts of honing your memory: look for memorable associations between the name and the person's permanent characteristics (shape of head, size of nose, mouth, eyes, etc.) and avoid associations with transient characteristics such as clothes, eyeglasses, or hairstyle (all of which could change by the next time you see the person).

At the end of the session, Frank again went around the large conference room, this time remembering each person's name from the introductions he had orchestrated an hour earlier.

"I'm sure you'll find this useful when meeting with clients and prospects whom you haven't seen for months. Won't you, Jean-Claude Vignerole? Won't you, Hans-Peter Wolframshause? Wan Cho Lee? Jose Carlos Lopez? Dieter Schmidt? Ahiko Tanabe?

"How about you, George Foster? Dirk Hendrik van Loon? Olufemi Oyewole? Giorgio Ambrosetti? . . ." and so on.

There were 100 names. Frank remembered 99 of them, missing the easiest one: Eric Bell. That didn't stop the class from standing and giving Frank a large round of applause. "Evidently this stuff works," commented the fellow sitting next to me.

After IOS closed its doors, Frank stayed on in Geneva, where he established his Memory Training Institute. He began to successfully market his unique memory systems to major corporations based in Europe and Asia. When Frank finally decided to return home to New York City, I invited him to join forces with me at my prospering management training company, Training House, Inc. He was consistently one of our most successful marketing consultants and worked closely with major Fortune 500 companies. You see, each sale of a management training program meant that Frank got to facilitate each workshop, and he is a superb instructor, speaker, and humorist. (In truth, it is the lure of an audience that is Frank's prime motivation in making a sale. Ah, the smell of the greasepaint, the roar of the crowd!)

Indeed, during the several years that Frank was with Training House, memory training had become a major request of corporate clients. Since Frank was the only one who could provide such training, and since I was moving our offices to Princeton, New Jersey, we agreed to go our separate ways.

Seven years ago, Training House held its annual associates meeting in Princeton. I invited Frank to be our main speaker and to give us a lesson on memory. Since associates come from around the world, we provided name tent at each seat. What could Frank possibly memorize?

He provided the answer: Send a list of their names, along with their addresses, phone numbers, hobbies, favorite restaurants, and the names of their spouses, kids, and pets. I sent him the list a week before the meeting.

Of course, Frank dazzled our associates. He used the demonstration to illustrate his guidelines for developing memory of all types of vital business information. He then taught everyone how to do the same thing! As I watched him perform, I had flashbacks to a day in Geneva some 30-plus years before. It was, as Yogi Berra said, "déjà vu all over again!"

More recently, I've watched Frank on PBS television interacting with his host, Alan Alda of *M*A*S*H* fame. It was fun to see these two consummate communicators playing off each other. The subject? Sharpening your memory, of course.

That's what this book will do for you. Enjoy!

Scott B. Parry, Ph.D.

Scott B. Parry, Ph.D., is professor of communication at Mercer County Community College in West Windsor, New Jersey. He is a member of the Human Resources Development Hall of Fame, and he serves on the board of directors of the American Society for Training and Development. Dr. Parry is the author of four books on management development and train-the-trainer techniques and of many published courses in instructional technology.

INTRODUCTION: HOW I BECAME THE "INDIANA JONES OF MEMORY"

I took my first step on the road to becoming a memory expert when I was still in college—and for a very simple reason: I was afraid of failing.

For me, high school was a breeze. With only minimal effort, I could master the material, do the basic amount of studying, and get good grades. College, though, was a different story. I started out confidently enough, but soon I felt overwhelmed by the amount of material I was suddenly expected to deal with. My grades started falling. Since I had to keep my average up to stay in school, I naturally became concerned.

I now realize that my situation was no different from that of thousands of other students who face a temporary struggle as they make the transition from high school to college. But at the time, I was nervous and wanted to take some kind of positive action. I'd seen an ad for the School of Memory and Concentration, and I had a sneaking suspicion that improving my memory might bring my grades up. So I enrolled.

It was a decision that would change my life.

As it happened, the school was run by the late, great Bruno Furst, Ph.D., the original memory guru in the United States. He'd brought the system over from Europe and turned it into a 10-week program consisting of just one 2-hour class a week.

My confidence in my own powers of memory and concentration improved right away, and I could see an immediate difference in my performance at school. Still, I didn't expect what happened next. About halfway through the course, Dr. Furst came over to me and told me that he considered me the perfect memory student. Would I be interested in continuing beyond the program, working with him to expand the field of memory training?

At the time, I had just switched my major from engineering to cognitive psychology, the study of how we learn, so Dr. Furst's offer couldn't have come at a better time. I was thrilled to accept his invitation, especially because I found the field of memory more exciting than any other subject I'd ever studied. The minute I saw what a powerful tool memory could be, I became totally entranced by it. Sometimes it seemed to me that I ate, drank, and slept memory!

What I liked most about taking Dr. Furst's initial course was that it made me feel successful, so I said to myself, "Improving the memory must make other people feel successful, too." Perhaps that was the moment when I had my first inkling of what was to become my life's work: applying the power of memory to the world of business.

I went on to appear with Dr. Furst on his television program and demonstrate his techniques with him at various universities. I did graduate work in New York City and later at the University of Geneva in Switzerland. There, I had the privilege of attending lectures given by world-renowned cognitive psychologist Jean Piaget, Ph.D., famous for his studies on children's memory and head of the department in which I was enrolled.

I enjoyed the academic world, but I think I knew even then that I wasn't particularly suited to it. I found business a much more satisfying and exciting field of study. I went to work first as a sales manager, then as director of training and development for a major financial services firm based in Geneva, a position that enabled me to travel worldwide and learn about marketing, strategic planning, and training technology. With this international business experience under my belt, I was then prepared to establish and apply my memory systems and techniques to a corporate environment.

I began to develop my own niche in the memory field, which eventually became the "business of memory." After I developed the business applications for my technique, I started my own memory-training institute in Geneva. Now that Dr. Furst had left, there was virtually no memory training in Europe, and the methods I taught at the institute caught on quickly. I worked with many international companies based in Geneva, giving presentations that were simultaneously translated into three or four languages. (I had to learn to slow down my speech and control my New York accent so the translators could follow me!) I also took my system on the road, traveling around the world to share my discoveries with employees at corporate outposts in Asia and Africa, often giving programs in countries torn by famine, riot, and revolution. I've given my workshops in the midst of jungles and in cities where my presentations were punctuated by the not-too-distant sounds of gunfire and explosions. Wherever my clients needed me to go, I went.

I vividly recall the workshop I gave in Indonesia in 1969, during the weeks when President Sukarno's rule was being threatened by riots and massive uprisings. As bombs went off in one part of Djakarta, I was in another neighborhood, wearing my three-piece suit in the 110-degree heat and training a hundred Indonesian sales reps in a tiny room cooled only by the faint breeze of a single fan. On that assignment, I had a bodyguard sleeping outside my room each night, and I breakfasted each morning on 100-year-old eggs and chicken saté cooked for me on an open fire in the courtyard.

Another client took me to Kenya to meet with his sales reps in a hunting lodge not far from the lodge owned by movie star William Holden. Somehow, the local people discovered I was there, and I ended up developing a program to help a nearby tribe preserve the memories of its own history, as modernized young people were beginning to forget the remarkable oral-memory techniques their community had developed over the centuries.

It was somewhere around this time that I started to be called the "Indiana Jones of memory"—and I have the hat to prove it! But beyond the adventures of traveling and meeting new people, I found it terrifically exciting to discover how well memory enhanced virtually every aspect of the business world. Sales training, management development, time management, negotiations—these fields and many others benefited when people's memories improved. I began to see that memory was at the center of virtually every business activity—communication, supervision, strategic planning, and more. When a few people's memories improved, their individual performances took a giant leap forward; when many employees' memories improved, the whole company was transformed.

I loved those early years of developing my program, but by the mid-1970s, I realized that my kids were getting older, and I wanted them to grow up in the United States. So my family and I returned to New York City—just as the "training revolution" was beginning here. Suddenly, every corporate entity was starting training programs, so offering memory training fit right in. I worked with Scott Parry, Ph.D., chairman of Training House, Inc., a business-oriented publisher and consulting firm, and he became my second mentor. Then I went on to set up my own corporation, offering the Business of Memory Training Program and the Three-Dimensional Memory Training System that I use today.

As I worked with thousands of clients in virtually every type of business, I began to realize that the problem wasn't so much that people's memories were bad. They were simply overwhelmed with information, much as I had been when I was in college. Throughout the past three decades, I've seen people's workloads increase exponentially. If you compare corporate practices of today with those of the 1970s, you see immediately that employees, managers, and executives are expected to deal with double and triple loads of work, vastly increased amounts of responsibility that likewise increase their stress. In today's current climate of downsizing and corporate cutbacks, people's careers depend on how well they handle enormous quantities of information—and once again, the key to doing well is memory.

In my years of working with sales reps, CEOs, middle managers, and a host of other professionals, I've come to see that memory is a catalyst that affects all other capabilities, energizing and enhancing virtually every business skill. Our ability to communicate, negotiate, sell, solve problems, make decisions, serve our customers, market our wares, create new products, formulate strategic plans, budget, and manage our departments is directly dependent on how much data we can remember and apply to the business world around us. Moreover, in today's world of huge conglomerates, we need our memories simply to remain aware of the vast amounts of vital information that must be disseminated within companies. I was pleased to see that in a recent article in the *Harvard Business Review*, appropriately titled "Change without Pain," Eric Abrahamson argues that every organization needs a chief memory officer. He writes, "Only by remembering the past as we tinker and kludge can we avoid making the same old mistakes—and take advantage of valuable opportunities."

I couldn't agree more. All I can add is that my program will do wonders for your own ability to remember the past—and anything else you want to remember. With just a little time and the willingness to try something new, you'll be amazed at what you can accomplish.

I'd like to conclude with one of the most inspiring stories I've ever encountered in the course of my nearly 30 years in the field. It took place about 10 years ago, but naturally, I've never forgotten it!

The story began when I was teaching my memory program to a group of a hundred lawyers. Even in a large group, I like to get to know as many of my students as I can, so when one of the lawyers called me six months later, I immediately recalled his angular face and bright red hair—although I was surprised when I found out why he was calling.

"Frank," this high-powered attorney said cheerfully, "what are you doing for lunch? I'd like to take you out to the best French restaurant in town!"

"Why?" I asked, bewildered. Granted, I'd gotten along well with this guy, but why in the world would he want to take me to an expensive lunch?

The lawyer, whom I'll call Al, simply laughed. "I'll tell you while we eat," he promised. "See you at one."

So off I went to Lutèce, which at that time was New York's top French restaurant. Al was an expansive and generous host, ordering the best items on the menu for both of us, with plenty of champagne, wine, and even an after-lunch liqueur.

"I have to know," I said finally, as the waiter cleared the last of the dessert settings from the table. "Why are you treating me so well?"

Al smiled. "Do you remember when you taught us that memory is based on *paying attention*? Specifically, you said—and I'll never forget it—that we had to learn how to observe things very carefully and notice the patterns, the things that jump out at us."

I nodded. *Paying attention*, along with *visualizing* and *associating*, are the cornerstones of my memory system.

"Well," Al continued, "I was working on a contract, and it was 100 pages long—a length I would have found pretty intimidating, let me tell you, before I took your course. There was a lot of money riding on this contract, too, and I was in charge of the account. Talk about pressure!"

I nodded again. These were exactly the types of situations for which I had designed my memory system—applying the principles I had learned from my mentors to the daily challenges and demands of the business world.

"Well," Al went on, "by paying attention to the contract, I noticed that the crux of the deal was contained in a particular seven-page section. So I took your system and processed every single element of that section—each piece of information, all the connections between the information, how this information mattered to each side. Just as you showed me, I turned the information into a story so I could hold it all together in my head.

"The meeting began. I just sat there. I let everybody else talk about everything else, while I didn't say a single word.

"Then, when this crucial section came up, I got up and started quoting word for word from the contract—numbers, phrases, dates, everything. I recited it all so easily and so well, it looked as though I'd had it in my memory for years. At that point, I noticed that everybody in the room was staring at me. And I knew I had the power! I had information power! Because I knew this part of the contract so well, they assumed I knew the whole contract this way. They perceived me as this all-powerful attorney who probably had a photographic memory and could remember anything and understand it and use it effectively.

"Well, Frank, I'm here to tell you, we got the contract. It was worth $300,000 to me—and it's worth the best lunch in town to you!" And darned if he didn't take me out to lunch every year for the next three years!

I don't expect *you* to take me out to lunch, but I will be pleased to think that reading my book has helped improve your business memory, giving you the kind of information power that my workshop gave Al— and so many others. Welcome to the wonderful world of memory! I'm delighted to share with you the fruits of some 30 years of helping people in business learn, understand—and remember. I'll leave you with one final thought: If information is power, then memory is superpower.

GET TO KNOW YOUR BRAIN

CHAPTER 1

IMPROVE YOUR MEMORY— IMPROVE YOUR PERFORMANCE

Would you be surprised to learn that you have a photographic memory? Well, you do! The problem is that it lasts only one-tenth of a second—hardly long enough to do you any good.

That's the bad news; now here's the good news. With my Three-Dimensional Memory Training System, you can extend that retention time considerably, vastly expanding the amount of information that stays within your brain. You'll remember more information, more accurately, and for a longer period of time. You'll be able to access the facts you need when you need them. You'll be able to remember anything you want, from a client's name to the amount he spent with your company last year; from the gist of this morning's training seminar to the high points of last year's annual meeting; from the price of your company's stock last fall to the projected earnings of your competitor next spring.

And here's the best part: You'll never again worry about forgetting an important fact, concept, name, or idea. What you want to remember, you will remember. Just imagine how that simple ability to trust yourself will exponentially increase your effectiveness at work.

Lou, for example, was a business development executive at Turner Corporation, a multimillion-dollar, New York City–based firm that builds hospitals, hotels, and office buildings. When he enrolled in my Business of Memory Workshop six years ago, he was already doing well, but he—and his company—thought he could do better.

"It's not that I have a bad memory," Lou told us during the round of greetings on the first day of the workshop. "But there are times when I'm working with a client, and I have the feeling that there's something else I should remember. Some special need they have that would help me clinch the deal. Or, on a personal level, remembering the names of my client's kids. That kind of thing makes a big difference."

Around the room, Lou's colleagues were nodding. They, too, were all successful, but improving their memories might give them that extra boost that makes the difference between a good year and a great year.

Obviously, their employer agreed—that's why I was there. Turner is only one of nearly 200 major corporations where I've taught the secrets of my Three-Dimensional Memory Training System to some 200,000 employees, managers, executives, and small business owners in a wide variety of enterprises. The series of workshops I held at Turner helped Lou and his colleagues recall and apply information about their clients and prospective clients, which in turn made them more effective negotiators. Not only did the Turner staff go into negotiation sessions better prepared, they also impressed their negotiating partners with the care the Turner side had taken to master the issues.

Or consider my experience at Hauppauge Industrial Association (HIA), where I've conducted numerous programs since 1997. This Long Island–based business organization includes more than 1,000 local companies engaged in a wide variety of industries. Under the auspices of former executive director Marcy Tublisky, I offered workshops to HIA members that helped them recall data, remember regulations, assimilate written information, and improve their recall of names and faces. It wasn't only that my workshops helped HIA members remember more facts more quickly and more easily. It was also that developing these new memory resources gave employees an enhanced sense of confidence and power, enabling them to work more efficiently, take more initiative, and exercise more responsibility on the job.

Here's some more good news: My system is easy. It's fun. And it takes very little time. All you need to do is master the basic concepts and practice them. You'll be amazed at how much you can accomplish once you begin.

THREE SIMPLE STEPS
TO A BETTER MEMORY

Improving your memory is easier than you think. All it takes is three simple steps.

Step 1. Concentrate and experience an event fully (pay attention). Walk into every important event with your eyes open and your brain on alert. You'll learn to notice key people, facts, and concepts—and noticing is the first step in remembering.

Your mind can operate with all the power of a laser—but you have to focus your brain and bring your mental energy to bear. If you pay attention to the people you meet, the facts you learn, and the words you read, you'll be astounded at how rapidly your concentration grows.

Step 2. Convert the experience to a form that can be stored (visualize). Our mind's eye is more powerful than we imagine, but if you want to take advantage of that power, you have to use it. Once you convert an item into a visual memory, you're far more likely to retain the memory.

Step 3. Connect the experience to other information (associate). We remember information that means something to us—and forget information that doesn't. Connecting new data to facts, feelings, and ideas to which we already feel connected is the key to remembering what we learn.

Scientists estimate that most of us use only 1 percent of our conscious brainpower. Staff at the New York Marriott Marquis soon learned about the awesome results they could achieve when using more of their brainpower. I taught them techniques that enabled them to remember every guest, their likes and dislikes, and their needs and interests so that the staff could go the extra mile to provide a wonderful hotel experience. In response to my training, management came to realize the importance of guest recognition and incorporated some of my approaches into their reservations software. As a result, during the eight years since my workshops, the New York Marriott Marquis has had the highest corporate sales in the entire Marriott system, along with one of the highest occupancy rates and most profitable hotel operations generally. Employees are clearly happier as well, since the New York operation has one of the lowest rates of employee turnover in the chain. Michael J. Stengel, the hotel's general manager, noted that he was able to recall the names and faces of more than 1,000 of his employees thanks to my training.

Another alumnus of the Business of Memory Training Program is Dan Flannery, vice president and area general manager of the exclusive Ritz-Carlton Hotels in New York and Boston. Flannery has taken the use of my system to the next level, training members of the Ritz-Carlton Battery Park Hotel arrival team—the door staff, bell staff, concierge, and front desk personnel—to recognize every guest and recall specific information about them in order to create an immediate feeling of welcome at check-in. We linked this training to the Ritz-Carlton's "20 Basics of Hospitality" and "Three Steps of Service," to reinforce their unique approach to their guests.

My hotel clients were primarily interested in remembering people. My student Theresa, on the other hand, was seeking a more integrated approach to memory in which she could pull together diverse facts and figures from many areas to boost her business effectiveness. Theresa worked at a Boston-based investment corporation, where my memory techniques helped her win a key promotion. While attending a weekly planning meeting, she brought to mind the details of a competitor's successful strategy to move into the international market—a "memory moment" that led to her spearheading the team responsible for proposing her company's new global department. She's now head of that department—and all because she could remember details precisely when she needed them.

Following my four-step program will not only enable you to remember more, it will also:

Vastly increase your overall efficiency. Like Theresa, you'll be able to bring up the facts, figures, and concepts that apply to a situation at exactly the right time. How often have you remembered necessary information an hour, a day, or even a few weeks after you might have used it? Well, say goodbye to those days—now the information you seek will always be at your fingertips.

Improve your communication skills. When you know how the brain and memory work, you know how to present information in the way that's most compelling for your audience. A few years ago, I went on a four-city tour sponsored by *Restaurant Business* magazine to teach some of the largest restaurant group owners in the country about menu design. What does a memory performance expert know about appetizers? Not much—but I do know how the human brain likes its information served up. A menu is no different from a business memo: Both present information in a way that's designed to stick in the reader's memory. The clearer the communication, the more crab cakes you're going to sell!

My techniques helped the restaurateurs organize information in clear categories so that customers could easily identify the types of food available. What had once been a confusing "appetizers" section was now broken down into hot hors d'oeuvres, cold hors d'oeuvres, soups, and salads, each described in appetizing language that modeled for the customers how they might remember the meal after they had finished it. Within weeks, the owners noticed increased sales of items that had never moved before—and all because my menu design helped customers grasp and retain the choices that were available. You can apply these skills to your own creation of memos, oral presentations, and written reports.

Enable you to argue more convincingly. Bryan was a television executive who'd been trying—and failing—to convince his boss to give him a raise. Using my system, he put together a bulletproof presentation that drew on key incidents over the previous two years, helping his superior recall just how many times Bryan's skills had made a crucial difference in programming decisions. Instead of a general set of arguments, Bryan came armed with a specific list of contributions he'd made, including the names of programs, dates they'd aired, costs they'd incurred, and ratings they'd won. Bryan's boss was impressed with both his past performance and his seemingly unlimited ability to talk about their company's recent history in vivid detail. She boosted his pay by an astonishing 30 percent—and Bryan went on to use his new powers of presentation as she expanded his contact with clients and producers.

Allow you to take full advantage of all your years of experience. What is experience, if not memory? When a lawyer with 20 years of experience looks at a tricky corporate tax problem, she sees something very different than does the associate sitting next to her. The veteran is able to apply her experience with all the other tax problems she's seen—but only if she can remember them. Increase your access to the events of the past, and your experience counts for more. Remember more about what you've learned, and your problem-solving skills skyrocket.

Position you to become a key player in your organization. When I started giving these workshops nearly 30 years ago, I'd mention "job security," and my students would nod respectfully. Now, when I say those words, it's not unusual for executives of all ages to burst out laughing. "These days, job security is only as strong as last quarter's balance sheet," one of my clients commented recently. The words were all the more striking because he was a highly placed executive at an apparently profitable company—yet clearly, he was worried about keeping his position. He felt considerably less worried, though, after taking my workshop.

"As long as I can remember so much about what my department is doing and bring it to bear at the right moment, I'm in good shape," he told me. "In fact, sometimes I'm the *only* one who remembers how a meeting proceeded or what a new client asked for—which pretty much makes me indispensable!"

MASTERING THE THREE BASIC MENTAL FUNCTIONS

One of my goals when I teach a workshop is to demystify the process of memory. I've noticed that many people consider memory a mysterious, almost magical operation, something that "happens" to you. If you're lucky, many people assume, you are blessed with a good memory. If you're unlucky, you've got a bad one. Either way, what you remember is what happens to "stick" to you. A good memory is simply more "sticky" than a bad one.

Nothing could be further from the truth. Memory is not a passive experience but rather an active process, something you consciously choose to do. People with good memories are simply more active than those with poor memories. They apply more concentration and attention to each new experience. They visualize the information they're given, making it real, concrete, and meaningful to themselves. Moreover, they associate the information they learn with other information that they already know, multiplying exponentially their chances of retrieving it. They take a positive, proactive stance toward their memories—and as a result, they remember more.

Of course, with my system, they—and you—could recall still more. Once you've taken hold of your memory's reins, so to speak, you can learn some helpful techniques for steering the wagon. But the first step is to review and become familiar with the three basic mental functions on which memory relies.

1. Paying attention. How can you remember something if you never even noticed it in the first place? How can you keep something in your memory if you didn't observe it closely when you had the chance? The first key to remembering is to pay attention to that which you seek to remember. In chapter 4, I'll show you what it means to actively observe, concentrate, and pay attention, along with exercises and practices that will help you understand and master this skill.

2. Visualizing. Did you know that the portion of the brain devoted to visual information is at least twice as large as each of the portions concerned with the other four senses? We take in information in all sorts of ways, but we remember it through our mind's eye. In chapter 5, I'll teach you how to convert a wide range of information into visual images so distinct and vivid that you'll never forget them.

3. Associating. One key way to retrieve new information is to connect it to old information. Then, when you want to pull out the new data, all you have to do is call upon the old. For example, if you're trying to remember someone's name, you'll have a far easier time recalling it if you remember that your cousin has the same name. You have myriad associations with your cousin but only a few with your new acquaintance. Once you link them, however, you enhance the new name with old memories. As a result, you'll be far more likely to recall it at will. In chapter 6, I'll teach you ways to do this as well as give you techniques for associating the visual images you created in chapter 5. The combination of visualization and association is unimaginably powerful.

THE FOUR ZONES OF INFORMATION

Once you've mastered the three basic mental operations that produce memory, it's time to apply them. In business, there are four zones of information in which you tend to operate.

1. People information. How many times have you wished you could remember the names of new clients or associates whom you meet or that you were better at linking names to faces? Don't worry—once you've read chapter 7, you'll easily be able to do this. You'll also learn how to relate key details about a person—such as job title, hobbies, and family information—to the new name and face.

2. Spoken information. Sitting in a meeting, talking with your boss, or even engaging in a brief conversation in an elevator—all of these are occasions on which it's highly useful to recall the words that somebody said. Many of us have trouble remembering oral information because words, once spoken, are so fleeting. That's precisely why we need good strategies for committing such words to memory. I'll share those strategies in chapter 8.

3. Numerical information. In our digital world, we're deluged by phone numbers, stock prices, sales figures, and a host of other types of numerical information. Whether you're a "word person" or a "numbers person," you'll find it helpful to recall figures when you need to—and in chapter 9, you'll learn how.

4. Written information. How many times have you found yourself trying desperately to recall the basic facts, concepts, or details in a report, magazine, or contract that you read only a few weeks ago? Well, once you've read chapter 10 and mastered the techniques there, you'll be able to call written information to mind whenever you like, with no worry about missing data.

HOW TO GET THE MOST FROM THIS BOOK

As you can see, I've organized this book according to mental operations first and then zones of information. I've also included a chapter on the science of memory (chapter 2) and a self-diagnosis (chapter 3) so you can see how you rate in each of the categories that the chapters cover.

My suggestion is that you read the chapters in order, since I've constructed the book so that each concept builds on the previous one. Although it's possible to isolate some of the material, memory works better as a synergistic whole, with each aspect reinforcing every other one. Thus, I encourage you to work your way through the book chapter by chapter. You'll get the most out of it if you do.

I've also filled each chapter with exercises and practices that demonstrate how each concept works and give you an opportunity to master it. *Exercises* are one-time efforts that are merely meant to make a point. *Practices*, in contrast, are intended to build up your "memory muscles." With each activity, I've suggested when to use it and how often to repeat it.

Finally, I encourage you to remember that while everyone's memory works according to the same basic principles, each person's memory is different. You don't face the same challenges that I do, nor does your colleague, your client, or your boss. Only you can really understand how your own memory works—and the more you do understand, the more you'll be able to improve.

There's a story I like to tell when I begin a workshop, concerning a conference I was invited to in Chicago. I was planning to be there for several days, so I thought I'd take two suits and two sports jackets, which I duly had dry-cleaned beforehand. I took the clothes home, put them in my suitcase, said goodbye to my wife, and took a taxi to the airport.

I got to JFK in plenty of time for my evening flight, but for some reason, I felt nervous. Almost without thinking about it, I checked my suitcase and realized suddenly that I'd packed the four jackets—but no pants. Although I usually keep my jackets and pants together, the dry cleaners had separated them, and when I'd grabbed one set of hangers, I'd somehow ignored the other. The clothes I was wearing to travel were not at all suitable for the business meetings I'd be attending, and I had only an hour and 20 minutes to attempt the roundtrip home.

I dashed out of the airport and into a waiting taxi. Breathlessly, I gave the driver directions to my home in Riverdale, a New York City suburb, promising him a super-size tip if he could get me there and back to JFK in time to make my flight. The driver rose to the challenge to a remarkable extent. He followed fire engines and tracked ambulances—at one point (though I didn't dare look), I think he was actually driving on the sidewalk. The driver took me to my door, and I dashed into my house. I snatched the pants out of my closet and bid a second goodbye to my astonished wife. The driver got me back to the airport in good time, and I made my flight with 10 minutes to spare.

I didn't enjoy the last-minute rush, but I do enjoy telling my students—and you—the story, with particular emphasis on the moral: *Even a memory expert can forget his pants!*

Now that you've learned my shameful secret, I hope you feel more secure about your own memory capabilities. As my little story makes clear, none of us is perfect, and all of us make mistakes. The challenge is in how much we improve—and I guarantee that if you read this book, complete the exercises, and perform the practices, you'll improve a great deal. So read, enjoy, and good luck!

CHAPTER 2

HOW MEMORY WORKS

Have you ever wondered why you can remember the phone number you had when you were in third grade even as you forget the name of that helpful woman in the human resources department? Knowing how your memory works will help you use it better, so here's a quick tour of the latest scientific understanding of our ability to remember.

YOUR AMAZING BRAIN

Whether you think your memory is good, bad, or in between, you can be sure of one thing: Everything you need to create a spectacular memory is right between your ears. The human brain is one of the most amazing information-processing devices ever developed—smarter, more complicated, and more creative than the fastest computer. Every day, you use your brain to solve problems, develop new insights, and create responses that no one has ever thought of before—something that no computer will ever be able to do. The better you understand how your brain works—and how your memory operates—the more effectively you'll be able to use this amazing capacity.

What makes your brain so special? Scientists are still working on that question, but part of the answer surely lies in the fact that from the day you're born until the day you die, your brain is always changing. We tend to think of the brain as a given, something we're born with that determines how smart we are and how good our memories are. The truth is very different, however, because the brain is actually a work in progress.

We do begin with some basic material: Each adult brain is endowed with approximately 100 billion *neurons* (nerve cells)—half of all the nerve cells in the body—but that's just the starting point. From the moment we commence thinking, remembering, observing, and learning, we are literally re-creating our brains.

For example, when you were an infant and first recognized your mother's face, you made a small but significant change in your brain. That moment of recognition created a new connection among some of your neurons, a connection that was reinforced each time you recognized Mama again. As you began to recognize other people, you made still more changes in your brain, creating still more connections. The day you figured out that it hurt to bump your head against the crib, the time you learned that your blanket was soft and warm, the night you saw the shiny silver moon—each of those occasions created new thoughts, images, and associations in your infant mind, with each new event recorded among your brain cells.

As you can probably tell, this process didn't stop in childhood or youth—it has continued right up to the very second when you're reading these words, and unless you isolate yourself completely from new experiences, thoughts, and emotions, it will continue until the day you die. Every time you remember a name, learn a new fact, or solve a problem, you are literally creating a new set of connections among your neurons. The more you learn, the more connections you create.

Scientists have estimated that each of us has the capacity to make up to 10 trillion connections among our neurons, although most of us take advantage of only about 1 percent of our potential brainpower. Regardless, each time we make a new connection, we actually make ourselves smarter. By increasing the number of connections within our brains, we're literally increasing our capacity to think. Just as using a muscle makes it stronger, using your brain makes you smarter, not just because you "know more" but also because your brain actually works better.

Think about the first time you learned to do something on the job—say, operate the office computer. When you're still learning how to do something or struggling to remember a new fact, your brain cells make the connections somewhat slowly and laboriously. When your ability to perform a function or answer a question becomes semiautomatic, that means you've established a well-functioning set of neural connections that fires up and operates almost instantly. In this case, learning to use the computer has actually altered your brain, adding a "computer-using" element that wasn't there before.

It's so important that it bears repeating: Forming a memory and learning something new is an *active* process. It's not simply a matter of storing information in your brain. Rather, it's about building neural connections, creating pathways within your brain that didn't exist before. By learning a new task, you literally change the structure of your brain. The more you learn, the more it's transformed.

There's a nice side effect of this process, too: The more you learn, the *easier* it becomes to transform your brain. The more pathways you have to draw upon, the more ways you have to get the party started, so to speak. If you already know how to operate your office computer, for example, it's a lot easier to learn how to use your daughter's laptop. If you've already mastered the strategies for remembering people information that I explain in chapter 7, you'll find it much simpler to use the techniques for remembering spoken information in chapter 8.

So if you're feeling a bit mentally out of shape, take heart. All you need to do to get in shape is to start learning. The more you know, the more you *can* know, and the more you use your brain, the easier it becomes to use.

CONNECTING AND CREATING

Once you can visualize the workings of your brain, you'll have a better sense of the amazing feats of which it is capable. You'll demand more of yourself, and as a result, you'll accomplish more. Moreover, if you understand how your brain operates, you'll find it easier to understand why I recommend the techniques and approaches that I offer throughout this book. So, although most of the book is eminently practical, bear with me while I offer you a short science lesson.

Let's start by taking a closer look at how we create the neural connections I've just described. A typical neuron consists of a tiny cell body (a few thousandths of an inch across). Out of this cell extends an *axon*— a fiber coated with a thin, fatty covering known as *myelin*, which both protects the axon and helps to conduct electricity along it. The axon branches out into smaller fibers at one end, like the twigs on a tiny tree.

Also extending from the cell body is a group of fibers called *dendrites*. Dendrites are smaller and finer than axons, but they're plentiful: Each of us has 100,000 miles of dendrites packed within our brain.

These axons and dendrites are crucial to conducting the electricity that enables neurons to communicate. When one neuron transmits an impulse to another, it usually sends an electrical charge along its axon, and another neuron receives the charge through its dendrites.

Axons and dendrites have to communicate, but like neighbors shouting to each other across a fence, they don't actually touch. Instead, there are tiny gaps between the neurons, known as *synapses*. (There are actually many different ways that axons, dendrites, and synapses can operate, but this simplified portrait is most useful for our purposes.) When one neuron wants to communicate with another—to create or recall a memory, to transmit the experience of pain or pleasure, to instruct a muscle to move, or to register an emotion—it generates an electrical impulse that must somehow jump across the synapse to reach another neuron.

How do these impulses make it across the gaps? They operate through *neurotransmitters*, chemicals that help transmit the electrical impulses and enable the brain to process and communicate information. The next time you solve a problem, recall something you already know, or even read a book like this one, you can picture the complex electrical circuitry within your brain, with different networks of neural connections in action. And the next time you learn something new, you can visualize the new circuitry you're creating, a new portion of your brain that will be there for you when you need it.

THE GEOGRAPHY OF THE BRAIN

Now that you know how the brain works, let's take a closer look at its geography. Throughout the rest of this book, I'll show you a wide variety of techniques that call upon different regions of your brain. Although you can learn these techniques without visualizing what's going on in your memory, I think it helps to be able to picture the different areas. That way, you can see how they work together to strengthen your memory.

Rising from the top of your spinal column is the *brain stem*, the oldest part of your brain. Some people call this the reptilian brain, our heritage from those early evolutionary days when we were still cold-blooded creatures. Indeed, the brain stem "remembers" how to do the most basic functions necessary to keep us alive, regulating our breathing, heartbeat, sleep, and waking.

Just behind the brain stem is the *cerebellum*, which processes information from muscles and joints to oversee balance, body position, and movement. When you've learned to do something physical so well that it becomes automatic—such as driving a car, riding a bike, typing, and operating a computer—that memory, known as *procedural memory*, is stored in your cerebellum. Some people refer to this as muscle memory, as if your muscles remembered on their own what they have to do. That's why you can, for example, turn on your computer while talking on the phone. Your cerebellum instructs your hand to reach for the "on" button, click on your user name, and so on, leaving the rest of your brain free to process the sounds, words, and thoughts that make up your phone call.

Sitting on top of the brain stem is the *limbic system*, also known as the old mammalian brain. A bit newer and more evolved than the reptilian brain, the mammalian brain is our heritage from our days as nonhuman mammals. Here is where our emotions reside—fear, sadness, anger, pleasure, and sexual desire—all the survival-oriented feelings we need to keep the species going and to recognize danger and safety (although we may also have developed more sophisticated uses for our emotions).

Here, too, is the part of the brain that interprets sensory data. Consider that in our animal days, sensory information—smell, sight, sound, taste, and touch—was crucial to survival, cuing us to eat nourishing food or to flee at the sight of a charging tiger and alerting us to the smell of an unfamiliar creature or the sound of approaching danger. Thus, it makes sense that our senses and emotions are so closely linked.

Moreover, because of this link, our senses can be powerful memory aids. The next time you're sitting in a business meeting, take a moment to key in on a specific, vivid sensory experience. It may be the scent of your hot, fresh coffee (smell is one of the most powerful memory aids) or the sight of the bright red tulips at the center of the conference table (sight is our second most powerful memory aid and is probably more useful than smell in a business context). If you're an auditory person, you might focus on the sound of traffic seeping in from the street outside. If you're lucky enough to be sitting by a window, you could enjoy the nice, warm feeling of sun on your shoulders. Or perhaps your most vivid sensation is the overly sweet taste of the stale cheese danish you just couldn't resist. The stronger and more vivid the sensory experience is, the better, and if you have strong feelings about it—Love those tulips! Hate that danish!—that's better still.

Now, the next time you want to recall what was said and done at that meeting, bring to mind that sensory key. You'll probably notice two things. First, along with the sense memory comes a wave of whatever emotion you were feeling at the time (pleasure in the tulips and distaste for the danish, along with whatever interest, confusion, or excitement you may have felt about the meeting itself). Second—and more important for our purposes—the sense/emotional memory will almost certainly carry with it a memory of what actually happened at the meeting, enabling you to recall what you learned, thought, or felt. (In the following chapters, I'll give you more specific suggestions for how to focus on key ideas so that you can use your senses and emotions to boost your memory.)

One of the most important elements of the limbic system is the *hippocampus*, a seahorse-shaped organ named from the Greek word for "seahorse." (Actually, you have two hippocampi, one above each ear, about 1½ inches toward the center of your head.) The tiny hippocampus performs a number of functions, including some of your most basic, survival-oriented memory tasks. In the old days, you'd have used it to remember where the nearest watering hole was, which trail would get you back to your home cave, or how long it had been since you saw the bear lie down to take a nap. Today, you're more likely to direct it toward recalling where you parked your car, remembering which guy in the copy department told you he'd rush your documents through, or knowing how long it's been since you told someone you'd call her "right back."

The hippocampus is also the part of your brain that handles logical expectation—what you should expect under normal circumstances. The expectation that hitting your computer's "on" button will cause your monitor to light up and your name to appear on the screen, for example, is created within your hippocampus. This process also has a primitive survival function because when things don't work as you'd logically expect, it may signal danger or perhaps unexpected opportunity. A monitor that goes dark without warning, a stock price that seems unusually high, and an uncharacteristically grumpy "hello" from your usually cheerful boss all register with you because you remember what you can expect under normal circumstances—and you know this isn't it! Your memory of old situations is crucial to alert you to new ones.

When an animal confronts a new situation, it's often at a loss. We've all seen a dog or cat return again and again to an empty bowl, simply unable to accept that their food isn't where it's supposed to be. We humans are supposed to be smarter, although we have enough of that old mammalian brain to share some limited thinking with our animal cousins. How many of us computer novices have continued to hit the "on" switch even when the monitor stays dark? Or to automatically call the extension of the old tech support person, who left the company two weeks ago, instead of dialing the toll-free number of the new guy at company headquarters? If we insist on doing the same old things in the same old ways, we're still relying on the animal portion of our brains.

When we start coming up with new solutions to unexpected problems, though, we're drawing on the uniquely human portions of our brains, the cerebellum and the *cerebrum*. The cerebrum constitutes about two-thirds of our brain, the "white matter" wrapped around the limbic system and hippocampus. Although there's still a lot we don't know about the cerebrum, we do know that it's where our personal memories are stored.

We also know that the cerebrum is divided into two hemispheres, which in popular jargon are the "left brain" and "right brain." Although brain function is more fluid and dispersed than these terms would suggest, we can say in a very general way that the left side of the brain handles logical thought, analysis, numbers, and words. In contrast, the right side of the brain recognizes patterns, intuits connections, perceives spatial relations, and tends to think in images and symbols.

Connecting these two hemispheres is the *corpus callosum*, a crucial link consisting of some 300 million nerve fibers. It's because of the corpus callosum that we can describe an image we've seen or draw a diagram of verbal directions we've received, moving back and forth between two modes of thinking.

On the surface of the cerebrum is the *cerebral cortex*, constituting some 70 percent of our brain cells. To borrow the colorful imagery of cell biologist and science writer Rebecca Rupp, Ph.D., if we unfolded our tightly packed cerebral cortex, it would be about the size of a bath towel—as compared with the typing-paper-size cortex in chimps or the postage-stamp-size cortex in rats. Folded, the cerebral cortex is about ⅛ inch thick, the so-called gray matter (actually, it's pink) that performs our most advanced mental functions—the ones that set us off from the rest of the animal kingdom and make us uniquely human.

BRAIN GEOGRAPHY AND MEMORY

As you can see, "memory" isn't a specific portion of the brain located in a single region. Instead, it's a number of different brain elements that work together in a wide variety of ways. This is good news for us. Instead of thinking of memory as an individual athlete with a more or less fixed degree of ability, we can start thinking of it as a team whose success depends on each "player" knowing a specific job and working well with the other players. If you consider yourself to have a bad memory, you might try thinking of it as a kind of "bad news bears." The problem isn't that the individual teammates can't play, it's that they've never had the right coach to bring them to victory. Now, I'll be your coach; all you have to do is make sure your players show up for practice.

One key player is the *visual cortex*—the part of your brain that processes information that comes in through your eyes. It's in the *occipital lobes* at the back of your head. Others include the *motor cortex*, which processes information relating to movement, and the *somatosensory cortex*, which tells us about touch, pressure, and body position. Appropriately, the parts of your body that are most sensitive to touch—the hands, lips, tongue, and genitals—are allotted the most space in this part of your brain, while your shoulder blades and toes get relatively less. Both the motor and somatosensory cortexes are found in the *parietal lobes* at the top of the head.

Over your ears are the *temporal lobes*, so called because they're near your temples. Here's where the *auditory cortex* is located, which processes information that comes to you through hearing. Here, too, is where your brain seems to change short-term memories into long-term ones. When you get a phone number from directory assistance, for example, you tend to remember it just long enough to dial it. Changing that number into one you'll remember for weeks, months, or even years involves moving the information out of your short-term into your long-term memory, a process I'll discuss further in the next section.

Behind your forehead are the *frontal lobes*, the biggest portions of your brain. They're the newest from an evolutionary standpoint and in some ways are the most human. These lobes occupy some 29 percent of the human brain, compared with 17 percent in chimps, 3.5 percent in cats, and almost nothing in rats. Here's where you cope with unexpected situations, create new solutions, set goals, and make decisions. The chilling frontal lobotomy operation of the 1950s was designed to calm unruly mental patients by removing part of this brain region. As a result, lobotomized patients became docile and indifferent, unable to create visions of the future and devise plans for how to get there.

As you can see, your brain is highly specialized, with different functions residing in different locations. Some regions of the brain, divided into segments that handle data from your eyes, ears, nose, taste buds, and skin, process sensory information. The part of your brain that handles language is subdivided into parts for nouns, verbs, people's names, and other linguistic categories. (People who have lost brain function in the "noun part," for example, may be able to tell you all sorts of information about, say, an elephant without ever recalling the animal's name.) Emotions are handled in one area of your brain and rational thought processes in another. That's why stroke victims, accident survivors, and those stricken with particular diseases of the brain often experience specific lapses and inabilities—because the parts of their brains that would normally handle those functions have been impaired.

Don't let this specialization fool you, though. The brain is actually very flexible in assigning duties. Although it's specialized to a certain extent, it's also very smart about protecting itself from diseases or accidents that might interfere with its normal function. There's a great deal of duplication of function within the brain and a lot of flexibility in what each part of the brain can learn to do. To continue our athletic metaphor, the brain is like a super-efficient baseball team in which many of the players can fill in at more than one position. That's why stroke victims who have lost some of their capacity can often regain some or all of their ability to function: Their brains simply assign the task of, say, walking, reading, or speaking to another geographic area that hasn't been affected by the stroke.

Remember, when you learn something new, you've literally created a new portion of your brain. An injury, such as an accident or a stroke, can destroy that part of your brain, leaving you unable to remember the skill, fact, or concept you've learned. But slowly, laboriously, and eventually successfully, another section of the brain can relearn the old information—learn how to play another position, so to speak—so that new systems of memory and ability gradually replace the old ones.

MAKING THE MOST OF YOUR BRAIN

Although "memory" isn't located in any single area of your brain, some specific memories do live in only one part of it—such as the word *elephant*, for example, or the automatic ability to remember how to tie your shoes. But the most interesting and important kinds of memory involve many different parts of the brain.

Let's say you're learning French. You look at a flashcard and see a line drawing of an airplane. You search your mind for the word, and finally, triumphantly, retrieve it: *l'avion*. That word is located in one little part of your brain, the language center of the cerebral cortex. If you lost that part of your brain, you would no longer be able to remember either *airplane* or *l'avion*.

Neither word, however, is the sum total of your associations with airplanes. It's not even your total experience of trying to remember the word. When you see the picture, you activate your visual memory, which reminds you how to translate the little series of lines on the page into an image that makes sense to you and then tells you what the image means. You may also remember the anxiety you felt on the flight to Omaha that ran into turbulence or the breathtaking view you saw from your window on the flight to Las Vegas. Perhaps you think fondly of your Aunt Bessie, who took you on your first plane ride when you were just a kid, or maybe you daydream for a moment of taking a private jet down to the Caribbean for a luxury vacation. You might remember that a flight to Europe from New York takes about 6 hours, that No-Frills Air has uncomfortable seats, or that you have a travel allowance for this fiscal year that you haven't used up yet.

All of these emotions, images, associations, and pieces of information are located in different parts of your brain. When you look at the picture of the plane on the flashcard, they work together to create a distinct electrical circuit—your association with airplanes. If someone were doing a PET scan of your brain as you gazed at the flashcard, it would show a complex set of flashing lights representing the electrical impulses zooming from neuron to neuron, connecting Aunt Bessie, your travel allowance, Paris, fear, awe, warm Caribbean sun, cramped muscles, and that spectacular view of the Grand Canyon.

Now, suppose you went on from this reverie to wonder whether you should call Accounting and find out when your travel allowance expires. The new thought would generate another set of memories and create another electrical circuit: the phone extension that you need to dial, that helpful Laura Midgely in Accounting with her bright red hair, your frustration last year when your travel allowance expired unused, and a host of other emotions, images, names, faces, facts, and stories. That's the process of memory, a process by which diverse areas and functions of your brain are linked in a complex circuit.

What does this mean for your efforts to improve your memory? The answer is a piece of very good news: *The more associations you have with an item that you're trying to remember, the more likely you will be able to recall it and use it in a number of different situations.* We'll learn more about the power of association in chapter 6, and we'll draw upon this powerful function in chapters 7 through 10. For now, let me just point out that the ability to call upon the information that's stored in your brain is precisely what being smart is all about. The more images, thoughts, and ideas that emerge in response to a problem, the more creative, thorough, and accurate your solution is likely to be.

TYPES OF MEMORY

Now that you've taken this little tour of the brain, you can see clearly that memory is far more than just a storehouse where facts and data are put away for future use. Instead, memory is an active, dynamic process in which old and new information, associations, and complex electrical circuitry all work together to synthesize everything we know into new responses.

In fact, memory isn't just one process; it's several. What we call memory is really many different types of functions that draw on many different abilities at once.

Declarative memory is what we know simply from living our lives as well as from learning a general body of knowledge. This is the memory that enables us to declare with certainty that "Aunt Bessie has white hair" or "France is located in Europe." We can make these statements because we remember seeing Aunt Bessie or reading about France.

Declarative memory would seem to be fairly straightforward, but watch out—we often remember things that simply aren't true. Sometimes they're not true because unbeknownst to us, the facts have changed since we first learned them—last year, Aunt Bessie dyed her hair bright red, or a few years ago, "Europe" became "the European Union." Sometimes, we've just remembered wrong—although we have a vivid image of Bessie's snow-white hair, a photo reveals that her tresses are a light golden brown; although we're certain that Monte Carlo is in France, it turns out to be in Monaco. Study after study has shown how unreliable our memories can be, even about events we've witnessed or participated in, particularly when emotions, wishes, and fears are involved.

Nevertheless, declarative memory is one of our mind's mainstays, important enough that scientists have divided it into two subcategories: 1) *episodic memory*, which concerns our personal reminiscences (that business trip to Taiwan; the first day at a new job), and 2) *semantic memory*, which concerns general information (the lamps won't work if they're not plugged in; the company president's name is John J. Jones).

Procedural memory, as you've already seen, is the ability to remember how to do something, a kind of memory that feels almost automatic. Driving, typing, using a phone, and a host of other daily tasks are conducted via procedural memory. If declarative memory is knowing *that* (France is in Europe), procedural memory is knowing *how* (to run the fax machine). People whose injuries or illnesses cause them to lose personal memories or even to forget words often retain a great deal of procedural memory, holding on to the skills they've acquired even as they forget certain types of information. When we speak or write, our vocabulary is rooted in declarative memory, whereas grammar—our ability to use the rules of a given language—is procedural.

Eidetic or photographic memory is the rare but significant ability to look at a visual image with such concentration that the viewer can return to the memory minutes or even hours later and derive additional details about the object that was viewed. Children with eidetic memories, for example, may be able to count the stripes on a photograph of a zebra simply by consulting their memory of the photo. Apparently, some 50 percent of all children under 10 possess this memory, but virtually all of them lose it during adolescence. Scientists are not yet sure whether the fading of this useful ability has biological causes—hormonal or biochemical alterations in brain chemistry—or whether social and psychological reasons are involved.

Short-term memory is the most immediate memory we have, the continuity that enables us to get through each minute without having to start over and over and over again. If you're working at your desk and put your pencil on a pile of papers, short-term memory will enable you to retrieve that pencil 5 minutes later. If you're copying figures from one list to another, short-term memory helps you hold the figures in your head as you go to write them down.

We use our short-term memories constantly—to hold the items from a menu in mind as we're deciding what to order, to keep a conversation with a coworker on track ("There are a couple of things I've been meaning to ask you about."), or simply to remember what we said a minute ago. Because it's in such constant use, short-term memory has a built-in limit—it can hold only a few items simultaneously. Numerous tests have determined that without a technique, most people can recall only from seven to nine items at a time.

However, memory experts know a number of ways to get around this natural limit, including an approach called chunking. Although we can remember only a limited *number* of items at a time, the *amount* of information contained in each item can be small ("7"; "airplane"), medium-size ("179"; "Boeing 747"), or relatively large ("1,234,567"; "The flight pattern of our Boeing 747 took us over Chicago."). Once we learn how to chunk little bits of information into larger pieces, we're able to hold more information in our short-term memories, even though we're still limited to seven items. (I'll talk more about chunking and how to use it in chapter 9.)

Long-term memory is the store of memories that we've decided to keep for a while. Although your short-term memory reminds you that you just put your pencil on that stack of papers, tomorrow you won't remember where the pencil was or even what you needed it for, unless it was something really important or exciting. You will, however, remember that you always keep a store of new pencils in your top desk drawer, a fact useful enough to have made it into your long-term memory. The transfer of facts from short-term memory ("I just heard the most fascinating presentation!") to long-term ("This bears on that useful presentation I heard last year; let me summarize it for you.") is one of the keys to successful memory—and one of the skills that the rest of this book will help you master.

Working memory is the process you use to combine short-term information with what you already know. If you need to look up a client's phone number in your address book, for example, you may read that it is 714-555-0055, a number that you're likely to hold in your short-term memory for only as long as it takes to press the buttons on your phone. It might be useful, though, for you to recall from your long-term memory that 714 is the area code for Orange County, California, so that when you reach your client, you can open with a friendly remark about the gorgeous weather they must be having there. Working memory enables you to juggle, combine, and reconfigure information stored in the past with new information coming to you in the present—a fruitful activity that often leads to new flashes of inspiration. ("Hey, *all* of my best clients seem to have West Coast area codes. Now what does that tell me about the kind of marketing we should be doing?")

Working memory is such an important part of daily problem-solving that researcher Alan Baddeley, Ph.D., professor of psychology at the University of York in England, has come up with a three-part model of it. In Dr. Baddeley's construct, a "central executive" processes input from two systems, known as slaves. One slave system draws on data from images and patterns, while the other works with words. Thus, as we try to envision how far San Diego is from L.A., we're invoking the visual aspect of our working memory; when we strain to recall the name of our best San Diego client, we're using the linguistic aspect.

The central executive in Dr. Baddeley's hypothesis helps us switch back and forth between the visual and the spatial. This switching process may take place as we marshal all our resources to solve a complex task—say, making a list of all our West Coast contacts, in geographical order, from south to north. Or it may happen as we multitask, gazing at a graph on the computer screen as we try to explain our new concept on the phone. Researchers have found that it's quite manageable to combine a visual and a linguistic task, but it's virtually impossible to do two visual or two linguistic tasks at the same time. In other words, you can look at a map while holding a conversation, but it's much harder to talk to someone on the phone while having a conversation with someone else at your desk, as most of us have already learned to our sorrow.

STORING MEMORIES
VERSUS USING MEMORIES

It may sound paradoxical, but it's true: Only by remembering the past can we figure out how to move through the present and create the future.

The rest of this book, then, is devoted to helping you figure out how to improve all the different aspects of your memory. You'll learn how to improve your short-term memory for facts, figures, names, dates, and places. You'll discover how to boost your working memory by accessing long-held information and combining it with new data. And you'll find ways of moving names, numbers, spoken words, and written information into your long-term memory, accessing the knowledge you need when you need it.

In their book *Intelligent Memory*, psychiatrist Barry Gordon, M.D., Ph.D., and Lisa Berger make an eloquent case for how improving our memory can actually boost our intelligence as well as our effectiveness.

> At any one time, most of the pieces of information in our heads, and the connections between them, lie dormant. Similar to a computer that has not been turned on, a part of our memory has not been awakened. . . . But if something triggers latent pieces and connections—like seeing a picture related to them—they become activated. Once activated, they trigger other pieces through the connections in Intelligent Memory.

How does this triggering process work? How do we turn on our mental computers and awaken our memories?

Sometimes all it takes is a new situation. Maybe you've just read about a new branch of your office-supply company opening in Hawaii. Suddenly, you recall an obscure item in last year's alumni newsletter reporting on a long-forgotten classmate who apparently has been in Maui for the past five years, happily running a small surfboard company. Although you can't remember your classmate's last name, you do remember that his favorite group was always the Beach Boys. Putting these disparate pieces of information together, you do a quick Internet search, and 5 minutes later you're dialing the number for the Help Me Rhonda Surf Shop, about to make a new sale. Who would have thought you'd ever make a connection among office supplies, surfing, and a Beach Boys tune? Life presented you with a new opportunity, and your memory pulled together the resources that enabled you to take advantage of it.

If Intelligent Memory is such a crucial element in business success, how can we improve that mental ability? According to Dr. Gordon, "The best way to improve your Intelligent Memory is to strengthen the mental processes that manage it." These are the very mental processes that you'll learn in this book: *paying attention, visualizing,* and *associating.* Learning how to improve your use of these processes will go a long way toward boosting your memory—and your intelligence. Moreover, this effort has a cumulative effect. The more you strengthen one aspect of your mind, the stronger other parts will become. Sharpening your powers of observation and concentration will mean that you notice and remember much more (paying attention). Learning how to create pictures and stories in your mind (visualizing) will strengthen your ability to make more and richer connections among your memories (associating). Sharpening all of these skills will help you apply the techniques I've developed for remembering people, spoken words, data, and written information.

The techniques you'll learn are based on more than 30 years of working with executives and employees, helping them master the memory skills they need to succeed in the world of business. They're also based on the latest scientific understanding of how our minds work and how we can make the best use of our mental processes so that we can learn, remember, and recall what we need to know. And, I will admit, they are rooted in my own experience as well, from years of seeing how powerful stories and associations can be in helping to support our memories.

To show you what I mean, let me share a personal story that illustrates the power of memory. It begins about two years ago, when my brother, Harvey, was watching a New York Yankees/Boston Red Sox game on TV. That's not so unusual—except that Harvey lives in Rome, and it's actually very rare to see American baseball on European TV. Harvey, a longtime baseball fan, was riveted, and as he watched the game, the visual image of bright green grass at Yankee Stadium triggered a 50-year-old memory. As many of us do, he had allowed an important event in his life to drift out of his daily thinking and remembered it only when a new event, linked to the old one, reminded him. Although he'd never actually forgotten the following incident, he hadn't thought of it in years—until seeing this game.

Back in 1947, Harvey—then a kid of 17—was playing baseball with his friends across the street from Yankee Stadium. They were interrupted by a man who introduced himself as the trainer for baseball legend Joe DiMaggio. Joltin' Joe was recovering from heel surgery, the man told them, and needed some practice to get back into shape, but the Yankees were on the road, so he had no one to practice with. Would my brother and his five friends be interested in catching fly balls from Mr. DiMaggio? Although the boys probably would have forked over a year's allowance to play ball with DiMaggio in Yankee Stadium, the trainer even offered them two bucks apiece.

The trainer took them into the stadium, which was completely empty, absolutely beautiful, and awe inspiring. He introduced them to DiMaggio, and for the next 2 hours, they caught and threw balls hit by the great one. After they finished, DiMaggio asked if they would like to take a photograph together to commemorate the occasion. The photograph was taken, everyone shook hands, and the boys went home, stunned almost into silence by the amazing events of the day.

After that batting practice with Harvey and his friends, DiMaggio went on to have one of the most amazing seasons of his career. In his first at-bat after coming back, he hit a home run; he hit .315 for the season, and he won his third Most Valuable Player award. The Yankees went on to beat the Brooklyn Dodgers in the World Series, and DiMaggio blasted two home runs in that series. Clearly, he had a lot of positive associations to link to the experience with my brother.

One year later, Harvey and the same five friends sneaked into Madison Square Garden to watch the Rocky Graziano championship fight. The security guards spotted the boys as they headed toward ringside, so the little group hunkered down in front of the ringside seats to hide. Suddenly, my brother felt a tap on his shoulder. "Why don't you sit on the floor so you don't block our view?" said a deep, familiar voice. Harvey turned around, and there was Joe DiMaggio sitting with Ernest Hemingway, the great sportswriter Jimmy Cannon, and famed restaurateur Toots Shor.

My brother, of course, recognized these celebrities right away. To his surprise, DiMaggio recognized him and his friends, too, asking if they were the same teenagers who had helped him get back into shape a year earlier. Amazed at DiMaggio's memory, the boys were just saying yes when the security guards appeared, demanding that they leave immediately. "But these are my special guests," DiMaggio told the guards, and they all watched the fight together.

Fast-forward to more than 40 years later, the early 1990s, when Harvey was living in Rome. Somehow, he heard there was to be a special celebration dinner at the American Embassy in honor of Joe DiMaggio. He managed to wangle an invitation to this big event and was even seated next to DiMaggio. Many speeches were made, and good food and wine were served. About halfway through the dinner, Harvey got up the nerve to say, "Mr. DiMaggio, I don't know if you remember me, but I was one of those kids who caught fly balls from you in Yankee Stadium after your heel surgery recovery."

DiMaggio turned to him with recognition on his face and said, "I remember you as clearly as if it happened yesterday. In fact, I even have a large photograph of you and your friends on my wall at home in Florida."

"Wow!" said Harvey, completely amazed. "Joe DiMaggio has a photo of *me* on his wall."

I tell this story in my workshops to illustrate the power of a story as a memory structure to which you can attach all sorts of information that you can retrieve later—even years later. If the story is good enough, you'll remember it forever, along with all the associations it contains. As you enter the fascinating world of memory, prepare to be surprised at how much you can remember—and how smart, creative, and effective you really are.

MY THREE-DIMENSIONAL

MEMORY TRAINING SYSTEM

CHAPTER 3
────────────

HOW WELL IS
YOUR BRAIN WORKING?
A SELF-DIAGNOSIS

Do you know how well your brain is working? I've devised a pretest to give you the opportunity to test yourself on the three mental powers on which memory relies.

• Paying attention (which involves subpowers of observing and concentrating)

• Visualizing

• Associating

I've also included some questions to help you evaluate your ability to recall the four types of information.

• People information

• Spoken information

• Numerical information

• Written information

If you do well on this test, terrific! Read the rest of the book to learn how to do even better.

If you have trouble with one or two areas, though—or even all of them—don't despair. No matter what kind of memory you think you have, I guarantee that you can make it better. All you need is the time to read this book and a few extra minutes each day to practice the exercises I'll give you. (You should prepare by gathering a timer, some paper, and a few different-colored pens.) By the time you've finished chapter 10, you'll be amazed at how much your memory has improved—perhaps even without your realizing it. In fact, just so you can see how far you've come, I've included a posttest in chapter 11, where you'll get another crack at the kinds of questions I've included here. Compare your scores on the two exams and marvel at your own improvement!

PRETEST

Paying Attention

Think of a room you know well, such as your bedroom, living room, or office. Set a timer for 5 minutes and begin to jot down, as quickly as you can, everything you recall about that room. Note the colors of the walls, ceiling, and floor; the pictures or other objects on the walls; every piece of furniture; every object on each piece of furniture; and any other characteristics of this familiar place.

When the timer goes off, rate yourself. What percentage of the room do you believe you "covered"? What percentage did you simply not have time to write about?

Next, evaluate yourself. Go into the room and look around carefully, comparing it with the description you jotted down. Did you basically remember the important things about the room, or did you leave out key objects or other important details? Use the following scale to rate yourself.

Everything or nearly everything—10 points

Most of the information—8 points

Half of the information—6 points

One third or less—4 points

Hardly anything—2 points

Your score for paying attention: _____

Observing

Find a relatively unfamiliar environment, such as a new coffee shop, a part of your office building you don't usually visit, or a block in your neighborhood that you rarely stroll down. Give yourself 5 minutes to observe this environment closely, noticing every detail you can.

When 5 minutes is up, find a place to sit and make notes on what you saw. Jot down every detail you recall.

Next, evaluate yourself. Return to the new place and compare it with your notes. How much of the environment did you notice and recall? Again, use this scale to rate yourself.

Everything or nearly everything—10 points

Most of the information—8 points

Half of the information—6 points

One third or less—4 points

Hardly anything—2 points

Your score for observing: _____

Concentrating

Go to a drawer with a number of objects in it and remove 20, then place them on a desk or table. Set your timer, giving yourself 3 minutes to remember as many objects as you can.

When the timer goes off, turn away and write down as many objects as you can remember without looking at the table.

Next, turn back and evaluate yourself. Give yourself ½ point for each object you recalled.

Your score for concentrating: _____

Visualizing

Set the timer for 5 minutes, then look at the following list of names and come up with a visual image for each one. I've done a couple of examples for you, sharing my thought process so you can see how I came up with the images, but don't write down your own process. Just name or draw your image.

Name	Thought Process	Visual Image
Mr. Harry Harmon	(harmony)	hairy harmonica
Dr. Lydia Ross	(Betsy Ross)	led a marching band with a stethoscope-wearing doctor draped in a U.S. flag
Ms. Karin Mitchell	(mid-shell)	a SHELL located MIDway up a beach IN a CAR

Name	Visual Image
Mr. Conrad Parker	_____
Dr. Mary Colbert	_____
Ms. Shirley Scharf	_____
Dr. Nicholas Theodorakis	_____
Ambassador Hugo Janheim	_____
Mrs. Barbara Bettany	_____
Mr. Gregory Zukav	_____
Rabbi George Feldman	_____
Ms. Amina Mustafa	_____
Mr. Jaime Silvero	_____

When the timer goes off, evaluate yourself. How many names could you visualize in the 5-minute time limit? Give yourself 1 point for each name.

Your score for visualizing: _____

Associating

Again, set the timer for 5 minutes. Use the time to create a story that incorporates as many of the visual images as possible from the previous list.

Example: If I were creating a story from my three names, I would imagine Mr. Harmon playing a saxophone from which harmonious musical notes emerge. Suddenly, in walks Dr. Ross, wrapped in an American flag. She drags Mr. Harmon off to the seashore, where they find a shell located midway up a beach.

Now it's your turn. See how many images you can incorporate into a single story.

When the timer goes off, evaluate yourself. How many images could you associate in allotted time? Give yourself 1 point for each image.

Your score for associating: _____

Recalling People Information

Set the timer for 5 minutes. Look at the pictures below and see how many of the people's names, faces, and identifying details you can memorize in that time.

Roger Burnett
Senior vice president
of an electronics firm,
reads science fiction
novels

Anna Gonzales
Construction engineer,
coaches Little League

Sanford Shapiro
Honors student,
tennis player

Elizabeth Merzon
TV news anchor,
likes art museums

Herbert Yamamoto
Architect, loves to
play billiards

Candace Bartholomew
Marketing manager,
enjoys swimming

Charles Ellenport
Stockbroker, plays chess

Michael McBride
Taxi driver, terrific
darts player

Nancy Powell
Retired teacher with
six grandchildren,
enjoys travel in Asia

Next, without looking back at the previous page, see how many people you can identify and what you recall about each one. When you've finished, check back to see how many you got right. Since you haven't yet learned my system, I'll give you a break. Give yourself 1 point for each name you recalled correctly, then give yourself a bonus point for each identifying detail you got right.

Your score for recalling people information: _____

Recalling Spoken Information

Arrange to tape 5 minutes of TV or radio news and set the timer. Listen to the program carefully while you're taping it, without taking notes. If you tape a TV broadcast, shut your eyes or avert your head so you respond to only the spoken information, not to any visual cues. Then take the time you need to jot down as many of the main ideas as you can remember.

Next, listen to the broadcast again, comparing your notes with what you hear. How many of the main ideas did you recall? Use the following scale to rate yourself.

Everything or nearly everything—10 points

Most of the information—8 points

Half of the information—6 points

One third or less—4 points

Hardly anything—2 points

Your score for recalling spoken information: _____

Recalling Numerical Information

Set your timer for 5 minutes. Use the time to memorize as many of the following phone numbers as you can in any order you wish. If some seem easier to memorize than others, you can start with those if you like. Your goal is simply to memorize as many numbers as you can.

212-564-3049

404-549-3201

704-221-0009

323-477-5545

401-669-0123

201-390-5600

207-455-8876

904-678-4578

512-307-7767

714-537-6737

When the timer goes off, stop. Then take a clean sheet of paper and, without looking at the numbers, write down as many as you can.

Next, check your work. Give yourself 1 point for each number you recalled correctly.

Your score for recalling numerical information: _____

Recalling Written Information #1

Choose a page from your favorite business magazine or newspaper and pick an article of about 500 words to read. Set your timer for 5 minutes—the amount of time you have to read the article and memorize its key ideas. Feel free to do anything you want to help absorb the article, including underlining, taking notes, or any other system you like. Be aware, however, that when you're asked to recall the article, you won't be allowed to use any visual aids; you'll have to recall it entirely from memory.

When your time is up, take a blank piece of paper and, without looking at the article or any of your notes, jot down the main ideas and key details that you remember.

Next, evaluate yourself according to the following scale.

Everything or nearly everything—10 points

Most of the information—8 points

Half of the information—6 points

One third or less—4 points

Hardly anything—2 points

Your score for recalling written information #1: _____

Recalling Written Information #2

Choose a business document from your job. It might be a memo, a contract, a report, or some other business-related material. Identify a 500-word section from the document.

Set your timer for 5 minutes—the amount of time you have to read the document and memorize its key ideas. As before, feel free to do anything you like to absorb the article, knowing that you'll eventually have to recall it entirely from memory.

When the time's up, take a blank piece of paper. Without referring to the document or your notes, jot down the main ideas and key details that you remember.

Next, evaluate yourself using the following scale.

Everything or nearly everything—10 points

Most of the information—8 points

Half of the information—6 points

One third or less—4 points

Hardly anything—2 points

Your score for recalling written information #2: _____

Evaluation

Add up your scores. In theory, the highest you could get is 99 points, although you may have racked up some extra points in the People Memory section. How did you do?

Your total score: _____

GET READY TO IMPROVE YOUR MEMORY!

Whatever your score was on the pretest, I hope you'll pause to give yourself a big pat on the back. Tests of any kind are never easy, and this one was purposely designed to be difficult. That's because if you could already perform every one of these functions easily and quickly, you probably wouldn't need to read this book!

In fact, I'm betting that you're like the vast majority of the businesspeople who enroll in my workshops and training sessions, whose scores dipped into the twenties, teens, and even lower. Like these other students, you probably have some areas of strength and some of weakness—or maybe even several areas of weakness. That's okay, because you're ready, willing, and able to learn—and you're going to be amazed at how different this test will look to you after you've read the next few chapters.

So get ready to improve your memory! If you got a high score, you'll soon learn how to make it even higher. If you scored low—as is the case for most of my students who take pretests—get ready to witness an even more dramatic improvement. There's nowhere to go but up!

CHAPTER 4

STEP 1: PAY ATTENTION

The art of memory is the art of attention.
—Samuel Johnson

The employees of the health and safety department at New York's Con Edison are trained to monitor a number of different volatile situations, particularly accidents involving oil spills. Over the years, I've done a number of workshops and training sessions at Con Ed under the auspices of W. Alan Homyk, who was then director of environment, health, and safety and is now general manager of operations services for Bronx/Westchester electric operations. One of our major goals was to help employees memorize the 24,000 safety regulations created to govern energy-related environmental health and safety.

One day, a former student showed up at a workshop in which he wasn't even enrolled. "I just had to stop by and tell you," he said. "Last week I spotted a potentially hazardous situation just in time to avert a problem. It's all thanks to you—I would never have noticed the problem if my observation skills hadn't been so acute. Because of what I learned in your workshop, I got my brain and my eyes to such a level that I now see things that before I would have just ignored."

OBSERVATION: THE FIRST KEY TO MEMORY

I'm going to start with a remark that seems so simple, you may be tempted to ignore it: *Before you can remember something, you have to notice it.*

Sound obvious? Maybe—but you'd be surprised at how many of us spend most of our waking hours *not* paying attention—particularly when we think we don't have anything new to learn.

Before we go any further, let's try an exercise that illustrates the power of observation. To do this exercise, you'll need a bag of lemons—ideally a full bag of over a dozen, but a half dozen will do. (When the exercise is over, you can always make lemonade!)

Exercise #1: Looking at Lemons

Step 1. Put the bag of lemons on the table. Close your eyes and pull out one lemon at random.

Step 2. Set a timer for 3 minutes or put a clock or watch in a prominent place so you won't be distracted by continually checking the time.

Step 3. Turn your back on all the other lemons and concentrate on yours. If your attention wanders, don't worry. Just keep bringing your focus back to the task at hand.

Step 4. When 3 minutes is up, avert your eyes and put your lemon back in the bag. Without looking at the lemons, mix them up, then spread them out on the table and find *your* lemon.

(continued on page 54)

Three Keys to Sharpening
Your Powers of Observation

1. Recognize patterns and anomalies. If I write the letters aaaBaaa, it's pretty easy to tell which letter doesn't belong and why. A longer sequence of letters, numbers, or data may require more concentration, but the principle is the same. Try to notice patterns—the ways that things repeat and remain the same. Also seek out anomalies—the thing that doesn't belong, the item that diverges.

Former clients tell me that this point alone is worth the price of the workshop. I've been thanked by hundreds of newly observant employees, from a money manager who caught an embezzling employee just by noticing a particular pattern in his spreadsheets to a paralegal who alone spotted the missing zero in the $90 million contract to the midlevel manager who snagged a major promotion by isolating a consumer buying trend that nobody else had seen. There's more to this skill than simply paying attention, and we'll focus on what else is involved in chapters 9 and 10. But paying attention—observing closely and concentrating on what you see—is the first step.

2. Experience each moment to the fullest. This sentiment may seem to be more appropriate on a greeting card than in a book on business memory. Nevertheless, I promise you that becoming fully aware of your experience—using the kind of focused, detailed observation that enabled you to find "your" lemon—will not only make your life richer and fuller, it will also boost your productivity, efficiency, and effectiveness in the workplace.

Think about what happens when you're confronted with a new problem. If you pay close attention to what you're doing and what you've learned, you'll carry the fruits of your problem-solving experience with you the next time you encounter a challenge. That's precisely the experience that makes you more valuable than a total newcomer—that rich, detailed memory bank of many different situations on which you can draw, using your past to navigate your future.

On the other hand, if you approach each new experience in a half-hearted, hurried, or distracted way, you're far less likely to remember either the problem itself or the solution you came up with. You'll be like those people who keep making the same mistakes time after time, simply because they're not paying attention. Not focusing on your experience makes you far less likely to remember it—and in that sense, you might as well not have had the experience in the first place.

3. Draw on your social skills. I once met someone at a professional conference, and as I was shaking his hand, he said, "I never remember names. Trust me, I'll have forgotten your name by the time you're finished telling it to me."

I'm sure he was only trying to save himself some embarrassment. Perhaps he was also worried that if he focused on my name, he wouldn't have enough mental energy left to follow the rest of our conversation, but what I—and all the onlookers—heard was, "You don't matter enough for me to even *try* to remember your name."

Ironically, if that man had brought his social skills to bear on the situation, and if he'd been applying his powers of observation and concentration, he would not only have been able to remember my name, he also would have remembered much more about our entire conversation. Once you start observing and concentrating, your whole mental capacity expands. Far from draining your overall ability to think and remember, committing a person's name to memory actually improves your mind's functioning.

Here's where a few basic social skills come in. Take a real interest in the person you're talking to, make eye contact, repeat the person's name, and ask questions. For example, suppose you're at a meeting with 15 people you don't know. As the meeting begins, someone goes around the table and introduces everybody. You don't remember more than two names—and I'll tell you now that you're not the only one. No problem! Take the opportunity during a break to go up to someone and reintroduce yourself. You'll flatter the other person; you'll be in an ideal situation to collect a number of personal details, which will increase the likelihood that you'll remember the name later; and you'll give the other person the opportunity to remember your name as well.

We'll go further into this question of remembering names in chapter 7. Meanwhile, start practicing your social skills and begin paying closer attention to the people you meet. You may find that your memory improves surprisingly with little or no effort on your part!

When I do this exercise in my workshops, I bring three or even four dozen lemons so that each participant can have one. I give everyone a few minutes to observe "their" lemon, then put them all back into the bag. When I dump the lemons onto the table a few minutes later and ask people to find theirs, they're able to do it immediately. Lemons look alike, they smell alike, and, let's face it, most individual lemons simply don't stand out from the crowd, yet 40 people will unerringly locate "their" lemons, simply because they took the time to observe them closely. It's a real tribute to the power of paying attention.

So I'll repeat my first point: *Before you can remember something, you have to notice it.* Memory isn't some magic operation that's unrelated to all our other mental abilities. It's closely linked to observing and concentrating—the process of paying attention. If you don't notice something, you can't remember it, but once you start paying attention, you'll be surprised at how much you remember, often without even trying.

Observation That Produces a Memory

I once worked with a client named Natalie, a talented department store executive who had recently moved from a back-office job into a position where she had to deal with a wide variety of clients.

"You have no idea how bad my memory is for faces," she told me in despair. "I'd probably forget my own husband if I didn't see him so often! Now, suddenly I'm meeting dozens of people each month—and you know they'll be offended if I don't recognize them at the next business meeting, let alone if I'm meeting them in a restaurant and can't find their table. I've been this way all my life—I'm not sure there's anything I can do about it."

Natalie was so concerned about the demands of her new position that she hired me to work with her privately. I knew that the first step in solving her problem was improving her powers of observation. I started by doing an exercise with her that I often do in my workshops. I showed her pictures of famous people—but not their entire faces. Instead, each well-known image was reduced to a single feature: Mick Jagger's mouth, Ronald Reagan's raised eyebrow, Jackie Kennedy's eyes, Marilyn Monroe's lips. Although Natalie could see only a fraction of each face, she was able to recognize it instantly, and she was almost always able to put a name to the face as well.

"I don't get it," Natalie said after she'd successfully worked her way through several famous features. "How come I'm so good at recognizing these people and such a dud at knowing my clients?"

I explained that she'd had many more opportunities to view the faces of these icons, whereas with her clients, she was likely to have seen them only once or twice. The point was not how well she remembered these familiar faces but rather how little of each face she needed to see in order to recognize it.

"Now that you know what you're looking for," I told her, "you can use the same technique a bit more consciously." In my workshops, I explained, I usually pair up students and have them take a few minutes to observe each other. I ask them to analyze each other's faces, identifying the one, two, or three features that would trigger recognition of these ordinary folks as surely as Elvis's hair or Seinfeld's grin inspires recognition of the celebrities. Then, when it's time for their lunch break, I tell my students to observe at least five strangers on their way to and from the restaurant or cafeteria—to watch people on the street, in the elevator, or behind the coffee counter, scanning each face for that special feature.

When the workshop participants return from lunch, they're usually exhilarated. They agree that it now takes them only about 5 seconds to key in on a special feature for each new face. When I ask them to recall that feature, they discover that they're able to recall not only the face but also the place where they saw the person. Often, they remember a few significant details as well—the person's accent, for example, or the kind of food he was serving, or something about his clothing. They can readily see that this kind of recognition and recall would serve them well with clients and associates.

At first, Natalie was discouraged at the prospect of trying this exercise, but I pointed out that part of her problem was precisely that sense of defeat. "If you think you're beaten before you begin, then you *won't* observe closely," I told her. "You'll just be marking time when you meet a new person, waiting for the conversation to be over instead of using those precious first few seconds to inscribe their features in your mind. Don't worry about how successful you're going to be. Just focus on the task: identifying the one feature you need in order to recognize that face."

Nervous but determined, Natalie went off to practice what I had told her. Sure enough, when I saw her a few days later, she was as elated as any of my workshop students. "It's still not easy for me," she admitted. "I get embarrassed looking at someone else's face so closely—it feels funny to pay that much attention to what someone looks like. And to be honest, I'm not all that interested in people's faces. But it's a whole different way of thinking about it, to tell myself to get interested rather than to tell myself that I can't remember. If I feel like my memory is the problem, there's nothing I can do. If I understand that my lack of effort is the problem, well, then, I'll just have to make the effort!"

I was proud of Natalie for catching on so quickly. Many people take a defeatist attitude toward memory when instead they could make such great strides simply by changing their perspectives. If you, too, have trouble remembering faces, or if you'd simply like to improve your "people memory," try Natalie's approach. Focus not on how bad your memory is but on how committed you are to observing people closely. Look at each face with a clear objective: to select the one feature that would enable you to recognize the whole face. Congratulate yourself when you succeed—and keep practicing. Memory isn't magic (although it can sometimes seem that way!). It's a skill that can be learned.

Practice #1: Focus on Faces

Try this simple exercise for 5 minutes a day every day for a week. At the end of the week, evaluate your progress. You may feel that you've mastered this skill, or you may want to give yourself another week or two. Either way, you should notice a definite improvement in your ability to observe and recognize faces.

Day 1: Eyes. Choose a time of day when you're likely to come in contact with people with whom you don't usually interact but can conveniently see again. You might focus on people who work in a store you can easily visit, the stand where you buy your coffee, or the restaurant where you eat lunch. At your chosen spot, take at least 5 minutes to notice at least five new people. Focus on each person's eyes. Using your sharpest powers of observation, notice everything you can. What color, shape, and size are the person's eyes? Are they deep set or bulging? Close to the brows or relatively distant? Fringed with long lashes or relatively bare? Are they hiding behind glasses or relatively easy to see? Is the person wearing distinctive eye makeup? Do you notice frown lines, laugh lines, or crinkles? Anything else? Your goal is to notice as much as possible within the approximately 5 seconds you have before your observation becomes, well, conspicuous.

Day 2: Nose. On your next day of observation, repeat the process, focusing on noses. What size and shape are they? High bridged or relatively flat? Large nostrils or small? Distinctive or unobtrusive? How do they fit into the brow? The mouth? What do you notice about the skin color and texture, about any blemishes, moles, or distinctive markings? Become as aware as you can of the similarities and differences that you notice among noses.

Day 3: Mouth. Now you're starting to get the hang of the process, so you should be even more sensitive to all the nuances of the mouth: shape, color, size, and texture. Are the person's lips set in a particular expression? Do you notice the teeth? If so, what shape, color, and size are they? What about the corners of the mouth—how are they set? Are they wrinkled or smooth? Are both lips the same size, or is one noticeably fuller or thinner? What other details do you notice? Remember that you're looking for differences and similarities.

Day 4: Forehead. The forehead is a bit less distinctive than the eyes, nose, and mouth, but you've been doing this for three days now, and I'll bet you'll see a lot more than you would have on Day 1. Look for shape, size, color, wrinkles, and how the forehead relates to the hairline and eyebrows. Ask yourself what you'd have to notice to be able to pick that forehead out of a lineup!

Day 5: Chin. Size, shape, and angle are important here, as well as skin color and texture. Lots of people have dimples or clefts or unusual-shaped jaws. (Caricaturists often go for the jaw—think of George Clooney or Hugh Grant, to cite two memorable examples.) There can be a lot of personality in a jaw, too—does it jut forward or recede timidly? Is it clenched tightly or held loosely? Once you start to observe, you'll be amazed at how much you notice.

Day 6: Select a feature. Now that you know how to recognize individual features, you're ready to start choosing which feature to focus on. Each time you see one of your five new people, ask yourself quickly which feature is most distinctive, then focus on it. An hour or two later, try to recall all five of your people. See if you can use that one special feature to trigger first the whole face, then the circumstances of your meeting. (Of course, you may not have actually met—but what do you remember about where you first saw them?)

Day 7: Evaluate your progress. Well, how did you do? Do you see a marked improvement in your ability to pay attention to faces and an improvement in your memory as a result? Or do you still feel as though, like Natalie, you'd be hard-pressed to remember a client or colleague the next time your paths cross?

• If you're happy with your results, congratulations! Move on to the next exercise.

• If you'd like to get better, repeat the process week by week until your observation skills are as sharp as you'd like them to be!

CONCENTRATION: THE SECOND KEY TO MEMORY

As we saw in the lemon exercise, observation is crucial—but by itself, it's not enough. Observation works hand in hand with concentration to create that powerful process known as *paying attention.*

When I start talking about concentration in my workshops, some of my students become anxious. "You don't expect me to concentrate on *everything*, do you?" exclaimed Malcolm, a young marketing executive at a West Coast advertising company. "My brain would explode!"

I reassured Malcolm and his worried colleagues that concentration is essentially a selective process. When you concentrate on something, you are focusing on it—but you're simultaneously blocking out all other sources of information. A person who is fully concentrating on reading a report, for example, won't even notice the lively conversation going on at the other end of the office—and she's far more likely to remember what she's read. A person who is easily distracted, on the other hand, will probably remember very little of either the reading or the intrusive conversation.

That lack of concentration is part of why we think our memories are so bad. If we haven't concentrated, the information we've taken in is no longer available to us; we simply don't remember it. We think our memories are faulty, but often, we simply weren't paying attention in the first place.

I'd like you to see for yourself just how much paying attention can boost your capacity to remember—and how much a failure to pay attention prevents you from remembering. Grab a clean sheet of paper and pen or pencil, then complete the following exercise.

Exercise #2:
Paying Attention to Pennies

Step 1. Take a moment to recall what a penny looks like. For the moment, just bring the image of a penny into your mind; don't pull one out of your pocket. Using only your memory, recall every detail you possibly can.

Step 2. Set a timer for 3 minutes. Keep track of your "penny memories" by writing each of them down. Take notes in any way you like—the format's not important. All you need is some way to record your memories so you can check them against an actual penny. Your goal is to note as many specific details as possible, using every second of your 3 minutes.

Step 3. When the timer buzzes, check yourself. Get out a penny and compare it with your notes. How'd you do? Would you say you recalled nearly 100 percent of what's on that little coin? Or is your score closer to 50 percent? 25 percent? Less than that?

Step 4. Next, set your timer again. This time, give yourself 3 minutes to observe the penny, knowing that when your time is up, you'll repeat Step 3, once again noting as many details as you can remember. Clear your mind of all other thoughts, concentrate exclusively on the penny, and take 3 minutes to notice as many details as you can.

Step 5. Repeat Step 2: Put the penny out of sight, set the timer for 3 minutes again, and start taking notes. Take the full 3 minutes to record every detail you recall about the penny.

Step 6. When your time is up, check yourself again.

If you really want to surprise yourself, repeat this exercise in a week or so, taking yet another 3 minutes to write down every detail you can remember about a penny without actually looking at the coin. Because you've already invested the time and energy in paying attention, you're likely to retain a lot of your memory. In fact, you may remember more about the penny you observed last week than about, say, the restaurant menu you read only a few hours ago at lunch.

When I ask my workshop students to perform this exercise, most of them are surprised twice. First, they realize how little they could recall about a coin that they handle almost every day of their lives. Then they discover how much they *are* able to remember after only a few minutes of effort.

Focusing Your Concentration

Of course, sometimes we can concentrate too hard on a narrow part of a problem, blocking out something that we should be taking in. Consider the case, all too common in business, of a negotiator who focuses only on *what* is being said, ignoring the *how*. The opposing negotiator's tone of voice, facial expression, and choice of words all may communicate a message that's very different from the "official" content of a statement, so the person who concentrates only on the words may miss the equally important information inherent in the "music." A negotiator whose focus is too narrow may remember a proposal made by the opposing side but may lose an important business advantage by not recalling how upset, triumphant, or confused the opposing side seemed to be while making it.

I can see how blocking out such crucial information might cause problems, but concentration per se is not at fault. The problem is that the negotiator chooses to limit his concentration too narrowly. In fact, learning to define our area of concentration—the range of our focus—is an important part of this skill. That's because, by definition, concentration is a kind of filtering process, something that tells the mind what information is important and what can be discarded or ignored.

Practice #2: Defining the Boundaries of Your Concentration

Try this simple exercise for 15 minutes at a time once a week for three weeks. I'll bet that by the end of the third week, you'll notice a significant shift in your ability to define and focus on a problem. The benefits will be particularly great if, during the three weeks, each time you sit down to work or to meet with a client, you ask yourself "Where should my focus be?" For still greater benefits, repeat this question to yourself every time you take a break. Pretty soon, defining and re-adjusting your focus will become automatic, an internalized skill that helps maximize your effectiveness at every task you undertake.

Preparation. Find a piece of artwork that you like—preferably a relatively complicated and detailed picture. It can be a photograph, a painting, a poster, or a collage, and you can view it on the wall, in a book, or on your computer screen. The only criterion is that you and the work should be positioned in such a way that you can comfortably view the entire image. Alternatively, you can do this exercise using a view from your window—but don't try it with an internal view, such as your office or bedroom. You want a relatively neutral image whose details carry no personal associations or memories.

Step 1: Identify the task. As you glance at the entire image, choose a particular portion of the painting or view on which to focus. You will observe and concentrate on this area for 5 minutes, so try to choose a portion large enough to hold your interest for that period of time yet small enough to allow you to view every single detail within the time allotted. Find some way to record which portion you've chosen. If you can make a photocopy of the work, you might mark out "your" portion with a colored marker (but don't use the marked-up work to observe). Or you can write down a few notes: "I'll look at the horse, the sword, and the flowers beneath the horse's feet." Note your choice in any way you want—but be sure to write down exactly what it is. Making the process of choosing as conscious as possible is part of what this exercise is all about.

Step 2: Observe and concentrate. Set your timer for 5 minutes and begin to observe. Focus on the area you've chosen and allow yourself to notice as much as you possibly can. If you find your mind wandering (as, for most of us, it will!) don't worry. Just take a deep breath and instruct your mind to return to concentrating on the task at hand.

Step 3: Remember. When the timer goes off, turn your head away from the image and jot down as many details as you can remember from the portion you chose. Work as quickly as possible—your goal in this case is not a painstaking effort of memory but an "off the top of your head" type of quick recall. When you think you've remembered everything you can, stop.

Step 4: Check yourself. Compare your notes with the image. How well did you do? You're looking at two different criteria:

- How many details you remembered
- How well you kept your focus within the boundaries you set

If you find that you recalled details outside your area of concentration, circle them in a different color—preferably bright red or green. If you find that you omitted important details, add them to your notes, again using red, green, or another color that will stand out.

Step 5: Evaluate yourself. Based on this exercise, how good are you at setting limits for your concentration? Did you pick an area that was too large or too detailed to absorb in 5 minutes? Too small to hold your interest for so long? Did you find the simple process of concentrating upsetting, exhausting, or anxiety provoking? (If so, you're not alone—lots of people react that way. Don't worry. With practice, you'll start to feel a lot more comfortable concentrating for longer and longer periods of time.) Complete this portion of the exercise by writing a sentence or two about what you've learned about yourself, your ability to pay attention, and your memory.

Step 6: Redefine your goals. Finally, write down a personal goal for the next time you do this exercise. Your objective might be as simple as "to feel more relaxed about concentrating" or as specific as "to choose a more appropriate area of focus." And of course, if you feel you completed the exercise perfectly, find a way to push yourself further the next time—choosing a larger area to concentrate on, for example, or trying to master the same amount of visual information in less time.

Note: This exercise can also be done with aural information, such as a piece of music, or with written information, such as a report, news article, poem, or story. For super-advanced practice, you can try it with a video or DVD, either of which gives you both visual and aural information to remember. However, developing your visual memory is so useful—and so much easier to check—that I suggest you do this exercise at least two or three times with a still visual image, even if you also try it with other forms of information. (For more on how important visualizing is to memory, see chapter 5.)

Now that you've had some practice choosing a focus, you may have noticed another benefit that results from improving your concentration: Because concentration requires so much energy, you really *can't* do it all the time. You have to decide consciously when you want or need to concentrate, and you have to choose when to start and stop. Becoming more conscious of when you need to pay attention and when you're free to let your mind wander will make you even more effective at paying attention, remembering, and getting your work done. Instead of feeling as though your mind is always wandering, you'll trust yourself to choose when to focus and when to relax—and you'll become far more productive as a result.

How Long Can You Concentrate?

Was it hard for you to spend 3 to 5 minutes concentrating on your penny or your picture? As Malcolm feared, most of us aren't capable of concentrating on any one thing for very long. We need breaks and respites, periods when our minds are allowed to play and wander freely, as well as times when they zero in, laserlike, upon a single task.

However, most of us *are* capable of better concentration than we tend to show. A few years ago, I came across a study of 50,000 managers across the country that surprised me considerably (although given the work I do, perhaps it shouldn't have). The study measured the average time during which these managers exhibited unbroken concentration on a single task.

Before I tell you how long these top managers were able to pay attention, take a moment to come up with your own estimate. When I ask the businesspeople in my workshops, their guesses tend to be in the range of 1, 2, or even 3 hours at a time. If I hadn't read the study, that's what I would have guessed, too.

In fact, the actual answer is 6 minutes. That's right. According to this study, most U.S. managers can concentrate for only *6 minutes* at a time.

Now, when I first learned this, I felt extremely discouraged. How, I

Multitasking: Memory's Enemy

Did you know that trying to do two things at once means that you're less likely to do either of them well? Multitasking not only leads to mistakes, according to a 2001 study at Carnegie Mellon University in Pittsburgh, it also interferes with the process of memory formation. If you're not fully concentrating on either of your two tasks, you're less likely to remember either of them.

Multitasking also takes more than twice as long as doing first one job, then the other. That's because our brains do better when they're fully engaged, concentrating totally on a single task. In fact, as psychiatrist Dr. Barry Gordon and Lisa Berger report in *Intelligent Memory*, multitasking can impair memory formation as much as age, alcohol, or sleep deprivation. The Carnegie Mellon scientists discovered that when people divide their attention between two tasks, they can't expend as much energy on each one. As a result, each takes longer to complete, is likely to be less well done—and is less likely to be remembered.

wondered, could U.S. businesses compete in the world with such a poor showing? After all, 6 minutes isn't a very long time in which to get work done. I pictured a company full of frustrated and distracted managers, interrupted by others or even by themselves every 6 minutes, continually having to gear themselves up for the next short spurt of productivity—only to be interrupted again 6 minutes later. I couldn't imagine how anything ever got done!

When I thought about it a few minutes longer, however, I began to feel rather optimistic. I had seen from my own work with thousands of businesspeople that concentration can easily be improved as soon as people realize its value. Potentially, all of those 6-minute managers could extend their spans of concentration to 9, 12, or even 15 minutes—with consequent gains in productivity. Increased concentration meant, too, that they would be working "smarter, not harder"—that they could get far more work done in the same amount of time simply by expanding their powers of concentration.

That's good news for you, too, so let's take a closer look at some of the ways that you can extend your ability to concentrate. You may find that you can accomplish in 3 hours what you used to get done in 7!

Focusing Your Concentration

"Okay, okay, you've convinced me!" Natalie said the third or fourth time we met. "Concentration is important—I get it! But I still find it hard to do. I'll be sitting in the office, looking at a client list—and all of a sudden I realize that I'm thinking about picking up my skirts from the cleaners or wondering how I'll make time to help my son with his homework tonight. Maybe if I wasn't running a household as well as an office, I'd be okay—but I really do have a lot on my mind."

As a husband and father, I was ready to sympathize, but as a memory expert, I knew that Natalie's lack of focus wasn't helping her performance either at home or at work. When I suggested that she commit to focusing on one thing at a time—whether that one thing was personal or work related—she readily agreed that would be better. "I just don't think I can do it," she sighed.

Fortunately, I had a practice to share with her—and with you. If you feel your mind keeps wandering when you want it to stay on target, try it out.

Practice #3: The Focus Alarm

Try this simple exercise as often as you like, whenever you're working alone, but be sure to practice it at least twice a week. It's something you do while you are working, but when I say that it can take up to 90 minutes, don't worry. It will actually make that 90 minutes more productive.

Step 1: Start working. Set your trusty timer for 15 minutes and get to work. Concentrate on the task at hand as best you can.

Step 2: Check in with yourself. When the timer goes off, stop and ask yourself, "Am I focusing on my work or on something else?"

If your focus was on your work, terrific! Set the timer for 20 minutes and go back to work.

If your mind wandered, don't worry. Concentration is a skill, and you're going to master it. Just reset your timer—and your mind. Instruct yourself to focus on the task at hand and set the alarm for 5 minutes.

Step 3: Check in again. The next time the timer goes off, ask yourself again if you were focusing on your work or something else.

If you were focused on your work, bravo! Add 5 minutes to your focus time, set your timer, and go back to work.

If your mind was wandering, stay calm. Take a deep breath, instruct yourself to focus, and set your timer for the same amount of time during which you tried to concentrate but didn't yet succeed.

Step 4: Keep going for 90 minutes. Each time you succeed in concentrating for the time you set, add another 5 minutes to the timer, and each time your mind wanders, set it for the same amount of time during which you tried to concentrate but didn't succeed. Either way, keep going until you reach 90 minutes, then take a break!

As you can see, the goal is to extend the time whenever you succeed in focusing. If you can't yet concentrate for longer stretches, you can proceed more slowly up to 90 minutes by practicing with shorter amounts of time. Eventually, you'll work your way up to a 90-minute work session without a break, fully focused and alert.

INSTRUCT YOUR MIND

As you've seen by now, concentration is a kind of instruction you give your mind. You can magnify the effectiveness of this instruction by com-

Take a Break!

In our quest to improve our efficiency, many of us put a high premium on working continuously without a break—but breaks are not only good for our health, they're crucial for our memory. According to the latest scientific research—cited in Dr. Rebecca Rupp's book *Committed to Memory* and elsewhere—short sessions with lots of breaks spaced out over time lead to far better retention of information than one long cramming session.

Indeed, if you're trying to master new information, Dr. Barry Gordon and Lisa Berger, the authors of *Intelligent Memory*, recommend working for short, intense periods of less than an hour. This allows, they say, for the formation of distinct memories that have a chance to live within your mind, whereas longer work sessions mean that the information you acquire later on crowds out the knowledge you gained when the session began.

"Also," they write, "spacing [taking breaks] gives your brain time to replenish nutrients and chemicals that build memories that are depleted during learning. The additional time lets new connections gain strength." And taking time between study sessions allows what we're learning to be absorbed by more different areas of the brain, so we make more connections to the new information and have a better chance of retrieving it. (For a more

bining physical movement and mental intention. This simple practice works because when you use your mind and body at the same time, you create synergy that significantly maximizes your ability.

Practice #4: The Memory Trigger

Try this simple exercise once a day, every day for 21 days in a row. For maximum effectiveness, perform it at the same time each day—ideally when you begin work. It takes less than 3 minutes—and you'll discover that those few moments are time well spent!

Step 1: Relax. This exercise is all about instructing your mind, and your mind hears instructions better when it's relaxed, so take a moment to get comfortable. Sit in a comfortable position, relaxed but alert. Take a few slow, deep breaths, breathing in and out first on a

detailed explanation of this connection-making process, see chapter 6.)

There's plenty of new research to support the value of taking breaks, but the notion that breaks are helpful was actually one of the first breakthroughs in memory research, the brainchild of Hermann Ebbinghaus, Ph.D. Dr. Ebbinghaus, a 19th-century German scientist, was the first person to study memory from a scientific point of view. He found that people were actually able to remember more right after a break than they could just before they took the break, an improvement that he called the reminiscence effect.

However, for the reminiscence effect to occur, you need a real break—a complete chance for mental relaxation. If you switch from trying to memorize portions of a contract to, say, answering your e-mail, your mind will be cluttered by the two types of information you've taken in, and your break won't be nearly as effective.

If you're just doing routine work, a 90-minute session can be effective, but when you're especially concerned about memorizing new information, work in 15- to 45-minute increments and take a real 2- to 10-minute break after each session, preferably including a walk in the fresh air or some deep breathing to feed your brain with nourishing oxygen. Many athletes use the same "rest and recovery" principle to guide their training.

count of 2, then 4, then 8. Allow your mind to ignore all of its other duties and simply be present and aware.

Step 2: Choose a gesture. Look for something simple and distinct, something that you'll be comfortable doing in front of other people, such as bringing the fingers of both hands together, tent fashion, or placing the palm of one hand over the back of the other. Find a simple gesture that you'll perform only when you want to trigger your memory, one that's distinct enough to repeat easily and exactly, again and again. This gesture will be your memory trigger.

Step 3: Give yourself an autosuggestion. As you bring your hands together in the gesture you've chosen, repeat these words aloud: "I am able to focus my mind like a laser beam. I am able to take in all the information that is being presented to me. I am able to store that information for as long as I need it. I am able to recall that information with ease."

I think it works best to say the words aloud, but if you're more comfortable repeating them silently to yourself, that's fine. In either case, feel free to vary your "mantra" based on your own needs. For example, you may want to say, "I will be able to recall the sequence of events that occurred during the meeting" or "I will effortlessly recall every major point made during the negotiations." Once you've chosen your autosuggestion, however, don't vary it. Repeat it to yourself in exactly the same way, with the same gesture, once a day for 21 days.

Step 4: Use your memory trigger. After you've used your autosuggestion for 21 days, you're ready to try the gesture by itself, without any conscious attempt to say the mantra. You'll discover that a sense of power comes over you, assuring you that you will be able to listen very efficiently, process information, recall everything with ease, and use all the information effectively. You can make this gesture before a meeting, a round of negotiations, or any other situation where you need to recall information quickly and accurately.

Practice #5: The Great Mandala

A mandala is a wheel-like design developed in Asia. It represents the unity of life, but it's also a very effective memory aid. In my workshops, I usually bring in a set of mandalas and show them on an overhead projector. Practicing the technique I'm about to show you for just 2 minutes a day for 21 days in a row will do wonders for your concentration and focus. I recommend doing the practice every morning, either when you get up or when you start work, to begin your day in a focused, effective way. You can also use this 2-minute exercise whenever your concentration starts to fail. Instead of taking a coffee break, try a "mandala break"! Whatever other exercises you are also doing, I recommend starting your mandala practice as soon as possible and then incorporating it into your regular routine. It will pay off in lifelong benefits.

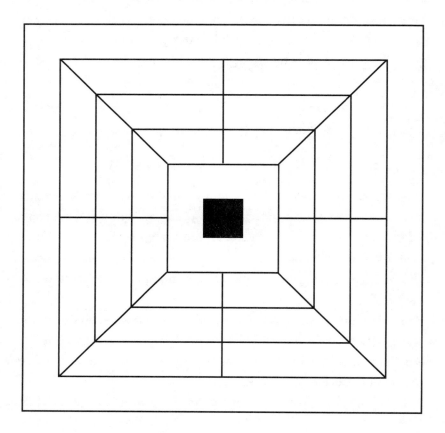

Step 1: Choose your mandala. You can find mandalas on the Internet (www.mandala.org is one good site) or look for them in a book, such as *Power Mandalas* by Klaus Holitzka. Once you grasp the concept, you can even make your own.

Step 2: Focus on the center of your mandala. By focusing on your mandala's center, you draw all your concentration in toward one point, excluding everything else. Practice this laserlike approach for 2 minutes, breathing deeply. Try to shut out all other thoughts. If a thought seeps in—as it does for most people—notice it and let it go.

Step 3: Notice the improvement. Within 21 days of working with a mandala at least once a day, you'll notice a significant increase in the span of your concentration. That's because failures of concentration generally occur when the eyes and mind are working separately. Your eyes and your mind are a team, and when they break up, your concentration goes awry. The mandala exercise reminds you to focus your eyes when you want to focus your brain.

KEEPING YOUR EYES AND MIND TOGETHER

As you've just seen, encouraging your eyes and mind to work together is one of the greatest aids to concentration you can employ. If your eyes are fixed on a speaker or client while your mind is worrying about your next appointment or your daughter's soccer game, you're going to lose concentration. Your goal is to bring your eyes and mind together to work as a team.

This eye-mind problem is usually easier to solve when you're reading, writing, or otherwise working by yourself. The practices I've offered in this chapter should help you increase the duration and intensity of your concentration during solo work.

What about when you're sitting in a meeting with colleagues, clients, supervisors, or employees, though? For many of us, that's when the trouble starts. We begin listening intently to whoever is speaking, but before we know it, our minds have gone off on their own recognizance, even if our faces are still set with attentive smiles.

There's a simple reason our minds go AWOL: Usually, when we're listening to another person speak, they just don't have enough to do. Typically, most people speak at about 150 to 200 words per minute, but

Make Breaks Pay Off

I think breaks are so important that I can't end this chapter without a few more suggestions for how to get the most from your break time. Here are some tips for making it more effective.

Go outside and run—or do something else that's physical. Even a minute or two of vigorous exercise can provide the glue that will help a memory attach itself to your mind. If you can't leave the office, consider running in place, doing a few jumping jacks, or trying some "deskercize"—isometric exercises that you can do behind your desk.

Sing a song. Okay, you'll want to keep your voice down unless your office comes equipped with a shower, but I'm perfectly serious. Singing employs a different part of the brain than speaking does (that's why stutterers can often sing perfectly even if they have difficulty speaking). Opening up another part of your brain will make the whole organ more effective.

Eat something healthy. You probably won't be surprised when I tell you that caffeine, sugar, and fat are no-nos when it comes to a healthy brain. On the other hand, eating a high-protein meal or snack before a business meeting or during a break is a terrific idea. If you're eating a meal that includes both protein and carbs, eat at least 20 percent of the protein first. That triggers the amino acid tyrosine, which energizes your brain. If you start with the carbs, you'll send some nice, relaxing tryptophan up to your gray matter, which may make it easier for you to nap but won't do much for your memory! Of course, since turkey is a protein that contains tryptophan, you should probably avoid it on occasions when you want to stay alert.

most of us tend to listen and think at 800 to 1,200 words per minute. As a result, when you're listening to somebody speak at a business meeting or conference, you're listening at only 20 percent of the speed of your thoughts. Naturally, your mind looks for something to take up the slack. At first, your brain is just filling in the gaps between the other person's words and your thoughts, but before you know it, your mind is busy elsewhere.

What's the answer? Use your eyes to help your mind stay focused.

Be sure your eyes move every few minutes. Giving yourself something new to look at encourages your brain to stay with your eyes and thus with you. If you're making a conscious effort to observe new and different details in the room, your concentration is likely to improve. Many people think that shifting visual focus may distract them, but in fact, looking at different items keeps you alert. Focusing on a single object can become almost hypnotic, and your mind soon begins to wander.

Keep your brain occupied with a related topic, not a distant one. Daydreaming about Jamaica or obsessing about your tax bill will pull your mind all the way out of your meeting. Wondering how this presentation would play in your Peoria office or whether your boss would be interested in the fascinating fact you just learned helps keep your mind on target. You're still having thoughts that go beyond the bounds of the conversation, but at least they're related to the topic.

Take notes if you like, but don't keep your eyes fixed on the page. Again, let your eyes wander a bit around the room, scanning different objects and noting various details in your environment. Otherwise, you may find yourself staring at the last word you wrote, off on a tangent, while the speaker has left you far, far behind.

If you can, take breaks. Often, of course, this isn't up to you. If your boss has called you in for a one-on-one, or if you're at a formal presentation, you can hardly excuse yourself for a bathroom break or a walk around the block. But at meetings and conferences where you can slip away for a few minutes, do so. The change of scenery will help you stay focused and alert—and the fresh air, if you can get it, will restimulate your tired brain.

THE POWER OF POSITIVE THINKING

My client Stanley was a soft-spoken man attending a two-day workshop I gave for midlevel managers at a Midwestern mail-order company. He said very little the first day, but I noticed him because he seemed so anxious and preoccupied. At the end of the second day, he came up to me and shook my hand, telling me, "You've taken a great load off my mind."

Stanley explained that his job involved reading numerous reports from his firm's many divisions and then coming up with company-wide policies designed to solve the problems that were being identified. "By the time I read the last report, I was always afraid that I'd completely forgotten what the first one said," he explained. "I felt like I was swimming in a sea of words and I was always about to drown. In fact, I worried so much, I couldn't even concentrate on what I was reading. I was just too worried about how much I was going to forget."

Then he smiled broadly. "Now that I'm not so worried, I'm able to pay much closer attention," he said happily. "And I can already see that by paying attention, I'll remember more. So you, Mr. Felberbaum, have just thrown me a lifesaver!"

I was happy to help—and I'm even happier to share his story with you. The moral is clear: The more you trust yourself, the better your brain will work. So relax, focus on the positive—and pay attention. You may be astonished by how much more you can remember.

CHAPTER 5

STEP 2: VISUALIZE

Jill was a sales associate at a New York City advertising firm that worked with a number of glossy women's magazines. When she began my workshop, she insisted that her memory was "hopeless, simply hopeless!" When we got to the section on visualization, she seemed even more discouraged. "I'm just not a visual person," she told the group. "That's why I'm on the sales side. I leave the visuals to the folks in creative."

Imagine Jill's delight when, after practicing the techniques she'd learned in my workshop, she found herself able to memorize huge chunks of visual information. She contacted me a few months later with a progress report. "Now I'm at the point where I can go into a meeting with a client and reel off the names of every magazine where their ads have appeared—along with the page number, the size of the ad, and all the other items on the page," she told me. "They're super-impressed—and it sure pays off in higher sales."

Brian was a salesman at a large Southwestern department store where I had been invited to give a morning workshop. Although he seemed a bit shy as the session began, he perked up as soon as I mentioned the concept of visualization. "I have always thought in pictures!" he exclaimed. "But I felt so foolish—I thought the smart people were the word people! Now I can trust the way my mind works naturally—I can't believe it!"

VISUALIZATION: A UNIVERSAL GIFT

Whenever I get to the visualization section of my workshop, I know I'm going to get two strong responses. There will be the participants who, like Brian, are thrilled to discover that one of their secret strengths is finally being recognized. Then there will be those who, like Jill, are certain that they're "just not visual people." "After all," people in this second group say to me, "that's why I have a job that focuses on words (or numbers, or interacting with people). *That's* what I'm good at—not that artistic stuff."

Well, I have news for both groups: Visualization is a basic attribute of the human brain. Everybody's brain. Unless we're blind or visually impaired, we all tend to rely on our sight more than the other four senses put together. If you have normal vision, more than 60 percent of your brain operates on a visual basis, and the channels connecting your brain and your eyes are 25 times more numerous than those that connect your brain and your ears. Whether you know it or not, you *are* a visual person. And when you learn to tap into the extraordinary power of visualization, you'll discover just how much you already rely on what you can see in your mind's eye.

In a moment, I'll show you what I mean, but first, let's start with a little quiz. I'm going to have you take the Visual IQ Test now, at the beginning of this chapter. Then you'll take it again when you've finished reading. Whether you think of yourself as highly visual, sort of eye-oriented, or someone who wouldn't know a visual image if it tripped you in the hallway, I'm willing to bet that your visual abilities will improve as you practice using the techniques I explain in this chapter. As a result, your memory will improve as well.

Exercise #1: The Visual IQ Test

Step 1. Find your favorite writing implement, or if you like, collect a few different kinds of pens, pencils, and markers. Set your timer for 3 minutes.

Step 2. Turn each of the circles below into a different image. You can either write directly in the book or photocopy the page. Draw whatever comes to mind: a smiley face, a clock, a coin, or whatever else you think of. The goal is to make each one as different as possible. Work rapidly, trying to complete each circle in 8 to 10 seconds.

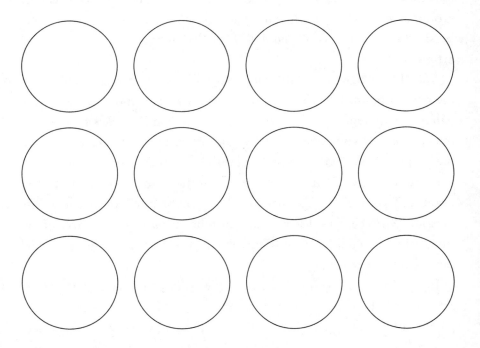

Step 3. When the timer goes off, stop working. Note how many you were able to complete. If you didn't fill in all 12, don't despair! Most people in my workshop can't do it—at first. You'll get another crack at this test when you've finished reading the chapter.

For bonus points: Take another few minutes to jot down what you learned about yourself and your visual abilities from this experience. Save your jottings—you may be surprised at how much your self-concept changes! Instead of thinking that you simply aren't very visual or imaginative, you may discover how rich and creative your mind truly is.

Visualizing the Past

What's your earliest memory?

Stop reading for a moment and think of the answer; don't start reading again until you have one. Let your mind sail back as far as it will go and see what you come up with. When you have your earliest memory firmly in your mind, read on.

When I ask about people's earliest memories in my workshops, I get a wonderful panoply of answers, from the birth of a brother or sister to an early birthday party to a first day at kindergarten. Invariably, the memories date back to the ages of 2 to 5. In fact, I've scored more than a few points with workshop participants by correctly predicting the time frame of their first memories. It's easy once you know that our ability to remember isn't completely formed until age 2 and that the power of our memories tends to grow for the next several years thereafter.

Once we've all shared our early memories, I ask the group what I'm going to ask you: "What happens when you remember? What goes on in your mind?"

Sometimes I get a range of emotional answers. "I feel bad," someone might say. Or "I remember being very excited." Or "I'm so happy just thinking about that day."

"All right," I say. "Those are the emotions you associate with your memories. But while you are remembering, what exactly is happening in your mind?"

"Oh," someone finally says, "I saw something. The memory is like a picture in my mind's eye."

Gradually, everyone comes to agree. In all the years I've been giving workshops, with all the thousands of participants, I've never had an exception. Everyone's earliest memory is a visual image. It might be a mini-movie or a blurry snapshot; it might be linked to other sense memories, like the heat of the sun or the smell of baking cake; it might be brightly colored or just a shadowy outline—but there is always some kind of mental picture involved.

Usually, this experience is enough to prove to my students that they are indeed visual people—and I hope I've convinced you as well. Every so often, though, I'll get an accountant or a salesclerk who insists, "No, I work with numbers," or "I work with people."

"I don't see pictures," this person continues. "I never visualize anything."

"All right," I reply. "Take a minute and think about Niagara Falls. Now—tell me what you thought." (What happens in *your* mind when you think about Niagara Falls? Take a moment to find out before reading on.)

In my workshops, the "nonvisual" people usually begin to describe an avalanche of water rushing down from tall cliffs. Maybe they mention a person going over the falls in a barrel, or perhaps they describe a honeymoon couple holding hands on the shore.

"All right," I say, "but was that in words or images? When you thought about Niagara Falls, did you think of words, or did you see mental pictures?"

"Oh!" comes the surprised answer. "I saw something!" That's usually the "aha!" moment. My students are surprised—but I'm not. As I said, we're all visual people. Some of us just don't know it yet.

Practice #1:
Extending Your Vision (Version 1)

Try this simple practice for 5 minutes a day for five days. At the end of that time, evaluate your progress. You should notice a definite improvement in your ability to visualize scenes, people, and situations in detail—and a corresponding boost in your ability to remember visually.

Preparation. Find a comfortable place to sit, somewhere you can count on not being interrupted. If you can, turn off your phone and allow your attention to turn inward. Take a few deep breaths, slowing your breathing to help you relax. Breathe in and then out on a count of 2, then 4, then 6, then 8. Then set your timer for 5 minutes and begin.

Day 1: School days. Choose a memory from your time in school. It doesn't matter which memory you select—in fact, it's best to let a memory leap spontaneously into your mind. Perhaps you remember the swings at your school playground, with their silvery metal frame and heavy chain links, or maybe you're thinking of the worn beige lockers lining the halls in your high school. Your memory may include people, objects, or special events, or it may simply be a visual scrap. When you've settled on a memory, bring your visual image into sharper focus. Notice the colors, textures, shapes, and angles. Direct your mind to home in on little details, such as the dull metal handles on the lockers, with the round holes in them, or the heavy leather seats of the swing. At this point, it doesn't matter whether you're remembering details or inventing them. The important thing is to allow your mental imagery to become as specific as possible.

Day 2: First home. Where was the first place you lived as a child? What visual images come to mind of that early home? Do you see the corner of the fuzzy blue blanket on your bed or perhaps the bright yellow curtains on the kitchen window? Maybe you remember the shiny white tiles around the bathtub or the worn spot on the linoleum floor of your big sister's room. Do you see someone from your family? Or maybe you see yourself, with a loved one or alone.

As on Day 1, allow your memories to become as clear, sharp, and detailed as you can.

Day 3: First job. When you hear "first job," what visual images spring to mind? Choose a mental picture and again, allow it to become more focused and detailed. Although you're thinking about work, try not to work hard now! Instead, relax into the memory, allowing your mind's eye to explore and play.

Day 4: Current job. Next, allow yourself to visualize a person, place, or object that you associate with your present job. This is likely to be something you have seen much more recently than the other images, so your mental picture will probably be even more specific and clear. Again, relax with the image, allowing rather than forcing it to come into focus.

Day 5: Your choice. Focus on any memory you choose. As always, allow your mental eye to zoom in on whatever interests you, discovering aspects of the scene that you may not have realized you noticed when you actually saw it. Maintain a relaxed, playful attitude about your mental viewing, allowing yourself to feel curious and discover new things.

How did you do? What kinds of changes did you notice in your experience as the week progressed? Did you start to become more comfortable with evoking visual images out of the past? Were you able to zero in on more detail? Did you remember things you thought you had forgotten?

To me, the most striking aspect of this exercise is how it helps us translate verbal information into visual images. This ability to go from the verbal to the visual is the heart of managing your memory. Because such large areas of our brains are keyed to the visual, it's far easier to recall something you saw than something that you heard or read. Thus, if you want to remember something your boss says to you, or information that you've read in a report, translate the key points into a mental picture. Then use the picture as a memory trigger to unlock your recall.

The more comfortable you become in translating information into visual images, the more quickly and easily you'll be able to access your memories. (In chapter 9, you'll even learn how to translate numbers into visual images.) In this chapter, we're going to focus on creating images. Here's another practice you can use to get your visual muscles in shape.

Practice #2: The Movie Drill

Try this simple exercise for 3 minutes a day two or three days a week. If you enjoy it, you may want to continue it indefinitely as a useful warmup for your mind's eye. It's also a good way to warm up for any situation in which you'll be called upon to absorb and remember large amounts of information, since this visual workout prepares your mind to create and retain still more images.

Preparation. Get one of those huge guides to movies and videos. Take your book to some private place—somewhere you won't be interrupted for at least a few minutes—and get comfortable.

Step 1. Begin to browse through your guide, pausing each time you come to the title of a movie you've seen.

Step 2. Take a moment to remember something visual about the movie. When you come to *The Godfather*, for example, you might remember the horse's head in the bed. For *Casablanca*, you may recall Rick standing in the fog at the airport.

Step 3. After you've had a mental picture of one movie, browse on to the next familiar title. Unlike the previous exercise, where you tried to develop extended, detailed memories, your goal here is to move quickly from one image to another, registering the first image that the name of the movie triggers in your mind.

What I like about the Movie Drill is how it brings home the power of your visual memory. Long after you've forgotten details of the plot or the names of the characters, you hold on to your mental images of the viewing experience. In the next few sections, you'll learn how you can consciously tap into that visual power, creating your own mental images to help you remember.

By the way, as your visual awareness improves, you may discover a striking side benefit. In my experience, when people begin sharpening their visualization skills, they also increase their ability to pay attention. They begin to observe the world around them more acutely, concentrating more easily on what they see. This synergy between paying attention and visualizing can lead to a dramatic increase in your memory.

Holding On to Memories

So far, we've focused on visualizing memories from the past, images that you stored long ago without even being aware of it. But visualization—and memory—can also be useful in the present, helping you cement words, names, thoughts, or plans in your mind so you can be sure of remembering them. Here's how it works.

Step 1: Identify something you'd like to remember. Let's say it's your sister's birthday, and you want to be sure to stop by the florist on the way home and pick up some flowers for when you join her tonight at her birthday dinner. Of course, you could write yourself a note, but what if you forget to look at it?

Step 2: Create a visual image that will stick in your memory. One obvious choice is to use a simple real-life image, such as opening the door of the florist's shop, or the florist handing you a huge sheaf of pink and purple lilies, or perhaps your sister smiling at you as she receives your gift. If you really like florists or flowers, or if you feel that your sister's response is unusually meaningful, that might work. For most of us, though, those images aren't so interesting—and therefore, not so memorable.

In that case, you may want to tweak the image a bit, making it more outrageous, funny, or just plain weird. Perhaps you see yourself holding an enormous bouquet of flowers like a handful of balloons, floating over the evening traffic on the way to your sister's house. Or maybe you see your sister's face at the center of every flower. Perhaps the flowers are growing up through the carpet in your sister's living room, surrounding her like jungle foliage. Your goal is simply to create an image that associates "sister" and "flowers" in an unusual way.

Step 3: As you visualize your image, say to yourself—silently or aloud—"Pick up flowers for Mindy after work." Your goal is to associate the visual and verbal messages. Of course, in this case, there's little doubt about what the image means, because getting flowers for your sister is an idea you've already mastered—you just need a little nudge. You'll be more dependent on the verbal/visual association when you apply this technique to situations in chapters 7 through 10, trying to memorize names, faces, numbers, and concepts that you don't already know. In that case, the visual image will act as a trigger for a more complicated piece of verbal information that may be a bit harder to retrieve. So start practicing the verbal/visual connection. It will pay off big time in preserving your memories.

Get More from Your Mind's Eye

Don't push. The fastest way to short-circuit a visual memory is to force it. Instead, encourage your mind to play freely, following its own natural curiosity. Think of the images you're seeking as shy, wild creatures. If you chase after them, they'll run away. If you become calm and receptive, you allow them to come to you.

Focus on details. Simply having the intention of bringing details into focus will encourage them to appear. Again, curiosity can help you here. If you allow yourself to wonder about details and specifics, your mind will supply them. In fact, your mind may even invent what it can't remember. This may be a problem if your main concern is accuracy, but since your focus now is simply to sharpen your visual abilities, don't worry about whether your memories are accurate. Just focus on making them detailed.

Relax. You'll do better—and remember more—if you're relaxed and open. Tension and anxiety tend to push memories away and interfere with visualization. A simple shift in breathing—slowly and deeply, from the diaphragm—can help put you in a relaxed, receptive frame of mind.

Practice #3:
The Pig with Wings (Version 1)

I recommend doing this exercise at times when you'd otherwise be bored—say, when someone has you on hold on the phone, when you're waiting in line, or perhaps when you're stuck in traffic. Use those "downtimes"—anywhere from 1 to 10 minutes—to exercise your brain, your mind's eye, and your creativity. You might even start looking forward to traffic jams! (P.S. Do try to play this game at least five times during the coming week.)

Preparation. Once again, try to relax. Slow your breathing from a 2-count inhale and a 2-count exhale down to 4, then 6, then 8. (If you're really frustrated with the traffic, work your way all the way down to 10 or 12.) This practice is all about creativity—and it's hard to be creative when you're tense.

Step 1. The goal here is to combine two things that ordinarily wouldn't belong together—hence its name, the Pig with Wings. Start by looking at some ordinary object within view. You might choose anything: the pen on your desk, the speedometer on your dashboard, an unlit elevator button, the corner cash machine. In fact, the more ordinary and familiar your object is, the better.

Step 2. Think of an item that doesn't belong with the one you're looking at. Animals are good (unless you're looking at an animal). Exotic flowers can be fun. Sloppy foods, glittering jewels, weird plants, some intimate item of clothing—you can choose anything as long as it wouldn't normally be associated with the original object. In other words, if you're looking at a pen, don't think of an envelope or even a checkbook. Think of a camel, a wedding cake, or a lace nightgown. Your goal is the most unlikely combination possible.

Step 3. Next, find a creative way to put the two objects together. Of course, you can be literal about it—placing the wedding cake on top of the cash machine or putting the pen in the camel's mouth—but push yourself to go further. Imagine a wedding cake with a cash dispenser as the second layer or visualize a camel whose tail is pen-shaped and with which you can write. The goal is to have fun playing with the images, so let your mind go. We remember the unusual far more easily than the ordinary, so the more unusual, unlikely, and just plain weird your image is, the more likely you are to remember it.

Step 4. At the end of the week, take a moment to jot down the images you've created. How many do you remember? How great a percentage do you think you recall of all the images you created?

Step 5. Take your evaluation a step further. As you look at your list of images, allow each one to come to mind. What other information does it carry? Can you remember where you were, what you were doing, or how you felt as you created it? Does your image inspire a second image, something you saw in real life as you were working on the visualization or a new thought that came into your mind? Does your image remind you of anything else? In the next chapter, we'll take a closer look at association, the process of linking memories or pieces of information, but you can see already that visualization and association are closely linked.

Practice #4:
The Pig with Wings (Version 2)

Try to alternate this version of the exercise with the first one as you move through your week, or spend a week on Version 1 and then devote a week to Version 2. Both approaches will give you good practice in creating memorable visual images—and both should remind you of the pleasure you can find in using your very creative mind!

Preparation. As always, try to relax, slowing your breathing from 2 counts in, 2 counts out, to 4, 6, 8, or longer, as you wish. By now, you should be getting really good at using your breathing to relax—a technique that will stand you in good stead throughout your career.

Step 1. Look at some ordinary object within view. Again, it may be an object on your desk, in your car, in the elevator, or somewhere you're waiting in line. You can also simply visualize an object in your mind's eye.

Step 2. Next, find some playful or fun way to distort the object. Expanding it to giant size or shrinking it to a tiny replica are obvious choices. You might also change the color, exaggerate a single feature, or add an unlikely feature (an elephant with a briefcase, a propeller on a pen, long blond hair on a cash machine). You're going for something weird and playful, so let your mind go.

Step 3. Find a word to associate with your distorted object—a word that wouldn't ordinarily belong. If you put a propeller on a pen, for instance, don't use *pen*—that's too close. But you could call it a "peneller." Likewise, using the word *money* for a cash machine isn't very interesting, but calling it glamorous—because of the long blond hair—might be a fun choice.

Step 4. Again, at week's end, take a moment to jot down a brief record of the images you've created. How many do you remember? Do you think you've forgotten any? Can you identify a reason why some images may be harder or easier to remember?

I have a memory like an elephant.
In fact, elephants often consult me.
—Noel Coward

Need a striking visual image? Picture an elephant consulting British playwright, songwriter, and performer Noel Coward about some important event in its elephantine life. Then imagine the elephant asking you about something you'd like to remember. Finally, when you want to remember the elusive fact, picture yourself sitting with the elephant and chatting about the information. The offbeat quality of that picture should help jog your memory—at least a little.

Step 5. Look once more at your list of images and see how many associated words or phrases you can recall.

If you practice each version of the Pig with Wings for a week, you should begin to notice an immediate improvement in your ability to create memorable images quickly and easily, almost without thinking about it. You'll also become used to linking images with words, phrases, and other information. Using an image to bring forth a word or phrase will be extremely useful to you when you start learning how to remember names and faces in chapter 7 and again when you start linking images to spoken words, numbers, and concepts in chapters 8, 9, and 10—so the more fluent you become in the language of images, the better. They are the basic language of memory.

FIVE-DIMENSIONAL MEMORIES: INVOLVING ALL YOUR SENSES

So far, we've been focusing on the visual, since that's the sense through which most business information comes. The other senses can also evoke powerful memories, as discovered by French novelist Marcel Proust. One day, Proust was biting into a madeleine, a small, sweet pastry. Suddenly, he was flooded with a series of memories connected to tasting this almond-flavored treat in his childhood. It seemed his aunt used to serve him madeleines, and the taste had the power to evoke many experiences related to his time with her. A three-volume novel was the result.

Most of us aren't likely to be so prolific, but we can call on our senses to enhance our recall. Here's an exercise that I actually adapted from the techniques developed by the great Russian director Konstantin Stanislavsky, who wanted to help actors recall and relive a wide variety of memories. Even if you're not planning to go on the stage, you'll find Stanislavsky's techniques helpful in a business setting.

Exercise #2:
Lemons in Five Dimensions

Preparation. For this exercise, you don't need access to actual lemons—in fact, you shouldn't be anywhere near a real lemon while you do it! You should, however, be in your usual private and comfortable place, somewhere you won't be interrupted for at least 5 minutes. As always, you should begin by taking a few slow, deep breaths to help you relax and clear your mind.

Step 1. Close your eyes and visualize a lemon. See yourself holding the small yellow fruit in your palm or between your hands. Feel the rough texture of its skin. Notice its shape as you hold it—the curve of the middle portion, the pointy part at the end. Drop it lightly on the table or floor and notice the sound it makes. Hold up the lemon and look at it, first up close, then at a distance. Notice every detail— the green streak on the rind; the little indentations; the warm, bright color. Hold it to your nose and smell the rind. Let the lemon fill your senses: sight, hearing, touch, and smell.

Step 2. Next, imagine cutting the lemon open. How do your senses respond? What do you see, hear, touch, and smell? Hold the imaginary lemon to your nose and breathe in its pungent aroma. Feel the juice running down your hands.

Step 3. Finally, taste the imaginary lemon. Drink a few drops of the juice or bite into the fruit. Continue to smell, see, and feel the lemon you are tasting.

Step 4. Open your eyes. Is your mouth watering? Have you managed to awaken your senses?

To me, one of the most interesting aspects of this exercise is the way it combines two types of visualization—drawing on memories you already have and creating an image that has never existed before. To imagine the lemon, you have to remember other experiences with citrus fruit. You also have to create an entirely new experience, not a lemon you've actually tasted but a lemon you can only imagine.

This combination of experience and invention will come in handy as you use visualization to both remember old information and grasp new concepts. One of the best ways to improve your memory is to link what you already know to something you've just learned. As you'll see in the next chapter, linking old and new information allows you to call up the new information simply by remembering the old. That's why people tend to pick familiar names for their computer passwords and to use familiar dates for their combination locks. The old information ("What's my wife's name?" "When was I born?") helps them recall the new ("What's my password?" "What's my combination?").

In technical terms, information such as your spouse's name and your birth date lives in your long-term automatic memory. You know this material so well, you can always remember it without effort. In fact, your memory for this information is so good that it doesn't even feel like "memory." It's simply something you know.

When you choose a password or set a combination, on the other hand, you are creating new information whose life begins in your short-term conscious memory. As you've seen, most of the data in that part of your brain tends to evaporate so you're not burdened with a lifetime catalog of meaningless names and useless numbers. Any data you want to keep must be moved into your long-term memory before it evaporates. One of the best ways to make the transfer is to link the new short-term information to something that's already in long-term storage—and one of the best ways to make that link is through your senses, which are already powerfully associated with memory. So take a leaf from Proust's book and begin to pay attention to your sensory experiences. Not only will your life be richer—your memory will improve.

Practice #5:
Extending Your Vision (Version 2)

Try this simple exercise for 5 minutes a day for five days. At the end of that time, evaluate your progress. How does combining your vision with your other senses further extend your ability to visualize?

Preparation. Find a comfortable place to sit where you can count on not being interrupted. If possible, turn off your phone so you are free to concentrate on the practice. Slow your breathing, set your timer for 5 minutes, and begin.

Day 1: School days. As you did in Version 1 of this practice, choose a memory from your time in school. As before, you can choose any memory you like, although it's best to let a memory burst spontaneously into your mind. Maybe this time you see the school playground, with its gravel-strewn dirt and challenging jungle gym. Or perhaps you're sitting at your desk, a sheet of clean white paper in front of you. As before, your memory may include people, objects, or special events, or it may be simply a visual scrap.

When you've settled on a memory, begin to call upon your other senses. Do you hear any sounds? What kind? How loud? Are they changing, such as voices rising and falling, or constant, such as the buzz of a machine or the ticking of a clock? What about smells? Can you smell the paint in your art room or the food in the lunchroom or the crisp new paper? What about physical sensations—are you warm? Cold? Are you holding anything in your hand? Perhaps you're wearing a scratchy sweater or a furry hat. Stay with the image you've chosen—just gently extend your senses into the image until your recall of the moment is as complete as you can make it.

Day 2: First home. Where was the first place you lived as a child? What visual images come to mind? Settle on an image and extend your hearing, smell, taste, and physical sensations until the image is as complete as possible.

Day 3: First job. When you hear "first job," what visual images spring to mind? Choose a mental picture and again, allow it to become more complete by bringing in the other four senses. Again, relax into the memory, allowing your sense memories to awaken.

Day 4: Current job. Next, allow yourself to visualize a scene that you associate with your present job. Most of us turn off our senses when we're at work, but try to turn yours on as you extend your image from the visual to the aural to the tactile, and then bring in smell and taste. Don't force anything; simply relax with the image.

Day 5: Your choice. Focus on any memory you choose. As always, start with a clear visual, then bring the other senses into awareness one at a time—hearing, touch, smell, and taste.

VISUALIZATION AND STORYTELLING: A POWERFUL COMBINATION

So far, your work with the five senses has focused on recalling images from your past. In a way, you've reproduced reality within your own brain, retrieving experiences that you've actually had.

Creating your own images is even more memorable than reproducing existing ones. Something about the active nature of the creative process, the extra effort required to invent rather than remember, seems to engage the mind more deeply and completely—and thus to produce results that you're more likely to remember.

Moreover, when you create a scene or image yourself, the entire scene is in some way "you." You feel a sense of ownership and responsibility, a sense of personal investment. You may have noticed this process when you've tried to remember a joke someone told you. If you've only heard the joke, and you simply try to reproduce what you've heard, you're in danger of forgetting the punch line. If you can relate that joke to yourself in some way, however, embellishing it with your own creative touches, you're far more likely to remember it. Making the joke your own cements it into your memory.

Recently, I worked with Howard, a young law student who found himself overwhelmed by the number of cases he was supposed to assimilate. "After a while, they all blend into one another," he complained. "How am I supposed to remember the difference between Smith *v.* Jones and Morgan *v.* Rogers and all the rest of them? I try to sit and study, but after a while, the words just blur."

I encouraged Howard to draw on his ability to visualize. I suggested that he create mini-movies for each case, casting them with his favorite actors or even with people from his own family. If he could visualize an angry Harrison Ford–like Jones knocking over Smith's mailbox, and Smith, a shy, retiring Matt Damon, finally losing his temper and deciding to sue, he would have a far more personal investment in the case—with a consequent boost in memory. Or if he pictured the hapless Morgan as his plump, cheerful Aunt Rita, slipping on a patch of ice outside the grocery store owned by a Rogers who was a dead ringer for his nasty eighth-grade teacher, he would find that his emotions, memories, and personal responses helped enhance his ability to remember.

Once Howard had created his mini-movies, he had to find a way to link the stories and images to the actual names in the case, a technique I'll share with you in chapter 7. The first step, though, was for Howard to become his own mini-movie director so he could bring his cases to life. Visualizing the cases as vivid stories in his mind's eye would make it much easier for him to remember each one. Here's a practice I developed to help him do just that.

Practice #6:
Make Your Own Mini-Movies

Give yourself 5 minutes a day three days a week to work on your movies. Start this exercise the week after you've finished Practices #1 through #4, when your visualization skills should be all warmed up. As with all the activities in this chapter, taking a playful, carefree attitude will get you further than bearing down and forcing a result. Remember, everything you need is right there within your mind. You only have to open up and allow it to emerge.

Preparation. Find a comfortable, private place and turn off your phone. If you have a list of storylike material that you're already working with—legal cases, business profiles, or even reports on how various divisions in your company have done over the past year—have them with you. Otherwise, just bring your imagination.

Step 1: Choose your material. Start with something short. Later, you'll be able to extend this technique to more complicated material, but for now, keep it as simple as you can. If you've got cases or case studies to work with, choose an easy one. If you don't have written material, think about some work-related information that you'd like to be able to remember. Maybe you wish you could recall more specific personal information about a client, such as what city she's from and what her hobbies are. Or perhaps you'd like to recall a set of market trends for a product your company sells, markets, or advertises. Whatever material you're using, write down as succinctly as you can the key points you want to remember, such as Morgan/Rogers/sued/slipped on ice/negligence, or Leandra Toothpaste/did well in Midwest/did poorly in Southeast/sales went up in 1994, down in 1999. It's fine if your list of key points is longer than these examples, but do try to zero in on the main ideas.

Step 2: Choose your main character. The simplest definition of a story is that it's an account of a person who tries to achieve a goal and encounters one or more obstacles on the way. That's the definition we're going to use here, so decide who your main character is. In a legal case, it will usually be the person bringing suit. In a case study or market report, the main character will probably be the business or product. You can even invent a more abstract character, such as "Consumer Confidence" or "Print Advertising Sales."

Step 3: Make your main character come alive. Whatever character you've chosen, visualize him, her, or it as a person. (See how your visualization skills are coming into play?) If you like, picture a person from your own life, such as Uncle Nathan or your first girlfriend. Or cast your character as the appropriate movie star, rock star, newscaster, or other celebrity. Some people prefer to simply create a character from scratch, imagining a personality, physical features, and a whole way of being. Whatever your preference, make sure you can clearly visualize the person you've chosen.

Step 4: Choose your character's goal. For your story to take off, your character needs to actively pursue something, even if it's something simple. Morgan may merely want to reach the store as she slips on Rogers's ice. Leandra Toothpaste probably wishes to be the most popular toothpaste in the world. Consumer Confidence may want to feel—well, confident. Print Advertising Sales may want to grow to giant size.

Step 5: Identify your character's obstacle(s). Overcoming one or more obstacles is the heart of a story. Morgan, for example, wanted to go to the store, but then she encountered the obstacle of Rogers's ice and broke her leg. Leandra Toothpaste was on her way to popularity when a smarter, prettier toothpaste started stealing all her customers. Consumer Confidence kept hearing reports of an oncoming depression that scared him so badly that he was afraid to leave the house, let alone buy anything. And Print Advertising Sales was growing nicely when an opponent called Video Marketing began cutting him down to size.

Step 6: Visualize your story. Now that you have your character, goal, and obstacles in place, review the main points you want to remember, visualizing each one in terms of your story. Think of yourself as creating a mini-movie in which each point is a scene. Watch what happens to your characters. Key in to what they want. Visualize how they behave and react. See how their opponents treat them. Find out how the story ends.

Step 7: Review your story. If you want to remember a story, it helps to tell it over and over again (as anyone who's ever read bedtime stories to children can assure you!). Once you have the basic outlines of your story in shape, replay the movie a few times, seeing the images as you tell yourself the words. Remember, the association of words and images is one of the most powerful memory devices there is, so hear yourself telling the story (aloud or in your mind) as you see the characters moving from scene to scene. The more detailed, visual, and specific your images are, the more memorable they'll be. Likewise, the crazier, more outrageous, and more personal they are, the more easily you'll remember them.

Step 8: Revisit your story. Try out your technique. Come back to your movie two or three days after you've created it and try to recall it. Visualize your characters moving through their story as you hear yourself retelling it. (You're likely to find that the visual images help trigger the verbal part of the story.)

Step 9: Evaluate the process. Do you notice any aspects of your moviemaking that you might do differently the next time? Would you make your stories simpler? More complex? Would you choose more familiar characters or wackier, more outrageous ones? Can you add humor, suspense, or disaster to your stories? (Hollywood filmmakers know that these elements usually make for memorable movies!) As you practice this technique, you'll find yourself getting better and better at it—and your memory will improve accordingly.

Howard was thrilled with the way this technique boosted his ability to connect personally with each of the hundreds of cases he had to remember. "Once I know a case is important, I can look it up and find the specific details," he told me. "But I needed something to remind me of which case was which so I'd have some sense of how to tell them all apart. This technique took a blur of cases and made each one distinct. And it made studying a heck of a lot more fun!"

HOLDING ON TO HOLOGRAMS

One of the reasons visualization is so effective is that images operate like holograms. A hologram is created when two laser beams intersect on a photographic plate, producing an image, but a holographic image is unusual in that it is, literally, holistic. Any portion of the plate, even when shattered into a hundred pieces, contains the entire image.

Likewise, a visual image in your mind operates like a hologram. As you've seen throughout the exercises and practices in this chapter, one simple visual image can recall a wealth of sensory detail, powerful emotions, information about where and when you saw the image, and a host of other associations. When visual images are linked to verbal messages, the words become part of the image, too, holographically appearing each time the visual is "reseen" by the mind. When visual images coalesce into an entire story—especially a story that has somehow been personalized, exaggerated, or otherwise invested with strong feeling—one little image can carry a whole plateful of information.

Visual images are compact and rich in information. They enable your memory to work "smarter, not harder." If you've found a way to link visuals with other data, you'll never have to struggle to remember a whole list of facts. Instead, you can simply call up a visual image and find that the facts you seek come with it automatically.

I'm going to leave you with one final practice, a way in which visuals can help you ground abstract ideas within concrete, visual symbols—symbols that you'll find much easier to remember than the abstractions with which you began. Whenever I give this exercise to people in my workshops, they are always struck—as am I—by the power of visual information.

Practice #7: Create Icons

Give yourself 3 minutes a day three days a week to create your icons. Start this exercise the week after you've finished Practices #1 through #4, when your visualization skills should be at their peak. And don't forget to have fun!

Preparation. Find a private place with a comfortable desk. Gather a few clean sheets of paper and your favorite pen. If you like, gather several different types of pens, pencils, and markers in different colors. Keep your timer nearby.

Step 1: Review this list. As you read each of the following words, visualize it. Perhaps for *communication*, you see people talking to one another, while for *negotiation*, you see people sitting on opposite sides of a big table. Don't struggle; just allow the images to float into your mind.

Communication
Negotiation
Liaison
Proposal
Target
Sale
Risk
Influence
Performance
Strategy

Step 2: Create 10 icons. On a clean sheet of paper, doodle an icon—a little symbol—to represent each word. Don't recopy the word, just create a visual symbol. For *strategy*, for example, I once had a student who drew a little chessboard. For *communication*, I saw someone draw two little faces in profile, with arrows going back and forth between them. It doesn't matter what the icon is as long as it's yours.

Step 3: Take a break. That's right. Set your timer for 10 minutes and do something else. Put the list of words and the page of icons out of sight and clear your mind. You can read, send a few e-mails, or whatever else you like. If you'd like to take longer than 10 minutes, feel free.

Step 4: Review your icons. Now that your break is over, how many words do you remember? Without looking at the list, write the words near the icons and check them against the list.

Step 5: Continue the process. Choose another 10 words and repeat the process another day this week, then pick yet another set of words and repeat the process once more. You can choose terms or phrases that are significant in your business, concepts that you want to memorize, or key points from an article or document that you'd like to recall.

The first time I do this exercise in my workshops, virtually everyone gets 100 percent, simply because everybody created the visual memories themselves. This is the same process that you'll use in chapter 10 to convert complex business concepts into visual icons that your brain will happily store and return to you at a moment's notice.

VISUALIZATION: A POWERFUL TOOL

You've been practicing visualization techniques for quite a while, and you've had the chance to use visualization in a number of different settings. Now it's time to see how far you've come by taking the Visual IQ Test once again. I think you'll be pleasantly surprised!

Exercise #3: The Visual IQ Test

Step 1. Find your favorite writing implement, or if you like, collect a few different kinds of pens, pencils, and markers. Set your timer for 3 minutes.

Step 2. Turn each of the following circles into a different image. You can either write directly in the book or photocopy the page. Draw whatever comes to mind: a smiley face, a clock, a coin, or whatever else you think of. The goal is to make each one as different as possible. Work rapidly, trying to complete each circle in 8 to 10 seconds.

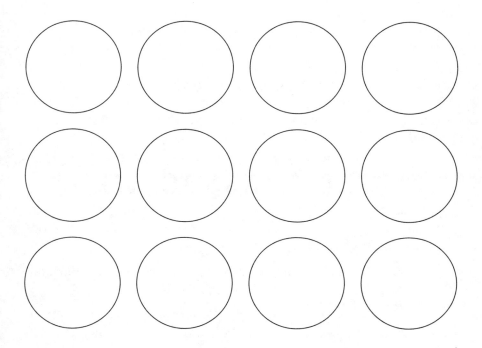

Step 3. When the timer goes off, stop working. Note how many you were able to complete. How does your score today compare with your first try?

For bonus points: Take another few minutes to jot down what you learned about yourself and your visual abilities from this experience. Compare your notes with your first set of jottings. Do you see yourself differently now? How?

Now that you've completed the chapter on visualization, I'm going to let you in on a little secret: There's a way to make this skill even more powerful. If you combine the visualization you practiced in this chapter with the association skills you'll learn in the next chapter, you'll have an extraordinary combination at your disposal. Each skill separately, I've learned, is extremely powerful—but together, they almost take on a life of their own. When you've mastered each one and learned to combine them, your memory will be virtually unbeatable.

CHAPTER 6

STEP 3: ASSOCIATE

Isabel ran the human resources department at a major midwestern company. When she took my workshop, I was struck by what a positive, optimistic person she seemed to be. As far as Isabel was concerned, there was no problem that couldn't be solved—except one. Almost tearfully, she took me aside during the first break at our workshop and confessed that she just couldn't remember anything. "I have a mind like a sieve," she told me. "I protect myself by writing everything down, but I'm always afraid that one day, I'll let something really important just slip through the cracks."

Yet when Isabel learned about the principle of association—improving your memory by learning how to link different kinds of information—she experienced a dramatic increase in her ability to remember. As she continued to practice the exercises I had taught her, her memory—and her confidence—continued to improve. Isabel's experience was the perfect example of a principle I try to teach every one of my students: Mental activity is something that every single one of us can get better at. It just takes practice.

ASSOCIATION: MAKING MENTAL CONNECTIONS

Isabel had a common problem—the sense of being overwhelmed by detail. With what seemed like a million little isolated bits of information, she felt as though she couldn't remember anything. Worse, she was never quite sure how much she was failing to remember, whether she had omitted a few minor details or several major obligations.

What she didn't realize at first was that it's virtually impossible to remember isolated facts, but it's the easiest thing in the world to remember information that means something. The key to making memories is making meaning—and this chapter will tell you how.

First, though, I'd like to show you how the process of association works and how individual the process is. No one in the world makes the same connections that you do. Drawing on the personal quality of your memories and the unique way you link one fact, scene, name, or image to another will give your memory an extra boost of power.

I learned the following process from the remarkable Tony Buzan, Memory Olympics coach, chairman of the Brain Foundation, specialist on the brain, and creator of the World Memory Championships. He uses it to prepare people for a technique he calls Mind Mapping, a term he has actually trademarked.

Exercise #1: The Mind Map

Preparation. Ideally, you'd do this exercise with several other people, but one friend or family member will do. See if you can find someone who's willing to share 5 minutes to help you complete the exercise. When you get together, give each person who's participating a clean sheet of paper and something to write with.

Step 1. Have everyone turn their paper sideways—so that it's wider than it is tall—and draw a circle in the center. In the middle of the circle, have everyone write the word *business*.

Step 2. Set the timer for 3 minutes as each of you maps out your associations to the word you've written. Each time anyone thinks of a word that relates to business, he should draw a line from the circle, like a ray from the sun, and write the new word on the line.

Step 3. If any word you write sets off a new chain of associations, write them down on a separate line extending from the new word. The word *business*, for example, might trigger the word *profit*, which in turn might inspire the word *loss*. Let your chain of associations flow.

Step 4. Don't look at each other's work—this is supposed to be a personal process. Don't stop to censor your thoughts or judge your associations. Simply keep adding as many words as you can until the timer goes off.

Step 5. When the timer goes off, stop working. Count how many words you have in all and ask your fellow mind mapper(s) to do the same. Record your total.

Step 6. Next comes the interesting part. Compare your associations with your partner's or those of fellow players. How many words are the same?

When I do this exercise in my workshop, I match people up in pairs and ask them to tell me their total number of words—usually somewhere between 40 and 80. Then I ask them to compare answers, just as I've done with you, so they can tell me how many of their words match.

When I first started doing this work, the answer surprised me, but not any more. Typically, the partners discover only 1 or 2 matching words, although sometimes they get as many as 3 and *very* occasionally, 4 or 5. Often, not a single word matches. When I have an unusually large workshop, and I put people in teams of three, the results are comparable: Although the three teammates are likely to have at least 100 words among them, typically, fewer than 5 will match.

I find this absolutely remarkable. Most often, the partners or teams are colleagues in the same company, maybe even the same department. They live in the same city, socialize with the same people, and share a common culture. Perhaps they are close friends, husband and wife, or even siblings who grew up together. Yet however close they think they are, each one's mind is different. Each has developed a unique mental world in which everything is connected in a different way. That is the power of association: an entire universe of individual connections, there in the privacy of your brain. Thanks to Tony Buzan, I have developed a new respect for the uniqueness of every human mind—even my own!

Becoming Conscious of Your Associations

Association is something that we all do automatically, all the time. When we learn that a colleague's office is on the 7th floor, for example, we might say, "Oh, seven is a lucky number!" Or when we meet a customer named Bob, we might think, "That's my son's name, too." We associate the new information (a colleague's location, a customer's name) with the old information (the luckiness of seven, our son's name), and because of its associations, we may find the new information easier to remember.

This is how the process works when it's unconscious and automatic— but if you make it conscious and purposeful, deliberately associating new information with old, you can maximize your memory. Association is so powerful, in fact, that just associating two types of information, even if they're both new, can make both items easier to remember. Here's an exercise I do in my workshops to drive home that point.

Exercise #2:
The Task-Location Hookup

Preparation. Get a clean sheet of paper and something to write with. Give yourself about 5 minutes to complete this exercise.

Step 1. Read through the list below. With each item, visualize yourself doing the task just as I describe it. Don't linger on any one item, but give yourself enough time to see yourself doing it. Be sure to include in your visualization the places and circumstances that I describe.

1. Read the newspaper. Afterward, put the paper on the dining room table.

2. Make a call on your cell phone while you're in a department store, then leave your phone on a sales counter.

3. Take some vitamins. Afterward, put them on the nightstand by your bed.

4. Choose a birthday gift for someone you love. Wrap it up, put a card with it, and place it on your bookcase.

5. Write a letter to a business associate. Put it in an envelope, stamp it, and put it in your bag or briefcase.

6. Buy some movie tickets online and print out the confirmation page. Put the page by the door so you'll take it with you when you leave the house.

7. Pick up the photos from your vacation, then put them in your photo album.

8. Renew your subscription to *Business Week*. File the invoice with the rest of your paid bills.

9. Purchase a new computer. Put it on your desk and get it ready to use.

10. Complete your tax returns, and don't forget to mail them! Be sure you put them in a mailbox before the deadline.

Step 2. Next, take a blank piece of paper and, without looking at the list in Step 1, complete the following quiz. If I give you the task, you tell me the location; if I give you the location, you fill in the task.

1. Task: Read the newspaper.
Location: _____

2. Task: Make a call on your cell phone.
Location: _____

3. Task: _____
Location: The nightstand by your bed.

4. Task: _____
Location: On your bookcase.

5. Task: Write a letter to a business associate, put it in an envelope, and stamp it.
Location: _____

6. Task: _____
Location: By the door.

7. Task: Pick up the photos from your vacation.
Location: _____

8. Task: _____
Location: The place where you file your bills.

9. Task: _____
Location: Your desk.

10. Task: _____
Location: A mailbox.

How'd you do? When I give this exercise in my workshop, most of the participants score 90 percent, and some score 100 percent. That's how well they do without even using a system. Just the skills of *paying attention* to what I said (or wrote), *visualizing* the task, and *associating* the task with a location are enough to create a substantial increase in memory power.

I have one more example to show you the power of association. When I first read about this exercise in *The Memory Workbook* by Douglas Mason, Psy.D., and Michael J. Kohn, Psy.D., it concerned the John F. Kennedy assassination, but I've adapted it to a more modern tragedy.

Exercise #3: Calling Up a Memory

Preparation. This exercise will only take 2 or 3 minutes, and you don't even need to use a timer. Just find a comfortable place where you will be free of interruptions for a few moments. Have a piece of paper and a writing instrument available.

Step 1. Read through the following phrases. Don't try to do anything special; just read the words and allow your mind to do whatever it would naturally do.

Two towers. . . Plane crash. . . 2001 . . . New York City . . . Terrorism . . . World Trade Center . . . Osama bin Laden. . .

Step 2. Without stopping to think, jot down the first few words and phrases that come to mind.

Step 3. If you like, take a few more minutes and write down other memories associated with the words you've just read.

When you came to the second step, did you find yourself writing—or thinking— "9/11"? If so, you've had a powerful experience with the process of association. The various elements of the tragedy on that day are so closely linked that it's virtually impossible to think of any one of them without thinking of all the others.

In the last step, you had the chance to recover some of the other memories that may be associated with that awful day. You probably had strong visual images of where you were when you heard about the disaster, how you felt, and a whole host of other facts, feelings, and associations. That's because all these different pieces of information—from the personal to the nationally known—are inextricably linked in your mind.

Again, that's what happens when the process of association is unconscious and automatic. As you can see, even then, association is pretty powerful! When you learn how to make the process conscious—as you'll do in the rest of this chapter—your memory will benefit enormously.

STRENGTH THROUGH STORYTELLING

As you saw in the previous chapter, stories are powerful memory aids. You also saw that part of their power comes from visualization. Stories help us picture actions, events, people, and places, turning words into the images that our brains are geared to recall.

A story's power comes from association as well. It connects people, actions, and events, forming a deep and indelible association between, say, Snow White and the Wicked Queen, or Darth Vader and Luke Skywalker. Those characters are forever associated in our minds because of the power of the story within which they live. Simply saying the name of each story—*Snow White* or *Star Wars*—brings up a whole host of associations. When you read the words *Snow White*, you probably think automatically of seven dwarfs, shiny red apples, and handsome princes. Reading the words *Star Wars* conjures up images of wookies and androids, the interiors of spaceships, and the vast deserts where Luke first met Obi-Wan. Look at how many associations are inextricably linked to just two words! That's the power of stories.

Sometimes, though, I have a hard time convincing some of my students that stories are serious business tools that can actually make a significant difference in their work lives. My client Ferris, for example, was pretty skeptical at first.

"Look, I'm a lawyer," he told me impatiently. "I help people solve their problems. I don't see why you're having me waste time learning about stories."

I thought for a moment. "When something important happens to you—either good or bad—what do you always have to do?" I asked him.

"I tell my wife," he answered promptly.

"All right. And how do you tell her? Give me an example. Think of the last big contract you landed. How did you tell your wife about it?"

Ferris looked more skeptical than ever, but he had hired me, and I suppose he figured he might as well get his money's worth. At my urging, he picked up the phone and pretended to be making a call. "Hey, honey," he said, a bit awkwardly. "You'll never guess what just happened. This guy came into my office without even an appointment; my secretary was at lunch, and I was here alone, so I had to at least talk to him. At first, I thought he was just wasting my time—he had question after question like you wouldn't believe. So finally I said, 'Look, I'll be happy to help you, but I've got work to do,' and the next thing I knew, he was signing me up for a major deal. I think he liked it that I dealt with him directly, didn't make him go through a secretary, that kind of thing. He says if this deal works out, there's plenty more where that came from."

"You see," I told Ferris. "You just told your wife a story, and I bet she remembered the incident almost as well as you did, because it was in story form. If you had just given her the bare facts—new client/contract/very direct/big deal—she wouldn't have remembered it nearly as well."

Ferris was skill skeptical until I pointed out to him that many of the legal cases he worked with could be translated into stories. I told him about Howard, the law student you met in the last chapter, and how turning his cases into mini-movies had helped him remember the plethora of cases he had to assimilate. By this time, Howard had graduated from law school and was working as an associate in a large firm. Much of his work consisted of doing legal research for the partners, and he had recently called and told me how grateful he was for my memory training. As I explained to Ferris, Howard found that stories were much easier to recall than any other type of information. Putting important information into a story was a surefire way to make sure he wouldn't forget it.

Reluctantly, Ferris agreed to try the Make Your Own Mini-Movies practice that you read in the previous chapter. He promised to spend 5 minutes a day three days a week creating little movies for himself, turning the information into stories, then visualizing the stories and retelling them to himself.

To Ferris's amazement, every case and client history that he turned into a story stuck with him, and he found himself able to refer effortlessly to details in his clients' pasts that he previously would have had to keep looking up. His clients were quite impressed—and so was he.

If you like, turn back to the previous chapter and review Practice #6: Make Your Own Mini-Movies. When you've refreshed your memory, move on to the new exercise I've included here.

Practice #1: Connecting and Creating

Give yourself 5 minutes a day three days a week to practice this technique. Start this exercise the week after you've finished Practice #6 in the previous chapter.

Preparation. Find a comfortable, private place and turn off your phone. Although your goal is eventually to make up stories quickly and effortlessly in your normal working conditions, you're still learning this technique, so give yourself the advantage of privacy and quiet.

Step 1: Warmup (part 1). Look at the following list of words. Work your way across each set of words or phrases, visualizing the first and third term on each line. Then, as quickly and automatically as you can, supply the second word or phrase, something that links the other two. Although there are no right answers—the goal is to develop your own associations—I've completed the first two just to get you started.

Computer	Paper	Printer
Window	Rug	Wall
Money	_____	Pocket
Law	_____	Rule book
Conference	_____	Speaker
Contract	_____	Customer
Coffee break	_____	End of day
Client	_____	Presentation
Report	_____	Cover
Supplies	_____	Equipment

Step 2: Warmup (part 2). Repeat the process with the next list of words. This time, the missing term may not be so obvious, so encourage your imagination to stretch and take chances. While Step 1 encouraged you to make literal and ordinary connections, use Step 2 to make weirder, more outrageous, and more personal associations. For example, if I gave you *umbrella* and *elephant*, perhaps you'd find yourself choosing *pelican* as the middle term. Although perhaps no one else in the world would understand that particular train of thought, you have just pictured a pelican with an umbrella in its beak, settling on an elephant's back and trying ineffectually to keep the huge animal dry. As when you were creating unusual visual images, your goal is to give your mind free rein to supply playful, humorous, and unique combinations.

Briefcase	_____	Piccolo
Palm pilot	_____	Monkey
Cell phone	_____	Martian
Stock market	_____	Swamp
Pie chart	_____	Bananas
PowerPoint	_____	Fire alarm

Keyboard	_____	Laundry
Law book	_____	Bicycle
Videotape	_____	Palm tree
Photocopier	_____	Volcano

Step 3: Create your connections. Choose a few facts that you'd like to remember. It may be some information about a client, data about a company, the names of three legal cases, or any other pieces of information that you want to keep together in your mind. Write each bit of information in a line across the page, just as the words were organized in Steps 1 and 2. Then find a way to link the facts.

Step 4: Add a dash of creativity. You'll remember even an ordinary story more readily than a collection of isolated facts. Here, though, your goal is to turn your run-of-the-mill story into as unusual a tale as you can, because that's the story you're most likely to remember. For example, if you want to recall that your client Sam Ellison enjoys golf, has three children, and takes vacations in the Bahamas, you could simply create a visual image of Sam playing golf in the Bahamas while three children carry the golf bag and chase after the balls. But I encourage you to go for something more playful and memorable.

Perhaps Sam starts playing golf on the roof of his company building (which gives you yet another association, since you can imagine the company name on a big sign flashing in the background). He swings his club so hard, the force of his drive carries him over the ocean to the Bahamas, where one by one, three children emerge from the holes on the course, their heads popping out like gophers. Odd? Yes. Bizarre? Certainly. But which image are you more likely to remember? When you have invested your own energy and creativity in a story that draws on your own associations, you'll be even more able to recall the links you've made.

Step 5: Improve your technique. Repeat Steps 3 and 4 as often as you like. As you return to this exercise throughout the week, feel free to skip straight to those steps. When you're ready, skip Step 3 and go straight to Step 4. See if you can work both more playfully and more quickly. Your goal is to make up outrageous, funny, and personal stories at the drop of a hat so you can link any information you choose.

Step 6: Expand your technique. When you feel you've mastered Steps 1 through 5, try creating stories with more pieces of information. Instead of 3 or 4, see if you can link 5, 6, 10, 12, or even 20 bits of data in a complicated but memorable story.

I hope you're starting to see how powerful story making can be, particularly when it combines the power of both visualization and association. I hope you see as well that you've got lots of choices for making stories, from the more elaborate visual mini-movies that you created in chapter 5 to the simpler stories you just came up with in this chapter. Now you can choose an approach that suits the kind of information you're seeking to recall. If you need to remember a legal case, a history or case study, a process, or an event involving several people, you may want to take the mini-movie approach. If you have a few pieces of information that can all be organized around a central person, company, or theme, you may prefer the simpler approach presented in this chapter. Or perhaps you'll come up with your own combination or some new variation that suits the way your mind works. Two things, though, are certain: Your associations will be unique to you, and your story making will vastly improve your memory.

YOUR PATTERN-MAKING BRAIN

Part of the reason association is so effective is that your brain loves making patterns. It thinks in patterns, sees in patterns, and of course, remembers in patterns. Association is the process of creating a pattern, so when you're trying to remember something, you can use association to consciously create a pattern to evoke that particular piece of information.

So far, I've talked about using association to ensure that you can remember information that matters to you. You create a pattern, story, or emotional association that will guarantee your recall of the data you're concerned about. You can also use association to retrieve an apparently long-forgotten fact simply by calling upon as much information as possible that's connected to your lost data. Here's how it works.

Practice #2: The Memory Circle

Use this practice whenever you want to bring forth an elusive fact, such as the name of a person you once met at a conference, the title of a report you need, or a particular legal case you've read about but whose title you cannot recall. Practice using it for 5 minutes a day three times a week so that when you really need to find a lost piece of information, you'll be proficient.

Preparation. For this activity, it's extremely helpful to relax. Information is more likely to float into your mind when you allow it to enter rather than try to chase it down. Slow your breathing from a 2-count inhale and a 2-count exhale down to 4, then 6, then 8, 10, and 12. Then take a clean sheet of paper and your favorite writing implement and begin. (No timer for this one. Take as long as you like!)

Step 1. Draw a circle in the center of the page. Leave the circle blank; that's the fact you want to fill in—the mystery guest, so to speak. Below the circle, jot down a brief label, such as "The name of the person I met at the marketing conference."

Step 2. Begin to recover all the associations to this missing fact that you possibly can. Just as when you practiced Mind Mapping in Exercise #1, draw rays out from the circle in the center, labeling each ray with an association: *I met her on a break . . . She was standing* *with George Rodriguez...She was wearing something blue, maybe with gold jewelry?...It was at least five years ago...I was wearing a brown jacket...We talked about the weather in Miami. . .* Any piece of information, no matter how trivial, may be linked to the elusive fact that you're seeking, so continue to allow every detail to emerge in your mind.

Step 3. If you're having trouble dredging up information, or if the associations you're discovering aren't working, try asking yourself questions: "Where did we meet?" "How did we meet?" "Why did we meet?" "What was the purpose of the conference?" "What was I wearing?" "What did we talk about?" "Who else was involved in this meeting?" Keep going until you've asked at least 20 or 30 questions.

Ideally, you'll be successful with the Memory Circle and discover the fact you sought. If you can't find it by searching through your associations, though, you'll almost certainly never be able to remember it, so if you come up empty, take heart. At least now you know you've done everything humanly possible to recover the lost data.

THE IMPORTANCE OF CUES

As you've just seen, it's far more difficult to recover a piece of information when you don't know which trigger might bring up the elusive fact you seek. When your memory operates unconsciously—when you just happen to remember something without consciously deciding to do so—you probably don't know which cue is going to bring it back into your mind. When you consciously encode something, however, you're far more likely to remember it because you're laying down a set of cues. When you want to recover the data you've stored, all you have to do is use the right cue, and presto! You've got the fact you were looking for.

Practice #3: Creating Cues

Practice creating cues for 5 minutes a day five days a week, after the week you spent mastering Practices #1 and #2. When we get to the next four chapters, you'll learn specific techniques for mastering four different types of information: people, spoken, numerical, and written. For now, though, just practice creating your own special cues, drawing on your unique set of associations.

Preparation. For this activity, too, relaxation will help. You want your mind to play freely, selecting and using cues easily and lightly. Forcing your mind to work hard is a bit like working hard on the dance floor—it will only make you stumble, and it won't even help you dance faster! You'll master this activity most quickly and fully if you approach it in a spirit of fun.

Step 1: Set your objective. Read through the following list.

A client's name

A legal case

A medical fact

A statistic

An address or phone number

An important fact about a client

An important but difficult-to-remember concept in your field or a related field

A task you must complete tomorrow

A task you must complete later in the week

A task you must do regularly but often forget

A location that is important to you

A fact you often forget but would prefer to remember

Choose an item from the list that you'd like to work with, or create your own category. Write the item at the center of a piece of paper. This is the item you'll be seeking to remember.

Step 2: Choose your cue. Think of a cue you can use to remember the elusive item. Association is an extremely powerful way of linking old information to new, so if you're trying to remember, say, a new name, you might come up with a play on words that involves a familiar name. For example, if you were trying to recall the name *Arnold Prince*, you might choose as a cue the name *Arnold Schwarzenegger*. Or you might play on the sound of the words involved. For example, if you were trying to remember that tomorrow you have to make lunch reservations for an important client, you might choose as a cue the phrase *I have some reservations about this deal!* If you're having trouble thinking of an association with the fact you've chosen, take a look at the types of associations listed earlier in the chapter.

Step 3: Extend your cue. Now elaborate on your cue to extend its association with the fact you want to remember. For *Arnold Prince*, for example, you might say "That Arnold Schwarzenegger is a real prince of a fellow!" For your lunch plans, you might say, "I have some reservations about this deal—and I'd like to have them at Abingdon Square Café!" Feel free to come up with more outrageous and playful associations— just make sure that your cues include all the information you need.

Step 4: Add visuals to your cue. As we've seen, the combination of visualization and association makes both activities even more powerful, so add a few visual images to your cue. When you say, "That Arnold Schwarzenegger is a prince of a fellow," see your client with huge Arnold-like muscles, wearing a prince's crown. When you think about your reservations, see *reservations* as some kind of tempting lunchtime fare, such as oysters or French fries, and picture yourself eating them. Even very simple cues will work, but as always, the wilder and more creative, the better.

Step 5: Practice using your cue. Say your cue to yourself a few times—aloud if possible—while visualizing first the image you've chosen, then the information you're trying to evoke. Here's where you link the cue and the important information, associating them in your mind as closely as possible.

Step 6: Test yourself. The next day and, if possible, the next week, try to recall the information you've encoded, using your cue. How did the process work for you? How would you change it the next time? Keep trying out the process until you've developed your own special cuing system. (You'll learn still more about various types of cues in chapters 7, 8, 9, and 10.)

THE MEMORY PALACE

One of the most colorful memory aids ever created is the so-called Memory Palace, also known as the Roman Room. This system was developed some 2,000 years ago by an ancient Greek poet known as Simonides. According to legend, the poet once gathered with his friends and relatives for a drinking party at a famous palace. By chance, he left the celebration just as the palace collapsed. Suddenly, all the guests at the party were crushed to death, unrecognizable even to their own families. Simonides, however, remembered where everyone at the party stood or sat, so he could identify each body. By his effective connection of place with identity, he demonstrated the power of location.

I draw a simple conclusion from this moving story: If you want to remember something, connect it with a particular place. Locations are visual images, drawing on the power of visualization. They're also spatial, drawing on our kinesthetic sense—the part of our sensory apparatus that tells us whether we're near or far, above or below, enclosed or in open space. A location is a far more powerful cue than a number or even a word.

Let's say you have to call your coworker Joe as soon as your meeting ends. Most of us would probably associate the task with a time: "I'll call Joe as soon as my meeting ends at 2:30." But time is made of numbers, and they're relatively abstract. Try associating the task with a location: Visualize the meeting room, see yourself coming out of that room, picture the phone you're going to find, and see yourself pushing the buttons on the phone. For extra associative power, picture Joe's face and hear his voice as he answers the phone. To take advantage of the "weirdness factor," picture Joe tangled in a giant telephone cord or imagine a huge, chartreuse-and-purple-striped phone cord linking you and Joe. Now you have a strong visual image to go with your task. The more visual connections you create, the more chances you have to remember what you need to do.

My client Carlos found the Memory Palace an extremely effective means of organizing the various tasks associated with his business. Carlos ran a restaurant in a small town in upstate New York. "I'm good with the people side of things," he told me when we first met. "But I have a terrible time keeping the whole business in my head—what supplies we need when, making sure the bookkeeping is done on time, all the little details that keep coming up, day after day after day. I feel like I can never get my head above water—I'm always bogged down in details."

When Carlos learned the Memory Palace technique, however, he felt an enormous sense of relief. "Now I have a 'room' for each type of work I have to do—ordering, billing, scheduling the workers, planning the menu," he said. "Whenever I want to know what my next task is, I just mentally go into the 'room.' "

Ferris, my lawyer client, had a similar experience. "Now, when I get a new client, I create a 'room' for him or her," he explained. "I spend some time visualizing the type of room that suits the client's personality, and I 'furnish' it with objects that remind me of the main points I need to keep in mind. Whenever I say the client's name, a detailed visual image of the 'room' comes into my mind—and all the information I need is right there."

Practice #4: Build a Memory Palace

Discover the power of location by creating your own memory palace. Spend 5 minutes a day for five days a week constructing your mnemonic edifice, adding a new room each day. At the end of the week, evaluate your progress. How does this technique work for you?

Preparation. Find a comfortable place to sit, somewhere you can count on not being interrupted. Ideally, choose a place where there is something beautiful to look at—a nice painting, a panoramic view, or some exotic plants. Although you don't actually need anything visually inspiring to do this practice, who knows? It can't hurt, and it might help!

Step 1: Design your palace. On the first day, choose the five rooms you will create over the course of the week. Like Ferris, you might choose a room for each of five clients, or, like Carlos, you might choose a room for each kind of task you have to do. You may have different rooms for the various territories where your company operates or for the different divisions you supervise. Don't agonize over this choice—just make a decision. You can always create a new palace next week!

Step 2: Furnish the first room. Once you have identified a theme for each of the five rooms, choose a place to start. Then take 5 minutes to visualize the first room. Fill it with all the associations that go with its theme. If your room is associated with a client, create an image for each aspect of the client that's important to you. If you're furnishing a room for Sam Ellison, for example, the client we met earlier, you might include a set of golf clubs, pictures of his three children, and a window that opens directly onto a beach in the Bahamas. Add a window on the other side of the room that opens into your office, for easy access. Then think of the other information about Sam that you want to remember and include it in your room. Or suppose, like Carlos, you want a room for a particular task—perhaps billing your clients at the end of the month. Fill the room with piles and piles of bills, with a big calendar on the wall reading "30," for the 30th of the month. Keep your images as visual and as playful as you can.

Step 3: Furnish the rest of the rooms. On the second day of this week, furnish the second room in your palace. Go on to do one more room on each of the next three days. In addition, briefly visit the rooms you've already furnished, perhaps embellishing or altering details as the spirit moves you.

Step 4: View your entire palace. On the last day of the week, take a moment to visit each room of your palace. See the images you've created in your mind's eye and enjoy the power of retrieving each piece of information in response to the cues you have created. Then step back and see the entire palace in your mind's eye. How does it make you feel to have created this palace? What are you able to do now that you couldn't do before? Do you want to add more rooms to this Memory Palace, tear it down and create a new one, or perhaps build another alongside it? Or maybe you'd like to keep your Memory Palace in reserve, deciding how to use it once you've mastered the techniques you'll learn in chapters 7 through 10. The choice is yours.

THE SYNERGY OF MEMORY: PAYING ATTENTION, VISUALIZING, AND ASSOCIATING

As you saw at the end of the last chapter, visualization plus association is a virtually unbeatable combination. And when you throw in paying attention—itself a combination of observation and concentration—you have real mental power at your disposal.

To some extent, dividing the process of memory into these different skills is a bit artificial. When you're actually exercising your memory and your mind, you tend to use the skills together. Certainly, when you move forward into the specific techniques of my memory system, you'll find yourself drawing on all three types of mental activity. If you've been doing the practices in chapters 4 through 6, you'll find yourself nicely warmed up and ready to take on more complicated tasks. Enjoy the use of your new mental capacity—and get ready to make some memories!

MY THREE-DIMENSIONAL MEMORY TRAINING SYSTEM IN THE WORKPLACE

CHAPTER 7

MASTERING PEOPLE INFORMATION

Nancy was a sales associate at a Bergdorf-Goodman department store, where I'd been giving two workshops a year for the past few years. Like her colleagues, she worked on commission, so she could see that it was in her best interest to recall as many customers as possible, along with the details of their likes and dislikes; preferences in style, size, and color; typical spending patterns; how often they shopped at the store; and other details about their occupations, families, and personal interests. From her first day on the job, Nancy understood how great a difference remembering this information would make in her popularity and effectiveness with her clients.

When she took my course, she decided to use the techniques I had taught to memorize all 500 customers in her client book. In effect, she became a walking client book, able to look at any one of her repeat customers and have at her fingertips all the information she'd ever learned about that person—previous purchases, favorite colors, and details about the customer's children, hobbies, and work history. As a result of her newly improved memory, Nancy's sales volume increased by 35 percent, and her income rose accordingly. Soon, she was winning sales awards and was made one of a select group of top salespeople.

"People really appreciate it when you remember them," she told me recently. "It makes them feel special, and it makes them trust you. I'd heard about those politicians who supposedly remember hundreds of people, but I never understood how they did it. After I took your course, I knew!"

MAKING PEOPLE MEMORY PAY OFF

Nancy's story is particularly dramatic, but it gives you some idea of the kind of success you can achieve when you, too, learn to remember names, faces, and important information about the people you meet.

The techniques for retaining such information are surprisingly simple, and I'll take you through them step by step. By now, you won't be surprised to learn that you'll be drawing on the skills you practiced in chapters 4, 5, and 6: paying attention, visualizing, and associating. To remember people's names, faces, and key identifying details, you'll closely observe their faces, concentrate on significant details, and create little visual stories to help you link names with facial features and other information.

Before we get started, though, I'm going to have you take a pretest in which I've done my best to reproduce the conditions of one of those dreaded cocktail parties. You know, the kind where your host says, "Bob, I'd like you to meet Mary Jacobs and Spiro Nikolopoulis. Oh, and this is Judy Kroll, along with her partners Bob Rosenthal and Janice Everett." Sound familiar? When you take my pretest, you'll meet 10 people within less than a minute. How many names do you think you can remember?

After you've evaluated your current abilities, I'll share my time-tested techniques for recalling names, faces, and other types of "people information." Then, at the end of the chapter, you'll take another test. Even in the short time it takes you to cover this chapter, I'll be surprised if your score doesn't double—and if your score was low to begin with, it may improve by even more. Thanks to paying attention, visualizing, and associating, you'll soon be able to remember people's names after meeting them only once—and keep them in your memory forever.

Pretest: Places to Go, People to Meet . . .

When I give this pretest in my workshops, it's an audio-video experience. I show slides or overhead projections of 10 photographs, lingering on each image for 5 seconds as I call out a person's name. Then I shuffle the photographs into a new order and show them again, giving participants 5 seconds to recall each name. If you can figure out a way to duplicate these conditions, perhaps by having a friend or colleague show you a series of photos from a magazine while saying a name for each, feel free to take the test that way. Otherwise, just look at the photographs and captions below. Allow yourself 5 seconds for each one—about the same amount of time you'd have if you met someone at a conference or cocktail party. Then look at the rearranged photographs on the next page and see how many you can identify.

Teresa Kwan

Spiros
Nikolopoulis

Barbara
Brazenor

Eric Cushing

Susan
Wasserman

Alexandra
Fitzpatrick

Ole Larson

Sharon
Sanchez

Robert
Marquette

Eileen van
Etten

How did you do? I'll let you in on a secret: When I do this exercise in my workshops, it's rare for anyone to remember any more than three names, and it's not unusual for many people to recall only one or two. I usually invite participants to share their feelings about the test results with me, and the comments are invariably the same: "I felt too stressed to remember anything"; "I seemed to be losing the information as it was given to me"; "I felt defeated before I began"; "I knew I couldn't do it—and I was right."

"Okay," I usually reply. "Now let's set some goals for ourselves. By the time you finish this workshop, how many faces do you expect to remember?"

In my experience, students don't generally expect to remember more than three or four people the next time they take the test—a figure I consider much too conservative. "Let me set the goal for you," I usually say. "By the time you get to the posttest, you're going to be able to identify at least 50 percent of these faces after hearing the names only once—and many of you will do much better than that." So don't worry. As you've already seen, memory is a skill like any other. To make dramatic improvements in a short time, all you need is a little practice.

I never forget a face—but in your case, I'll make an exception!
—Groucho Marx

"I KNOW YOUR FACE. . . BUT WHAT'S YOUR NAME AGAIN?"

If I had a nickel for every time someone has told me that they can remember faces but not names, I could probably retire right now. (Although I wouldn't—I love my work!) Even though people in my workshops readily confess that they have trouble recalling names, many insist that they have no such trouble with faces.

The Name Game

Recently, I had the pleasure of creating material for the Public Broadcasting Service (PBS) as part of two broadcasts on memory for *Scientific American Frontiers*, on which I appeared with actor Alan Alda: "The Memory Marathon" (first broadcast in October 2000) and "Don't Forget" (first broadcast in May 2004). If you'd like a little preview of this chapter, along with an audio-video version of the pre- and post-tests, visit the PBS Web site at www.pbs.org/saf/1102/features/name_game.htm. You may enjoy visiting the Web site twice—before you begin this chapter and after you've completed all the exercises you'll find here. You can also return to the site whenever you want to brush up on your people information skills.

"All right," I usually respond, "but do you know *why* you find faces so much easier than names?"

Usually, the only reply I get is a blank look, followed by an "aha!" moment when I start to explain the difference between *recognition* and *recall*. Most of the time, people who say they remember faces are talking about recognizing a face they've seen before—a relatively passive process. After all, information—the face's shape and unique features—is being presented to them. The only mental activity involved is realizing that they've seen that face before.

Recalling a name, however, is a far more active and therefore more difficult process. Rather than simply responding to information, we have to retrieve it, extracting a name and perhaps some identifying details from our memory banks. If we've met the person only once or twice before, we're likely to have very few associations to help us activate the connection. If, as is usual in business situations, no particular sensory or emotional experience is associated with the person, we're likely to have even more difficulty.

The difference between recognition and recall becomes even clearer when we compare picking a person out of a lineup with describing the same person to a police artist. In a lineup, we rely on recognition, responding to a face we've already seen. For the police sketch, we have to retrieve the visual information from our mental computers—and we may find that just as difficult as recalling an unfamiliar name.

There's another reason that we find recognition so much easier than recall. Recognition appears to be a primary survival skill for us humans, so Mother Nature has made sure we have a strong inborn ability to recognize people, places, and objects that might be important to us. Our brains seem to have a special region where our mothers' faces are imprinted at birth, along with those of any other primary caretakers whom we saw in the first few hours of our lives.

Our ability to recognize doesn't stop there. A study at the University of Rochester involved showing participants 2,560 slides over several days. Then they were shown 280 pairs of slides, with one slide in each pair from the original larger set. Remarkably, participants scored a 90 percent recognition rate. A similar study involved showing people 600 slides and then immediately testing their recall. In that case, recognition rates rose to 98 percent. In both cases, participants had never seen any of the slides before and viewed them for only a few seconds at a time— yet they were able to recognize virtually every image they were shown. These results suggest that most of us have very strong abilities to recognize what's familiar and what isn't—a capacity that must have come in handy for early humans trying to identify tiny but potentially dangerous changes in their environment.

Unfortunately, Mother Nature didn't anticipate our need to attend cocktail parties, business conferences, and client meetings, so she hasn't provided us with a similarly proficient built-in recall for names. To complicate matters further, the part of the brain that retrieves verbal information, such as names, is in a different location from the area that recognizes faces. Thus, if we want to improve our memories for people, we have to activate both parts of the brain—and then find ways to connect the two.

Fortunately, there's a very good way to do this, and in this chapter, I'll show you what it is. But just in case you're one of those people who think they can't remember faces either, I'd like to return briefly to our old friend the lemon. I often begin my workshops on people memory with the following exercise, just to drive home the point that our brains work better than we tend to give them credit for.

Exercise #1: The Face of a Lemon

Step 1. Start with a bag of lemons—as large a bag as you're willing to buy. Close your eyes and pull out one lemon at random.

Step 2. Give yourself 3 minutes on a timer to examine your lemon. Notice every detail you can—whether its color is even or splotchy, if there are any distinguishing marks, how it's shaped, and how its skin is textured. Use the relaxed, open, alert frame of mind you developed in chapter 4, remaining available to as many details as you can and calmly directing your attention to each.

Step 3. When time is up, return your lemon to the bag and mix it into the "crowd" with your eyes averted. Then spread the contents of the bag on the table and find your lemon.

How long did it take you to locate your lemon? Did you recognize it from a distance, or did you need to pick it up and examine it closely? What details did you use to check your perception? Were you surprised at how individual and distinct your lemon had come to seem?

When I do this exercise in my workshops, participants are invariably amazed at their own ability to pick out an individual lemon—an object, after all, that isn't nearly as distinctive as a human face. "Look," I usually say to my students, "you're introduced to people all the time, and you're telling me you can't remember their faces. So why are you able to pick out one single lemon from a sack of 25 or 30 even though, when you meet somebody at a conference, you don't recognize them 10 or 15 minutes later?"

"Well," someone usually says, "you asked us to look for certain characteristics in our lemons."

"And what difference did that make?" I ask.

"It meant that we really paid attention to the lemon's 'face,' and by doing that, we were able to recognize our own lemons out of all the other lemons."

Now you know what we're going to do with faces. By paying attention to particular characteristics and zeroing in on certain key details, we're going to learn how to recognize even the most ordinary-looking face after only about 5 seconds of viewing time. When we've mastered that skill, we'll go on to put names and other significant information with the faces.

Extra credit. After you've found your lemon, take a moment to check out the other lemons in the bag. Glance over the whole group, noticing all the little details that give them variety. How long do you think you'd need to recognize another one? Set your timer to a time of your own choosing, shut your eyes, and select another piece of fruit. How much can you improve your "lemon recognition rate"? What factors enable you to zero in on a particular lemon? How quickly can you pick your lemon out of the crowd? These skills will all come in handy as you begin to expand your recognition of human faces.

THOSE LIPS, THOSE EYES. . .

Remember back in chapter 4, when we met Natalie, the department store executive who couldn't remember people? If you recall, I introduced her to an exercise that I often do in my workshops, in which I showed her the standout features of famous faces: Marilyn Monroe's lips, Mick Jagger's mouth, Ronald Reagan's raised eyebrow.

Of course, recognizing celebrities is rarely called for in the business world, but using a single vivid feature to key in on a face *is* a useful technique, and one that will work just as well for recognizing the less famous folks you meet in the course of your job. Here's how it works.

Step 1: Identify Key Features of Famous People

Get a copy of a fan magazine, a book of Hollywood photographs, or some other set of images of famous people. Leaf through the photographs, pausing whenever you come to a face you recognize. As you glance at the face, ask yourself which feature is most distinctive. You can look at the face as a whole or work your way down from forehead to chin. Most likely, you'll want to follow Leonardo da Vinci's advice to beginning portraitists and focus on the central core of the face: forehead, eyebrows, eyes, nose, mouth, and chin. Continue to practice looking at famous faces until it takes you only 5 seconds or less to choose the "famous feature."

Step 2: Analyze "Ordinary" Faces

Next, turn your attention to more ordinary folks. Find a magazine or a book of photographs that portrays "regular people" rather than celebrities. Focus on one face at a time, working your way through each feature from the top of the head to the bottom of the chin. Ignore hairstyles, glasses, mustaches, and beards—you want to be able to recognize people even after they've cut their hair and gotten contacts. Keep your eyes on the stable, steady features of the core face: forehead, eyebrows, eyes, nose, mouth, and chin. I usually don't even look at the ears unless a person has really distinctive Clark Gable–type ears that stand out from the sides of the head.

As you look at these "ordinary" faces, analyze each feature, out loud if possible. Here's a chart of different facial aspects to help you enrich your visual vocabulary. As you read through these lists of features, try to apply them to yourself and the people you know. Can you visualize the faces on which such features might be found?

A Detailed Breakdown of Facial Features

Shape of head: Round, egg-shaped, square, rectangular, flat back, curved back.

Shape of face: Round, moon-shaped, square, rectangular, narrow, heart-shaped.

Forehead: High, low, wide, narrow, curving forward, receding.

Eyebrows: Arched, straight, thick, thin, separate, meeting.

Eyes: Large, small, close-set, wide-set, bulging, deep-set, almond-shaped, slanting.

Nose: Straight, Roman, "ski-jump," pointed, round, "button," flat and wide.

Nostrils: Flaring, wide, prominent, narrow, horizontal, turned down.

Mouth: Full, thin, lips the same size, upper lip larger, lower lip larger, pointy corners, turned-down corners, turned-up corners.

Chin: Round, double, pointed, square, jutting, receding, flat, "three-dimensional."

Now, here are some examples of how you might integrate your observation of facial features into a total analysis. As you read each description, try to visualize the person being described, as if you were sitting across a table from each other.

- Hmm. This man has a large, square head, and yet his face is long and narrow. I notice a high brow, bulging a bit, with a long, high-bridged nose that comes to a sharp point. His nostrils turn down a bit—it kind of gives him a snooty look, as though he had "his nose in the air"—and his eyes are small, deep-set, and narrow under thick, bushy brows that meet in the middle. He's got thin lips that come to a point and kind of turn down. He has a long, pointed chin; look at those lines curving down from his mouth to his chin.

- This woman has a big, round moon face with a double chin, a bulging forehead, and a round head that curves around in back (though it's hard to see the shape of her head under all that hair!). Her eyes are big and round and set far apart under thin, arched brows—it all seems to give her a surprised look—and her eyes are kind of bulgy, too, sticking out a little. Her nose is pretty ordinary, sort of round, and her nostrils are small. Her mouth is small, too—I think you'd call it a rosebud mouth—and her lower lip is bigger than the upper one. She has bulgy cheeks, too, so you don't really notice the corners of her mouth. Her chin is round and three-dimensional.

- This woman's face is small and delicate. She has almond-shaped eyes that are far apart and deep set. Her nose is thin and small, and her brows are thin and straight. She has a heart-shaped face—but look how her ears stick out! Her cheeks are a little round and bulgy, but her chin is small and square. Her lips are thin, with the upper lip a bit thicker than the lower one. Her face has a kind of pinched look, as though all the features are coming together.

Note that the descriptions include some emotional responses, judgments, and comparisons. I'll ask you to include these types of descriptions deliberately a bit later on, but if you happen to see faces in those terms now, that's terrific! Welcome any and all impressions, associations, judgments, and emotions—they will all enhance your ability to recognize a person. After all, which are you most likely to remember after all these years, the face of the class bully or that of the inoffensive kid who used to sit next to you at lunch? The face of the homeroom aide who collected your lunch money or that of the classmate on whom you had a crush from afar? We remember people who are important to us or to whom we have strong reactions, so the more vivid reactions you can generate with your facial analysis, the better. (And of course, no one has to know about these responses but you.)

Step 3: Choose the One Feature That Enables You to Recognize the Person

After you've analyzed each of several faces as a whole, go back to your book or magazine of photos. Look closely at each picture and let your

You Oughtta Be in Pictures. . .

If you like, test yourself by photocopying pictures of famous people.

Step 1. Make two 8$\frac{1}{2}$ x 11 copies of each picture.

Step 2. From one copy, cut out the famous feature you've selected.

Step 3. Put a blank piece of 8$\frac{1}{2}$ x 11 paper over the second copy.

Step 4. Using the image underneath as a guide, paste your cutout feature in its proper place on the blank paper.

Step 5. Make a new photocopy of the pasted-up feature on the blank page.

Step 6. Write the name of the famous person lightly in pencil on the back of the page.

Step 7. Follow the same procedure with the other photos, then put the "famous feature" pages aside. After a few days, look at them again. How many features can you recognize?

eyes zero in on each face's most distinctive feature, the one that would trigger the same kind of recognition as Monroe's lips or Gable's ears. As you choose the special feature for each face, describe it to yourself aloud, saying, for example, "small, pointy nose" or "big, fleshy chin." Again, if you find yourself associating the feature with some other person or image ("strong, jutting jaw, just like my Uncle Al"), or if you discover judgments and emotional responses ("She's got a really warm, wide, friendly smile—I think that's so attractive"), welcome these "extras" with open arms. They'll come in handy later.

Step 4: Close Your Eyes Briefly and Visualize the Feature

There are several ways you might perform this step. Some people like to start with the distinctive feature and then bring the rest of the face slowly into focus. Others like to see the whole face while directing their mental attention to the chosen feature, perhaps by shining a mental spotlight on it, causing it to glow with a golden light, or visualizing a bright red circle around it. I like to see the whole face with the special feature exaggerated way out of proportion. I find the humor and "weirdness" provide an extra little memory boost, and they also come in handy for the next few steps. You may want to experiment with a few different methods until you find the one that's right for you.

Whatever your preference, don't skip this step. It's important that you use your mind's eye as well as your actual eyes, particularly if you want to remember what people look like before you see them again. Natalie, for example, often had to meet clients for lunch after only the briefest of initial introductions. She was always terrified that she'd leave an important business contact stranded in a restaurant while she went from one table to another, hoping desperately to recognize her guest. After learning my system, she was able to relax because she entered the restaurant with an image of her lunch date firmly in her mind's eye. And while she hoped never to describe her clients to a police artist, she did appreciate being able to give descriptions to a maitre d'!

At this point in my workshops, someone invariably objects. "This is taking forever," my student is likely to complain. "I don't have this much time to remember somebody's face or name when I first meet them! By the time I've finished choosing a feature, they'll be gone!"

"Be patient," I'm likely to reply. "This is the learning stage. Think of when you first learned to access your e-mail—didn't that take a long time? But now you do it automatically, even while you're on the phone or talking to a colleague. This process will become equally automatic—but it takes practice."

In fact, now that you've learned the first portion of my technique, let's take some time out to have you practice it. In my workshops, I usually have everyone pair up and analyze their partner's face. Then I have them switch partners, switch again, and maybe even switch a third time. Here's a version of that practice that you can do on your own.

Practice #1: Focus on Features

Because this technique is so basic to recognizing people, I suggest giving yourself 5 minutes a day three days a week to practice it. If you're in a job where recognizing people is especially important to you, you may want to bump it up to five days a week.

Preparation. Find a place where you can observe someone's face for 3 to 5 minutes, such as at a coffee bar, diner, or restaurant; on public transportation; or while waiting in line or in a waiting room. You can also perform this practice with family, friends, or coworkers if they're comfortable being observed.

Step 1: Get an overview. Take a good overall look at the person's face. Talk your way through the face feature by feature—forehead, brows, eyes, nose, mouth, chin, and any other facial elements that leap out at you, including ears and cheeks. Ideally, you would perform this step while talking aloud to yourself—perhaps camouflaging your activity by using a memo-size tape recorder or a cell phone—but if you're not comfortable with that, take notes or talk to yourself silently. Be sure, though, to put your thoughts into words. Otherwise, it's too easy to get lost in your own musings without the sharpness of intention and focus that enable this technique to work.

Take as much time as you need to complete this step, which at first may require up to 5 minutes or even longer. Your eventual goal is to take in the whole face at a glance and move instinctively to Step 2.

Step 2: Choose a feature. Remember, your goal is to pick the one feature that would enable you to recognize this person again, a feature as distinctive in its own small way as Ronald Reagan's raised eyebrow or Bob Hope's "ski-jump" nose. Zero in on the feature you've chosen, firmly and decisively.

Step 3: Visualize the feature. Close your eyes briefly and see the person's face, focusing on the distinctive feature. In your mind's eye, exaggerate the feature or highlight it in some other way.

Choosing Distinctive Features

- Allow your mind to remain open and alert and see where your attention goes naturally. The feature that draws you first is probably the one you want to choose.

- Don't be distracted by superficial features—hairstyle, glasses, facial hair, or makeup. These may indeed be the most distinctive aspects of a face at a first meeting, but since they're things the person can easily change, they could sabotage your recognition the next time around.

- When you do choose, be decisive. Making a strong choice with lots of energy behind it will add some emotional "zing" to your memory, making it that much more likely to stick in your mind.

THE ANCIENT ART OF FACE READING

So far, you've been employing two major skills: paying attention and visualizing. To make your recognition and recall skills even more powerful, however, you need to bring a third skill into the mix—associating. Now that you've mastered the ability to see people's faces in detail and to choose distinctive features, it's time to start evoking your personal reactions and associations. When you start observing and analyzing faces, ask yourself the following questions.

- Is this a face that pleases you?
- Do you find it attractive?
- Do you notice any feelings of anger, annoyance, or frustration as you look at this face?
- Does it remind you of a friend, a relative, or someone else you know?
- Do any other associations—places, people, events, literary characters, actors—come to mind?

What you're trying to do is make the face more familiar. By asking these questions, you bring the face closer, becoming more involved with it and developing or heightening any associations it may hold for you. Remember what you learned in chapter 6: The more associations you have with a piece of information and the stronger your emotional response to it, the more chances you have of retrieving it from your memory banks. Thus, when you glance at strangers' faces, developing instant associations and emotional responses will give you a better shot at recognizing them a second time.

At this point in the workshop, I often bring out two useful and fascinating books, Mac Fulfer's *Amazing Face Reading* and Lailan Young's *The Naked Face: The Essential Guide to Reading Faces*. Fulfer is a lawyer who began to realize that reading faces would make him more proficient at picking jurors who might be sympathetic to his clients.

Young is an anthropologist who has studied both the Chinese tradition of face reading and more recent scientific studies on the topic. I mention these books not to encourage you to take up face reading (helpful though that may be) but because learning a bit more about the features that these authors analyze can help make you still more sensitive to observing the faces you encounter.

Moreover, if you come to believe that certain facial characteristics signify specific personality traits—whether you're correct or not—you've taken another step toward evoking emotional reactions to the faces you observe. Once again, you have a twofold goal: to observe facial features in detail and to develop strong emotional responses and associations with the faces you see. You don't have any trouble remembering what your family members look like, do you? In a sense, you're trying to make every stranger you meet as familiar as your brother, sister, parent, or child—as familiar and as unforgettable.

I personally believe that facial features do help us predict behavior—and lawyers like Fulfer who use face reading to help them select juries agree with me. Whether or not you go along with this idea, developing your personal associations with facial features will help bring each face you observe into your memory, making it, in a sense, your own. Becoming aware of your own ideas about a face—whether your ideas are correct or not—will help you remember that face.

Exercise #2:
Reading the Language of Faces

Just for fun, take the following pop quiz. There are no right or wrong answers here, just an attempt to help you identify your own associations and responses to various facial features.

Preparation. For this activity, it's extremely helpful to relax. Responses will float far more easily into your mind when you're open and laid-back rather than forcing yourself to come up with an instant answer. Slow your breathing from a 2-count inhale and a 2-count exhale down to 4, then 6, then 8, 10, and 12. Then, as you read each description below, allow yourself to visualize it. Don't push yourself to choose an emotional response or opinion; simply notice the ones you have. You may be surprised at how good a face reader you already are!

Face-Reading Quiz

1. A receding chin indicates someone who is _____.

2. Brows that meet in the middle suggest a person who is

_____.

3. A high forehead indicates _____, while a low brow means _____.

4. Small, close-set eyes make me expect a person who is_____, _____, and

_____.

5. A wide, full-lipped mouth causes me to think of

_____.

6. A tiny button nose suggests that the person will be _____ but not _____.

7. A double chin tells me that a person is _____ as well as _____ and _____.

8. High cheekbones and thin cheeks indicate a personality that is _____ but not _____.

9. When I see dimples, I think, "Here's someone who

_____."

10. List three more facial features and the associations you have with them.

    a. _____ means _____.

    b. _____ means _____.

    c. _____ means _____.

Well? What did you learn about yourself and your responses to facial features? Whatever your associations, your goal is to become aware of them and even to create them. Here's a practice that may help you do that.

Practice #2: Reading Faces

Practice reading faces for 5 minutes a day three to five days a week during the week after you've mastered Practice #1. Again, don't worry about how long it takes you to analyze each face. Once you've mastered this technique, you'll find that you can perform it almost instantaneously. It's only the learning process that goes slowly—the actual use of this technique goes very quickly indeed.

Preparation. For this activity, too, relaxation will help. Allow your mind to play freely, moving easily from one association to another. All of us respond instinctively to facial features—it's how we select our mates, choose our friends, and even decide which strangers to approach at a party. Let your built-in knowledge work for you. All you need is to become conscious of what you already do unconsciously.

Step 1: Find an observation post. As you did in Practice #1, find a place where you can observe someone's face for 3 to 5 minutes, or else find cooperative family, friends, or coworkers who will allow you to observe them.

Step 2: Get a first impression. Quick—ask yourself what your initial response is to the person you've chosen. Perhaps you're thinking, "What an attractive person!" or "He looks like someone you could tell your troubles to," or "She looks mean." In that case, make a mental note of your reaction and move on to Step 3. If your first glance seems to produce no response, prod yourself a little. Ask yourself if that's someone you'd like to date, work for, or work with. Picture asking this person to babysit for your kids. Imagine her sitting behind the desk where you've gone to apply for a loan, or see him standing alone at a party. How do you feel? Keep observing the person until you find yourself responding in some way.

Step 3: Identify the strongest feature. Next, glance at the person's face quickly and ask yourself, "What's the most outstanding feature?" Notice whether your eyes zero in on the nose, eyes, mouth, brow, forehead, or chin. Make a mental note of the facial feature that seems to leap out at you.

Step 4: Relate the feature to the response. Put the feature and the response together in a sentence, such as, "That's the strong chin of a very stubborn man," or "That's the wide, generous mouth of a warm, generous woman." Allow yourself to picture the person in a situation that shows off the outstanding feature, being stubborn, generous, mean, helpful, stingy, or any other quality you've chosen.

Step 5: Visualize the feature. Close your eyes for a moment and visualize first the feature, then the little situation you've created. As you envision the situation, keep the outstanding feature within your

What's in a Name?

Until the 11th century or so, societies around the world endowed their members with first names only. Perhaps some people had two or three first names, but the idea of a last name, surname, or family name didn't come into existence until medieval times in Venice. As the center of international commerce at the time, Venice was host to a wide variety of ethnic and national groups as well as a population magnet for Italians from the surrounding villages, towns, and cities. Eventually, there were too many people living in the city with the same first names, and differentiating among all the Paolos and Marias began to become difficult.

Enter the last name, a quick and easy way of designating family association as well as individual identity. When last names first came into use, they began very simply, with names designating men as the sons of their fathers. By the time the practice made its way over to England, it initially led to such easy name formations as John's son, Johnson;

mental vision, either by exaggerating it or by pointing it out to yourself in some other way.

Step 6: Check yourself. Return to your observation post a day, a week, or a few weeks later. Look for the person you observed by seeking out the feature you chose. How quickly can you recognize the person? Is there anything you can think of that might reinforce or improve your recognition skills?

REMEMBERING LAST NAMES

Now that you've seen for yourself how to look at a face and choose a feature, let's move on from faces to the more difficult part of the equation—names. You'll draw on the same old skills—paying attention, visualizing, and associating. Your ultimate goal is twofold: to create a vivid visual image that evokes a person's name and then to associate that name with the face it belongs to.

Ben's son, Benson; and so on. (Daughters' names were less important since female children were expected to marry and take their husbands' names.)

Eventually, though, using the "son of" names caused the same problem as the first names had: There were just too many similar ones. Then occupations came into play. In English, for example, you had Taylor, Baker, Fisher, and of course, Smith, the noble blacksmith. Alongside occupations came locations: Forest, Glen, River, Brook, Hill. Sometimes people were named for animals found around their homes: Wolf, Fox, Wren, Tiger, and so on. Mineral resources inspired such last names as Gold, Silver, and Diamond, while adjectives—especially colors—gave us Short, Long, Young, Brown, Green, Black, and White.

As you can see, last names originally had a simple, direct meaning that could be easily visualized if you paid attention to the word from which the name had come. Thus, when you meet someone with one of these easily envisioned names, your work is cut out for you: Create a visual image in your mind that stems from the logical meaning of the name.

Here's a little preview of where we're going. By the time you've completed this chapter, you'll have mastered each step of this process.

Step 1. Zero in on a face's distinctive feature.

Step 2. See that feature—exaggerated or distinguished in some way—in your mind's eye.

Step 3. Listen to the sound of the person's name, repeating it aloud as you learn it.

Step 4. Create a clear visual image—a kind of mini-movie—for the name.

Step 5. Integrate your "name movie" with an image of the distinctive feature.

Practice #3:
Visualizing Simple Last Names

Engage in this practice for 1 to 2 minutes a day two or three days a week. Because the names in this practice are simple, they shouldn't be difficult to visualize. Your goal is simply to become used to creating mental pictures as soon as you hear a familiar name.

Step 1: Read and visualize. Read the list of names below, aloud if possible. As you hear each name—aloud or in your mind—allow your mind to develop a picture from it. Your goal is to create a quick, vivid image that's linked to the name. When you first do the exercise, you may work more slowly, but by the end of the week, you should be visualizing quickly and easily.

Ms. Brown
President Benson
Mr. Glen
Mrs. Silver
Dr. Diamond
Professor Taylor

Reverend Smith

Vice President Short

Mr. Johnson

Miss Long

Step 2: Create your own list—and visualize it. Repeat Step 1, only this time, create your own list of simple names. Fill in the blanks below, then reread them, creating a quick, vivid visual image for each name.

Mr. _____

Vice President _____

President _____

Dr. _____

Mrs. _____

Miss _____

Reverend _____

Mr. _____

Ms. _____

Professor _____

Names with Preexisting Associations

There's another type of name that's a bit less concrete but is nevertheless easy to visualize because of your built-in associations. For example, if you meet a Mr. Reynolds, you might picture Reynolds Wrap, or aluminum foil. When you encounter Ms. Ford, you could picture a Model-T or an SUV. Here are some other categories of names that may have preexisting associations for you—associations that will help you create visual images relatively quickly.

Presidents. Washington, Adams, Jefferson, Roosevelt, Truman, Kennedy, Johnson

Brand names. Reynolds, Ford, Campbell, Kraft, Bayer

Objects. Keyes, House, Glass, Booker, Penn, Card, Page

Movie stars. Monroe, Redford, Crowe, Pitt, Lemmon, Roberts

Composers and musicians. Bach, Wagner, Jagger, Prince

People Memory at Work

In the 1980s, I taught a series of workshops at General Foods (now part of Kraft Foods, Inc.) that inspired an article in *Candid*, a corporate newsletter for employees in the Westchester, New York, headquarters. Although the article focused on the terrific job done by the telecommunications department in keeping the directory up to date, you can see the influence of my workshop in how employees' names were categorized.

It's about Those Names

Did you know that General Foods employs a Baron, Shah, King, Kaiser, and Prince? Actually, those are among the names of approximately 4,000 GFers. . . . Telecommunications follow the tracks of individuals . . . like Mole, Peacock, Fox, Pinto, Katz, Crow, Setter, and Lyon. And it will enable operators to keep tabs on their coworkers who are not only Fine, Grimm, and Hardy but also Ruff, Tough, and Meek.

Among the Westchester listings, there is no Costello for the lone Abbott, but there is a Burns and Allen, Day and Knight, Lewis and Clark, and Hill and Dale. There is an Easter and a Valentine, and although Christmas has left the director's pages, there is still a Klaus. . .

. . . [T]here are 20 Smiths, 13 Johnsons, and 12 Williamses.

For the most part, GFers are a colorful crew—there's at least one Black, Brown, Golden, Gray, Green(e), Rose, Silver, and White. They're also a busy bunch—not only is there an Archer, Baker, Barber, Brewer, Butler, and Judge but also a Carpenter, Currier, Cook, Cooper, Farmer, Hunter, and Miller. Not to mention a Packer, Potter, Porter, Scripter, Shearer, Singer, Skinner, and Tanner.

When it comes to Rhymaun, there is a Simon, as well as a Bopp and Popp, Norton and Morton, Main and Lane, and Heller, Keller, and Zeller.

Presidents are well represented, from Carter, Nixon, Johnson, Kennedy, Wilson, and Cleveland to Harrison, Arthur, Tyler, Taylor, Hayes, Jackson, Adams, and Washington. . . .

On the literary side, there's a Faulkner, Mann, Wolfe, Hardy, Teasdale, Shaw, Frost, and O'Neill. On stage, there is Hepburn, Holden, Swanson, Valentino, Kelly, Peck, Randall, Perkins, Taylor, Boyer, and Burton. Boxing buffs can point to Sullivan, Tunney, Dempsey, Jeffries, Johnson, Patterson, Armstrong, Leonard, and Lewis. For Superman comics fans, there's an Olsen, Lane, White, Kent, and Luther. . .

. . . the directory lists a Winter and Sommer, along with an April(e), May, and August.

They can be found near Brooks or Rivers, not far from Hill, Butte, Reif, and Shoreland, and sometimes fairly close to Dell, Field, or Glenn.

If all this has made you hungry, you'll be pleased to know there there's a Berger, Berry, Peach, and Quince (please cook first); a Wiener, Salmon, and Herring; Rice and Gum. You can wash it all down with some Coffee or a Stein of Mead, but we wouldn't recommend a Martini.

By the way, the Westchester listings open with Aaron and conclude with Zuckerman. There's no Beginning, Middle, or End, but fortunately, there is a Klose.

Used by permission of Kraft Foods, Inc., from "It's about Those Names," *Candid,* for General Foods Westchester People, vol. 30, no. 42, December 7, 1984.

Practice #4: Visualizing Last Names with Built-In Associations

Alternate this practice with Practice #3 for 1 or 2 minutes a day, two or three days a week. Again, your goal is simply to gain practice at creating mental pictures from these relatively simple last names.

Step 1: Read and visualize. Read the list of names below, aloud if possible. As you hear each name—aloud or in your mind—allow your mind to develop a picture from it.

Ms. Keyes
President Kraft
Mr. Scott
Mrs. Reynolds
Dr. Kennedy
Professor Truman
Reverend Monroe
Vice President Jackson
Mr. Angell
Miss Appleton

Step 2: Create your own list—and visualize it. Repeat Step 1 using your own list of names with built-in associations. First, fill in the blanks with names of your choice, then create a powerful visual image for each name.

Mr. _____
Vice President _____
President _____
Dr. _____
Mrs. _____
Miss _____
Reverend _____
Mr. _____
Ms. _____
Professor _____

Names with No Associations

Finally, we come to the most difficult type of name—those that at first hearing don't really mean anything to you. Because these names hold no preexisting associations, you'll have to create connections of your own, conjuring up mental pictures that can help you transform a meaningless name into a concrete visual image.

With these names, you can't go by what they represent, mean, or remind you of. You can only go by how they sound, syllable by syllable, then use the sounds of each syllable to help you create a little visual story.

Let's see how this process works with my own name, Felberbaum. You've got "fel," which sounds like "fell." The "ber" sounds something like "beer." And then maybe the "baum" reminds you of "bomb." Perhaps the image you create from those three words is "falling bottles of beer, coming down from the sky in the shape of bombs."

Three Steps for Remembering a Stranger's Name

Step 1. Repeat the person's name, making sure you've pronounced it correctly. Everyone loves to hear their name, and you'll gain points for being so attentive and focused. Meanwhile, you are giving yourself a chance to hear the syllables.

Step 2. Listen carefully to each part of the name. Look for the visual meaning you can create from its sound. Remember, every sound can evoke an image, so pay attention and let your imagination fly.

Step 3. Don't try to be logical as you create your image. There's nothing about the name Felberbaum, for example, that inherently evokes beer bottles falling from the sky, but it's a vivid, useful image that's likely to stay with you, especially after you've learned how to connect it to my distinctive face! Logic is fine when you meet a Mr. King or a Ms. Summerfield, but it won't work for Dyssegaard, Orloff, or Cisneros.

Or perhaps you've just met Mr. Moskowitz. Well, *Mosko* sounds like "Moscow," and *witz* is pronounced like "wits"—so you might say, "When you're in Moscow, you'd better keep your wits about you, or you might get into trouble!" As you say those words to yourself, you picture an international spy keeping his wits about him. A minute ago, *Moskowitz* was just a collection of meaningless sounds. Now it's a little visual story.

What about your encounter with Ms. Rodriguez? Well, *rod* could make you think of "gun," while *riguez* sounds similar to "regas." Visualize the charming Ms. Rodriguez keeping her gun in her car and making a quick trip to the filling station to re-gas. Once again, you've changed a set of sounds into a story.

Sometimes my students ask me whether knowing how to spell a stranger's name is helpful or whether they need to visualize the written version of the new name. If you're very spelling oriented, this approach may be helpful. Indeed, I've met some people with excellent memories who seem to need to know how a name is spelled before they can assimilate it. Most of us, however, will do better just focusing on a name's sounds and creating a vivid visual image.

Practice #5: Visualizing Last Names with No Associations

Start this practice the week after you've done Practices #3 and #4, and—because it's so important—work on it 5 minutes a day five days a week. Your goal is still to gain practice at creating mental pictures from these more complicated last names.

Step 1: Read and visualize. Read the list of names below, aloud if possible. As you hear each name—aloud or in your mind—allow your mind to develop a picture from it.

Ms. Mankiewicz

President Lopez

Mr. Kellman

Mrs. Jacobs
Dr. MacPherson
Professor Smemo
Reverend Wyatt
Vice President Berkeley
Mr. Jenkins
Miss Maddox

Step 2: Create your own list—and visualize it. Repeat Step 1 using your own list of names with no associations. First, fill in the blanks with names of your choice, then create a powerful visual image for each name.

Hint: For this part of the exercise, you may enjoy using your own name and those of people you know!

Mr. _____
Vice President _____
President _____
Dr. _____
Mrs. _____
Miss _____
Reverend _____
Mr. _____
Ms. _____
Professor _____

PUTTING THE NAME WITH THE FACE

We'll get to first names in a minute, I promise, but first I want to show you how to link last names with faces. That way, you can start using this system even before you're totally proficient at it. After all, in business, it's usually the last name that's most important. Also, because first names tend to be more familiar to all of us—names we've heard before and with which we already have associations—last names just take more work. The sooner you start practicing this approach, the faster you'll become good at it.

Let's use me as an example once again. I'll confess that I have quite a distinctive nose, with a high, narrow bridge and slightly flaring nostrils. Whenever I ask my students to practice this technique on me, this is the feature they choose. Presumably, if you met me, this would be something that you, too, would notice—especially if you've been honing your powers of observation. So use that detail to help me stand out from the hundreds of other people you meet over the course of a year. Zero in on my distinctive nose, create the image of "falling bottles of beer, coming down from the sky in the shape of bombs," and then put the two together, perhaps by visualizing the beer bottles landing on my nose and exploding, with all the beer running down my face. If you want to make the image even more personal, visualize the bottles with the label of your favorite brand of beer. It's an image you'll never forget—and when you run into me six months from now, you can confidently smile and say, "Mr. Felberbaum! So nice to see you again!"

If our Mr. Moskowitz has, let's say, a high, broad forehead, you might visualize the city of Moscow imprinted on that forehead and imagine his wits seething and bubbling behind his brow as Mr. M. tries to think of how to stay out of trouble in that Russian city. (Remember, weird, humorous, and exaggerated images stand a better chance of being remembered than something ordinary.) Or you might simply see the forehead itself dashing around Moscow, trying to muster its wits. Your goal is to visualize the name in a way that permanently associates it with the face in your mind so that you simply are not capable of remembering one without the other.

Likewise, if Ms. Rodriguez has a distinctively small, pointed chin, you might see the gun (rod) and handle of the (re-) gas nozzle clustered around that special feature. Or you might see Ms. Rodriguez herself, waving a gun in one hand and holding the re-gas handle in the other, her chin glowing brightly.

In my experience, each of us has our own distinctive way of linking name imagery with the facial features we've chosen. Your practice with creating mini-movies and weird images in chapters 5 and 6 will help you here as you draw on your own style of visualizing and associating.

MARY, MARY, NO LONGER CONTRARY

At last it's time to incorporate first names into the mix—and for the first time, you have an opportunity to cheat. Because so many first names are so common, you can actually prepare a mental list of images for many first names ahead of time so that whenever you meet someone with that first name, that portion of your mini-movie is ready to go. If you prepare to see a hot dog when you meet Frank, picture some jam when you meet James, or see a thief jimmying a lock when you encounter Jimmy, you're good to go. Likewise, a little advance work can make you ready to see the majestic *Queen Mary II* chugging into the harbor when you meet Mary, to visualize a seashell on the beach for the lovely Shelley, or to picture a bright red rose for your new client Rosa.

Personally, I like to use baby-naming books for this part of my memory work, browsing through these useful compilations of male and female first names from a wide variety of ethnicities. Pick up one of the many volumes of baby names available in your local bookstore or just make a list of the most common first names you can think of. Create some prefab images for each name, images that you'll then incorporate into your last-name mini-movie.

In my case once again, you might see a hot dog (Frank) among the falling beer bottles exploding like bombs against my prominent nose. Picture Ray Moskowitz illuminated by a huge, golden ray of sunlight as he tries to keep his wits behind his bulging forehead in the city of Moscow. Imagine a bright red rose in the barrel of Rosa Rodriguez's gun, or see a shower of roses falling around the filling station where she's re-gassing her car. The sky—and your own imagination—are the only limits!

Practice #6: Visualizing First Names

Start this practice the week after you've done Practice #5. Allot it 2 or 3 minutes a day two or three days a week. I've listed some names here to get you started, but as you practice this technique, you can use a baby-naming book to supplement the list or simply add names of your friends, family, and coworkers. Your goal, yet again, is simply to gain practice at creating an instant mental picture for any first name you hear.

Hint: *Some people like to use a name's meaning or history to help them grasp its image. If you're the kind of person who enjoys knowing that* Barbara *means "strange" (from the Latin word for "foreign") or that* Alexander *means "friend of the people," you can look up a name's meaning in your baby-naming book and incorporate that definition into your imagery. On the other hand, many of my students feel that the extra step is just too much additional work for their memories. They'd rather stick with how the syllables sound than go with what they mean. The choice is yours—feel free to experiment until you find the memory process that is right for you.*

Step 1: Read and visualize. Read the list of names below, aloud if possible. As you hear each name—aloud or in your mind—allow your mind to develop a picture from it.

Women's Names

Jenny

Laura

Rebecca

Ashley

Brittany

Eugenia

Tanya

Lakeesha

Luz

Carmen

Larissa

Mei Lee

Men's Names

Joe

Martin

Perry

Jason

Chris

Peter

Luke

Jacob

Malcolm

Charles

Jamal

Jorge

Step 2: Create your own list—and visualize it. Repeat Step 1 using your own list of first names. First, jot down a dozen male and a dozen female first names, then create a powerful visual image for each one.

Hint: For this part of the exercise, you can either use the names of people you know or start working your way through a baby-naming book.

Women's Names

1. _____
2. _____
3. _____
4. _____
5. _____
6. _____
7. _____
8. _____
9. _____
10. _____
11. _____
12. _____

Men's Names

1. _____
2. _____
3. _____
4. _____
5. _____
6. _____
7. _____
8. _____
9. _____
10. _____
11. _____
12. _____

Practice #7: Putting It All Together

Start this practice the week after you've done Practice #6. Because it's so important to your people memory, give it 5 minutes a day, five days a week. I've listed some names here to get you started, but as you practice this technique, you can start using the names of your friends, family, and coworkers. Your goal is to create a visual image associating a first and last name.

Hint: *If you have trouble creating images for any of these names, go to page 166, where I share some of my own ideas. You don't need to use my images, but they're there to get you started if you need help.*

Step 1: Read and visualize. Read the list of names below, aloud if possible. As you hear each name—aloud or in your mind—allow your mind to develop a picture from it.

Ralph Frasch

Spencer Barton

Gloria van Kamp

Carol Goldsmith

Maria Mendoza

James Cracchiolo

Jeannette McGowan

Frank Luciano

Teresa Hayakawa

Arnold Kiplinger

Step 2: Put the name with the face. Next, start incorporating your name imagery with your facial observations. Every day this week, make a point of meeting someone new. Focus on the person's face as you meet, zeroing in on the key facial feature you choose. Then create a visual image that incorporates first name, last name, and the special feature. Continue with this practice until you feel that it happens automatically every time you meet someone whose name you want to remember.

ADVANCED PEOPLE INFORMATION

By now, you've learned the most important aspect of people information: remembering people's names. Believe me, your clients, colleagues, coworkers, and business acquaintances will appreciate it! But you can do still more. Now that you have your mini-movie going, you can incorporate additional information into it, such as the names of people's spouses, how many children they have, the positions they hold in their companies, and any other details you think are important—or impressive!—for you to remember.

At this point, you can probably guess what I'm going to say next: Just incorporate imagery for any additional details into the basic mini-movie of the name and face. Put a little rattle in Mr. Moskowitz's movie to help you recall his newborn baby. Picture a giant rose visiting the local market—gun and gas nozzle in hand—to remind you that Rosa Rod-re-gas is head of marketing at her company. I'll let you figure out your own image to trigger your knowledge that Frank Felberbaum—a.k.a. Mr. Memory—is the author of a book on business memory!

"Wait a minute," my students are likely to object at this point in the workshop. "I'm already on overload with the names and the faces. How am I going to remember *more* information?"

Many people seem to think that the less you know, the better your memory will work, simply because there are fewer facts to recall. In fact, the opposite is true: The more you know, the easier it is to remember everything. Each additional piece of information can give you access to the rest. That rattle in Mr. Moskowitz's mini-movie offers you one more

People Memory at Work

When I worked with Pfizer, Inc., the world's largest pharmaceutical company, my student Rob paid particular attention to the portion of my workshop that concerns memorizing names and recognizing faces. Rob spent a lot of time at overseas meetings, and he'd often felt overwhelmed by the first day of each trip, which generally involved meeting several new colleagues at once. Since he was going to be working with those people, he wanted to make a good impression on them, and he knew that remembering their names was the first step toward doing that.

The names of his Asian colleagues were particularly challenging, since they were so different from the Western names he knew, so Rob devised a plan for boosting his memory, using techniques that he'd learned in my workshop.

1. He looked very closely at the person he was meeting, zeroing in on a particular aspect of the person's face or appearance.

2. He always repeated the name of the person ("Pleased to meet you, Dr. Chang."). If the name was complicated, he asked whether he had pronounced it properly and took the opportunity to say it again.

3. He broke the name into parts that made sense to him and found an image that linked the names and the person's unique feature.

Once, for example, Rob met the manager of a department in Thailand whose name was Oranut Arunatut. Rob translated the unfamiliar syllables of the name into sounds that he could remember.

chance to trigger the entire set of images, just as adding a market to Ms. Rodriguez's set of associations increases your opportunities for recalling her face and name.

If you create a vivid circle of information around a person's name and face, with each fact and image connected to every other one, you'll find that the total picture jumps into your mind whenever you think of any part of it—and there it will be, a mental movie that you created and that you can view anytime you like. As you continue using this technique,

---

- Oranut: The syllables were similar to *aura* and *nut*, so he pictured a bright, shimmering aura around a walnut.

- Arunatut: *Arun* sounded like "around", and *tut* made Rob think of King Tut.

With these similarities in mind, Rob pictured Ms. Arunatut, a short woman with glasses, in a King Tutankhamen outfit with a walnut glowing in its own aura and circling around her.

On another occasion, Rob met a Chinese manager whose name was Tang Xue, who was introduced to him last name first, the traditional Chinese way. He devised the following images.

- Tang: This was the same as the orange-flavored drink.

- Xue: Pronounced "schway," it sounded a lot like "sway" as uttered by someone who's had too much alcohol to drink.

Rob pictured Tang Xue leaning backward, drinking a glass of Tang but apparently tipsy, swaying back and forth. The eyeglasses he always wore had fallen and were perched on the glass of Tang.

Does Rob have more influence with his two colleagues as a result of reliably remembering their names? Probably, since they really enjoy working with him—and if you enjoy something, you're much more likely to want to continue it. When he told me about how he'd used my system, I was delighted that it worked both to help him remember names and to allow him to be more comfortable in the many cultures in which he worked.

you'll find that you have hundreds of circles in your mind so that whenever you meet someone again, a little collage of everything you know about the person will appear in your mind. These circles of information will prove invaluable as you access them, secure in the knowledge that whenever you need the knowledge, it will be there.

Practice #8: The Circle of Information

Start this practice the week after you've done Practice #7. Because it's so important to your people memory, give it 5 minutes a day, five days a week.

Hint: *If you have trouble creating images for any of these names and details, go to page 166, where I share some of my own ideas. You don't need to use my images—but they're there to get you started if you need help.*

Step 1: Read and visualize. Read the list of names that follows, aloud if possible. As you hear each name—aloud or in your mind—allow your mind to develop a picture from it. Incorporate images of the person's profession and hobbies as you create your mini-movie of the name.

Edward Montgomery: Professor of marketing, two sons in college, avid hiker

Take a Mental Snapshot

Years ago, I read Mort Herold's *You'll Never Forget a Name Again!* His book had an extremely useful suggestion, one I've incorporated into my own memory work. I offer my own adaptation of Herold's idea here: Whenever you meet someone, after you've identified the key feature and created a mini-movie for the person's name, take a moment to turn your head away and visualize the imagery you've created. Seeing the movie in your mind's eye will fix it there forever, enabling you to recall the image even when you're not actually looking at the person in question.

Elizabeth Ticino: Advertising copywriter, collects coins

Penelope Tennison: Designs Web sites, weekend painter

Carl Uslaner: Sales agent for a sporting goods store, leads a bowling league

Maureen O'Brien: Data programmer, enjoys pottery as a hobby

Ben Segal: Lawyer, married to a TV executive, vacations in Caribbean

Cynthia Anderson: Liquor company executive, daughter of a diplomat, born in Thailand

Abe Potansky: Financial planner, enjoys racquetball

Sharon Kanakaredes: Plastic surgeon, looking for help with marketing, does yoga

Robert Fleming: Sells bonds, huge baseball fan

Step 2: Create your own circle of information. Next, start practicing this skill in your own life. Each day this week, make a point of meeting someone new and learning two facts about the person: job title, marital status, hobby, or whatever you like. Focus on the person's face as you meet, zeroing in on the key facial feature you choose. Jot down the name and information after you've met, then create a visual image that incorporates the name, facial feature, and personal details. Continue with this practice until you feel that it happens automatically every time you meet someone whom you'd like to remember.

APPLY WHAT YOU'VE LEARNED

Here are two more practices that can help you carry your people information techniques into your business life. Give each one a try so you can see whether you find them helpful in keeping your memory sharp.

Practice #9: Using Your Appointment Book

Try this after you've mastered the techniques in this chapter. It's a good way to remind yourself to apply what you've learned to the people you meet every day.

Step 1. Each day, review your appointment book and notice the new people you've met. Take a few moments to come up with a little story for each name. Jot down a sketch or some visual image to remind you of each story.

Step 2. Once a week for four to six weeks, review the names and stories you've recorded. After you've gotten comfortable with the technique, you can review the names less often—once a month or perhaps once a quarter. Notice how, as you look at each name, the corresponding face seems to leap off the page into your mind's eye.

Practice #10: Preparing for a Meeting

If you try this technique before you attend a meeting or small conference, I guarantee that you'll astound everyone there with your prodigious memory. How do I know? I've often used this technique myself before meeting a group of students for a workshop. It never fails to amaze—and yet, when you know the technique, it's so easy!

Step 1. Find out the names of everyone slated to attend the meeting. Learn as much as you can about each person in advance. At the very least, you should be able to find out title, company or division, and telephone extension. You may be able to learn even more specific identifying details.

Step 2. Prepare your visual collage for each person. If you have access to a photograph—in a company directory or online—you can even link the collage to the person's face. If not, prepare a mini-movie with the information that you do have. (Later, you can integrate the mini-movie with whichever facial feature you choose.)

Step 3. When you meet each person, make a point of referring to the information you've learned. Since it's rare for anyone to attend a meeting with that level of knowledge, you'll come across as incredibly well prepared! Of course, you're not doing it only to impress others. Eventually, this kind of knowledge will make your job much easier, too.

CONGRATULATIONS—AND KEEP PRACTICING!

When we get to this point in my workshops, I usually administer a post-test like the one on page 167. As I predicted, my students usually remember at least 50 percent of all the names and faces they're given—and many do much better than that. Then we all applaud ourselves. I remind the participants that they got this far only by practicing, and I encourage them to keep working at this technique until it becomes automatic, expanding and improving their ability to recall large amounts of personal information along with names and faces.

I offer you the same kudos—and the same challenge. Now that you understand the process, it's up to you to use it. Repeat the practices that I've shared with you in this chapter, then apply the process to your daily life, focusing on the names and features of the people you meet in the course of your workday. Remember that your improvement will be directly related to the amount of energy you put into the process. After all, memory is a kind of mental muscle. Use it or lose it!

Image Suggestions

Here are some ideas for creating first- and last-name imagery for the two sets of names I supplied in Practices #7 and #8.

Practice #7

Ralph Frasch: Rough, fresh

Spencer Barton: Spend, Barton candy

Gloria van Kamp: Glory, van, camp

Carol Goldsmith: Christmas carol, goldsmith

Maria Mendoza: Marry, men-doze

James Cracchiolo: Jam, crash-hello

Jeannette McGowan: Join-net, make-go-wand

Frank Luciano: Hot dog, Lucky Luciano

Teresa Hayakawa: Terrace; Hiya, cow!

Arnold Kiplinger: Iron-old, Kiplinger's magazine

Practice #8

Edward Montgomery: Head, mount-gum-airy

Elizabeth Ticino: Queen Elizabeth, teach-in

Penelope Tennison: Pen-elope, tennis-sun

Carl Uslaner: Curl, U.S.-land

Maureen O'Brien: Marine, o-brain

Ben Segal: Bean, seagull

Cynthia Anderson: Sin, under-sun

Abe Potansky: Lincoln, pot-in-sky

Sharon Kanakaredes: Share-one, can-a-car-red

Robert Fleming: Robot, Ian Fleming

Posttest: The Final Challenge

Are you ready to see how far you've come? Look at each photograph and caption below, or ask a colleague to show you photocopies of each one, saying the associated name. Allow yourself 20 seconds for each one—about the same amount of time you'd have if you met someone at a conference or cocktail party. Then look at the rearranged photographs on the next page and see how many you can identify.

Hiro Matsuyama
Surgeon, plays Scrabble

Dolores Da Silva
Gymnast, enjoys arts
and crafts

Victoria Harrington
Criminal lawyer and
gourmet cook

Alan Perez
Film editor,
enjoys travel

Ruth McIntosh
R.N., crossword
puzzle fan

Joseph Brodsky
Ballet dancer,
martial artist

Lauren Armstrong
Magazine publisher,
collector of gold coins

Doris Katzenbach
Advertising executive,
plays golf every Sunday

Nat Birnbaum
Student, collector of
rare comic books

_____

_____

_____

_____

_____

_____

_____

_____

_____

CHAPTER 8

MASTERING SPOKEN INFORMATION

The strategic planning team at GE Capital was about to enter into a series of delicate negotiations with one of their top clients. Marc, their chief negotiator, was known for his charm, stubbornness, and creativity in devising new solutions—all terrific qualities that had enabled him to win agreement for many profitable contracts.

Marc was frankly skeptical about my workshop. He didn't see how improving his memory could sharpen his already superlative negotiating skills. What he didn't realize was that his memory for spoken information was not on a par with the rest of his abilities. Like many people in business, he knew how to speak, read, and understand numbers—but he didn't know how to listen.

After two days with me, however, his ability to concentrate, retain detail, and hold on to the flow of key points in a conversation had vastly improved. By paying attention, visualizing, and making associations, he was able to refer effortlessly to a specific detail that had come up a few hours ago or even on the previous day. Whereas before, he was bound by the facts and figures on paper before him, he now had a new mental dimension to work with—and he used it to full advantage. The negotiations, he told me later, were among the most successful he had ever conducted, and he could only look forward to more.

THE BENEFITS OF REMEMBERING SPOKEN INFORMATION

When I begin my memory workshops and training sessions, I typically tell my students that they can become human tape recorders, promising that they'll be able to recall crucial concepts, facts, and events from meetings, interviews, training sessions, and other encounters that center on the spoken word.

Like Marc, however, many of my students don't seem very interested in the benefits of improving their memories for the spoken word. "Why become a human tape recorder when I can just push the button on a *real* tape recorder?" a skeptical student might ask.

"I always take terrific notes," someone else might add. "In fact, that's the one time I don't *need* to remember anything!"

"Really?" I'm often tempted to reply. "But how often do you find yourself returning to that tape or those notes later on?" In my experience, listening to the tape of a presentation is an excruciating experience that everyone avoids if at all possible. Likewise, the notes we take during an oral presentation are often incomprehensible if we no longer remember the event. Even if your notes are better than most, how much does your note taking impede your ability to participate freely and confidently?

Over three decades of teaching memory to people in business, I've come to see that the advantages of retaining spoken information are enormous. Remembering what's been said at meetings, in seminars, in casual conversation, and on a thousand other occasions can exponentially increase your effectiveness at work. Not only will you do your own job better, you'll gain a subtle but unmistakable advantage over those whose memories are not as sharp. Knowledge is power, and the person who recalls key details, facts, and concepts has a considerable measure of power when compared with someone who can remember a conversation in only general terms.

The techniques for retaining spoken information are the same ones we've been learning all along.

Pay attention. Listen closely, focusing on the key concepts, words, and facts.

Visualize. Translate those key concepts into visual images.

How Much Time Do You Spend Listening?

Quick—take a moment to complete the following self-evaluation. What percentage of your time each week do you spend on the following activities?

Writing: _____ percent

Reading: _____ percent

Speaking: _____ percent

Listening: _____ percent

According to Madelyn Burley-Allen, author of *Listening, the Forgotten Skill*, most of us spend 9 percent of our time writing, 16 percent reading, 35 percent speaking, and a whopping 40 percent listening. Corporate training expert Scott Parry, Ph.D., also stresses how much of our working days we spend listening to information. Now, if you could *remember* what you heard, how much more powerful would it make you? Your potential power grows when you consider that most people in business never really learn to listen. Just think what an advantage your listening skills will give you!

Associate. Create a story out of the images and associate it with the stories you've already created about the speaker.

Of course, you can still take notes if you like, but with your new proficiency at my memory system, you'll be able to integrate your notes into the new matrix of memory that you're creating. I promise you that your new notes will be easier and more fun to take, and they'll trigger far more memories than your old ones ever did. (For specific suggestions on how to take effective notes, review the discussion of Tony Buzan's Mind-Mapping technique in chapter 6.)

WHEN YOU NEED TO REMEMBER WHAT'S SAID

Let's start by considering the many times it would come in handy to remember the information spoken aloud in a business situation. Note that in many of these instances, it may not be possible, appropriate, or desirable to take notes.

- One-on-one discussions, such as conversations, job interviews, and performance reviews
- Social situations with clients, colleagues, and potential business connections
- Meetings—small, medium, and large
- Negotiations
- Phone calls
- Presentations and conferences
- Demonstrations and instruction sessions
- Videotapes
- Audiotapes heard in your car or elsewhere
- Elevator talk

The challenge in each of these situations is to capture and transform spoken information into memorable information *as you hear it*—because in this domain, you don't get a second chance! Written information is always there for your referral, but spoken information disappears very quickly. You're required to pay close attention so you can capture and store it before it vanishes so completely that even the speaker may not remember what was said.

I'm reminded of a joke by offbeat comedian Steven Wright. He says something like, "I always try to put aside a little bit of time each day. Then, at the end of the year, I've got all that extra time."

Unfortunately, we can't actually use Wright's "method" to save time—but we can use our memories to save thoughts. Although we can't "save time," with my system, we can always capture it.

Techniques for Staying Focused

Why is it so hard to pay attention? Remember what you learned in chapter 4? Our minds work much faster than most people can speak. We tend to listen at 800 to 1,200 words per minute, but most people speak at about 150 to 200 words per minute. Believe it or not, your mind would rather be fully occupied, so it looks for something to take up the other 80 percent of its attention. Before you know it, your mind is completely absorbed in some other interesting thought—and you haven't heard a word for the last 5 minutes.

As you also saw in chapter 4, however, you can always use your eyes to help your mind stay focused by practicing some simple strategies.

- Be sure your eyes move every few minutes.

- Keep your brain occupied with a related topic, not a distant one.

- Take notes if you like, but don't keep your eyes fixed on the page.

- If you can, take breaks.

GETTING MOTIVATED

When I ask my students what's the biggest impediment to remembering spoken information, I'm always fascinated by the answers I get.

"Lack of concentration," one student might say.

"Poor memory training," someone else suggests.

"Physical problems with hearing," a third student calls out.

I agree that these are all obstacles to good listening and remembering, but my students are always surprised when I tell them that in my opinion, the greatest barrier to remembering spoken information is simple lack of motivation.

Think about it. When you're on an airplane, how closely do you listen to the safety information? If you travel often, you probably tune out the rather boring explanation of how the seatbelts work and where the emergency exits are.

Now imagine that the day before your flight, you've seen a harrowing account of a plane crash on the nightly news. How much would your listening improve?

Sometimes, just for fun, I ask my students to imagine that they've been unjustly imprisoned and are about to make a jailbreak. The next words they hear will be the instructions for how they might escape. "If you can listen as though your lives depended on it," I tell them, "I guarantee that you'll remember every word."

Of course, in most business situations, the stakes aren't usually so high—which is probably a good thing! Still, reminding yourself of the following possible motivations to listen will go a long way toward boosting your ability to remember what you hear.

- To save or acquire money
- To save time
- To preserve or improve your position in the company
- To acquire a new customer
- To improve relations with an existing customer

Exercise #1:
Identify Your Motivation

Step 1. Look over my list of possible motivations for listening on the previous page, then find a comfortable place to sit with a few blank pages and your favorite writing instrument. If possible, set a timer to go off at regular 2-minute intervals, or just put a clock with a second hand where you can easily see it.

Step 2. Look at the first item on my list on page 172 of business situations in which you need to listen. Since the first item is one-on-one conversations, visualize yourself having such a conversation. Imagine a situation in which this is the most important business conversation of your life, an encounter whose details can make or break your career. Who's talking to you? What is she saying? Why must you remember? Experience the urgency and focus of your listening as you mobilize your memory.

Step 3. As the timer goes off or the clock reaches the 2-minute mark, take a few seconds to jot down any key words that come to mind about your visualization, words that you associate with that imaginary experience of focused, urgent listening. Then move on to the next situation on the list. Repeat the process until you've worked your way through every example, making sure each time to envision a situation in which your memory of what you hear is crucial to your life or career in some way.

Step 4. When you've gone through the entire list, take a few moments to write about the experience. What have you learned about yourself and your motivations for listening? What will be useful to you as you return to the world of work?

DEFINING YOUR INTENTIONS

Getting motivated is a terrific first step, but motivation can be a fleeting thing—a brief stimulant that can evaporate without your even noticing. It's not enough to *say* you'll pay attention—you actually have to do it. More accurately, you have to take specific steps to keep your attention focused on the problem at hand.

Most of us aren't used to paying attention in such a concentrated way. As you've seen throughout this book, though, the skills that make up memory—paying attention, visualizing, and associating—are *learned* skills, abilities that you can practice until they become second nature. Your goal is to encourage yourself to pay attention so often and so effectively that it eventually seems natural to do so.

One powerful way to stay attentive is to *listen with intention*. Having a clear intention gives your listening focus, so as you listen, ask yourself questions such as the following.

How will I use this information? If you imagine a use for what you

Your Obedient Brain

Did you know you can give instructions to your brain?

In fact, you're constantly telling your brain what to do and how to behave, although you may not be aware of it. Each time you say something like, "I'm so forgetful!" your brain obliges by forgetting things. On the other hand, each time you tell yourself or others, "My memory is improving tremendously," your brain will obey that hidden instruction and give your memory a little boost.

This extraordinary power of self-instruction has been central to sports training programs, in which positive reinforcement and what's known as positive self-talk have come to be seen as crucial for top athletes. One famous study tested the efficacy of athletes giving themselves *only* positive reinforcement. That is, when they did well, they told themselves, "Good for me! Look how well I did!" and when they did badly, they told themselves, "Good for me! I'll do better next time!" Apparently, this constant round of positive "in-

hear, you'll immediately know what key elements to focus on and what you can afford to discard. Envisioning how you'll use the information will also keep you alert as you wait to hear about the questions you already have, concerns you're preoccupied with, and opinions you currently hold. Evaluating the information against your own needs and your own knowledge base will make you a far more active and attentive listener.

Where does this information fit in my business life? If you don't know immediately why you're listening, look for a place that this information might be useful. Is it something that will help you acquire more customers? Can it help you please the particular customer who is talking? Might you include a summary of the interchange in a memo to your boss? Will it enhance your performance at tomorrow's sales conference? Of course, if you truly believe you'll never find any possible use for the data, you're free to let your mind wander. (If you're like most of us, you've long ago learned the useful art of looking attentive while thinking of something else entirely!) But I urge you not to give up so quickly.

struction" to the brain got better results than positive self-talk for the good moves and criticism ("I shouldn't have done that!" "That was wrong!" "Oh, no!") for the bad ones.

Try it for yourself. Every day that you work on the memory programs in this book, tell yourself how great you are at every possible opportunity. Insist that you have a terrific memory that's getting better every day. If you can't manage that level of self-praise, focus on whatever positive qualities you can reinforce, telling yourself how much you're learning and how quickly your memory is improving. (I promise you these things are true, even if it doesn't seem that way!)

Then, when you've finished the program, evaluate the success of this positive self-talk. Did your brain help you by agreeing to remember more than you ever thought possible? Did you get better results than when you insisted on your poor memory and forgetful ways? You can take advantage of your brain's obedience to expand your memory and many other qualities as well—so don't ignore this powerful resource!

Often, there is a way to take advantage of something you hear—if only your mind is active and creative enough to find it.

Who else would be interested? Sometimes it's enough just to imagine yourself retelling the story of this encounter to an interested party—a colleague, client, supervisor, or even a friend. Ideally, you're hearing solid data that is crucial to an upcoming deal, and your motivation and intention will be obvious. If you're just marking time until your garrulous client lets you get off the phone, however, find something else interesting to focus on—his favorite turns of phrase or her revealing observations about her coworkers. All too often, someone will chat aimlessly for a few minutes and then return to crucial information. If you've been paying attention all along, you won't need to say, "Wait a minute—*what* did you just say?"

The next step is to visualize yourself using the information. Whether you see yourself regaling your spouse with an amusing work story or imagine impressing your boss with a cogent memo, visualizing your use of spoken information can help keep your listening focused and your mind alert. Knowing that you'll need the information will help you pay attention to it—and what better way to remind yourself how important the information is to you than to see yourself using it?

> *Speech is a joint game between the talker and the listener against the forces of confusion. Unless both make the effort, interpersonal communication is quite hopeless.*
> —Norbert Weiner, *The Human Use of Human Beings*

THE ART OF ASKING QUESTIONS

Your goal when listening to spoken information is to become an active listener, someone whose mind is working at top speed *while* you are paying attention. One great way to stay active and attentive is to ask questions, either aloud or in your mind.

Let's suppose you're listening to a presentation on sales figures in the Florida office. You're mightily tempted to zone out, but you know that your boss will ask you how the presentation went, and you'd love to impress her with a quick summary. So you decide to practice your new memory skills as you listen, and you settle on the strategy of asking questions. Here's what might be going on in your mind.

Presenter: The greatest sales gains were in the Naples region, while the St. Petersburg area saw relatively little improvement.

You: *Hmm. I wonder why Naples did better than St. Pete? Is the population base different? Or does it have something to do with the local economy?*

Presenter: We have attributed the discrepancy to the relatively untrained status of the St. Petersburg sales force...

You: *Oh, so that's it. But then why are the St. Pete people less well trained? Is that office newer, or is the manager just screwing up?*

Presenter: . . . which we believe is a result of the high turnover in St. Petersburg . . .

You: *And what's behind that high turnover?*

Presenter: . . . the reasons for which we have not yet been able to determine.

You: *I wonder if anyone has thought of doing a study on that? Maybe I should suggest it to my boss. Of course, I don't want to step on any toes. Where could I find out whether anything has been done? That's the kind of thing Nate always knows—or maybe I could ask Melanie to do a search for me . . .*

Presenter: Meanwhile, morale in the Naples sales force seems to be extremely low, despite the high figures . . .

You: *Well, I bet I know why that is! It must be that manager they have down there—now what was her name again?*

Presenter: . . . although the local manager, Ms. Martinson, has assured us that morale is improving rapidly . . .

You get the idea. The goal is to keep your mind moving at top speed while staying focused on what you're hearing. Asking questions and then listening to find out the answers gives your mind plenty to do while keeping your thoughts in the room. Your goal is to find a method of listening actively—and listening to find the answers to your questions is an excellent way to do that.

Strategies for Active Listening

Most of these strategies will work whether you perform them silently or aloud. Of course, sometimes it's not possible to talk back to a speaker, and in those cases, you'll just have to participate in silence. If you can actually speak as well as listen, that's likely to increase your ability to concentrate.

Ask a clarifying question. "Why is that problem occurring so frequently?" "Where are the areas with the biggest gains?" "Can you give me some examples of what you're talking about?"

This is useful because it both keeps you actively participating and helps you zero in on the ideas or facts that matter most to you.

Summarize what you've just heard. "In other words, you're concerned about morale even more than about sales figures." "If I'm hearing you right, you're excited about the overseas potential, but you're cautious about the Asian market." "What I'm getting is that things in your department couldn't be better—that's terrific!"

Again, summarizing the information keeps you active. It also makes the information yours. You're a lot more likely to remember something you've said than something you've heard, simply because saying words gives you an automatic investment in them.

Repeat exactly what you've heard. "Let me make sure I've got it straight: You need a 10 percent increase by the end of the year." "Wow. You're really going to convert all your plants to the new system in only three months?" "What I'm hearing is that you're all excited about the new guy—I'm glad he's working out so well."

Practice #1: Ask Questions

I suggest you practice this technique every chance you get. Look for at least one occasion each day when you can put it into practice. If you feel self-conscious or insecure trying it out at work, watch 5 minutes of TV news each night or, better yet, listen to a radio news broadcast and practice it there. As soon as possible, though, start doing this on the job—you'll be amazed at how your memory for spoken information improves!

People love to have their words said back to them, so you'll never go wrong with this. Although it's not as creative or analytical as some other techniques, it's a surefire way to keep you engaged in the conversation—and you'll gain big points from your conversation partners, who'll see you as hanging on their every word.

Repeat what you've heard to other people, either aloud or in writing. "So what Joe told me was . . ." "Have you got a minute? I'd like to fill you in on the presentation this morning . . ." "Memo re: This afternoon's sales conference. The key points were . . ."

There's no better way to learn something than to teach it to others. Either reconstructing a conversation verbatim or summarizing a presentation can ensure that you will remember the information you've shared.

Notice the speaker's facial expressions and body language. "Hmm, why does he always scratch his nose when he says 'sales figures'?" "Look how tense she is—her shoulders are all hunched forward. What's up?" "His face just lights up whenever he mentions the Oklahoma office—he must be really proud of those guys."

There are two reasons to keep a sharp eye on people's faces and body language as you listen to their words. First, you're more likely to remember what you hear if you can associate it with a visual image. Second, by keying in on facial expressions and body language, you engage your own critical faculties. You can use your observations to help you figure out how the speaker feels about what he's saying or to evoke how you feel about the speaker—and as you saw in chapter 6, those judgments and emotional responses will sharpen your memory.

Preparation. Identify a situation in which you listen to spoken information for 3 to 5 minutes without being able to respond. It can be any one of the business situations I've identified, or you can practice with an audiotape, videotape, or TV/radio broadcast.

Step 1: Identify your motivation. Figure out a good, clear motivation for why remembering this information is important to you. If possible, jot down your motivation before or as you start listening. Be as specific as possible about why you need to retain what you hear. Find a reason that helps you to feel as though your life depended on it!

Step 2: Instruct your brain. Before you begin listening, tell your brain what you'd like it to do. Say, "I intend to listen actively and remember everything important about this conversation" or "I will pay close attention so that I can write my boss a detailed memo." Tell your brain both what you expect (attentiveness, active listening, a good memory) and the actions you plan to take (recalling the information, writing a memo).

Step 3: Ask yourself questions as you listen. Even if it seems unnatural, force yourself to think of a question for every sentence the speaker utters. Find something you want to know about what is said, then listen to see if you can learn the answer to your question.

Step 4: Evaluate your progress. As soon as possible after the speaker finishes, excuse yourself and jot down everything you remember about the conversation. The following day, ask yourself how much you remember, then ask yourself again the following week. If you like, keep a little log, rating yourself on the percentage of key facts or ideas that you recall from each spoken encounter. If you're not making the progress you'd like, consider whether you are fully committing to every one of these steps or whether you're allowing your mind to wander.

Practice #2: Use Active Listening Techniques

Practice these techniques, too, as often as you can. Ideally, you should try out at least one each day over a two-week period. As with Practice #1, you can use them on the job or with your TV or radio—as long as you don't mind talking back to them!

Preparation. Identify a situation in which you listen to spoken information for 3 to 5 minutes while being able to respond. As before, it can be one of the business situations I've identified or simply listening to an audiotape, videotape, or TV/radio broadcast in a situation where you're not embarrassed to speak aloud.

Step 1: Identify your motivation. As you've done before, figure out a clear motivation for why this information is important to you. Then, before you begin listening, jot it down. The more specific and urgent your motivation, the better your memory will be.

Step 2: Instruct your brain. Tell your brain what you want, giving yourself a clear, focused, positive instruction. Avoid using negative constructions, such as "Don't let my mind wander!" Your brain will hear only "mind wander" and obey you accordingly. Instead, tell your brain in clear, simple terms what you do want: "Stay focused." "Hold on to all important information." "Remember everything I need to write a terrific memo."

Step 3: Use a technique from "Strategies for Active Listening" (page 180). Pick any one of the five techniques you like and focus on that. The next day, choose another, and so on, until you've used each technique at least one day this week. Don't worry if this approach seems unnatural at first. The more you use these techniques, the more comfortable you'll become.

Step 4: Evaluate your progress. After each encounter is over, excuse yourself and jot down everything you remember about what you've heard. Then check back with yourself the following day and the following week. Keeping a log of your progress can be a powerful reinforcement since it demonstrates that your memory is improving, even if it doesn't seem that way at the time.

CONVERTING VERBAL TO VISUAL INFORMATION

One way to fill in some of the mental gap between your listening speed and other people's speaking speed is to convert verbal to visual information—another version of what you did in chapter 7 to remember names and other identifying information. You have two main options for making this conversion. Experiment with each of them and then choose the one that seems right for you.

Draw on all your senses as you associate and make connections. One way to remember spoken information is to tie it to the visual and other sensory information associated with the experience of taking it in. As you converse with your boss, notice what color his suit is. Remark upon the scent of lilies from the vase of flowers in his office and take a moment to savor the warm feeling of sunshine flooding in his window. Then, when you want to recall the conversation, those sense memories will be available to help you remember the spoken information as well. (You saw how powerfully sense memories could evoke other memories in chapter 6.)

Anchor your memories with names and faces. If you're sitting in a meeting, conference, or negotiating session, chances are you'll hear spoken information from more than one person. Anchoring the information with the person's name and face will help you remember both the information you heard and the person who said it.

To employ this technique, go back to chapter 7 and review the process of creating a visual story—a mental mini-movie—that links a person's name, face, and other identifying information. Use the same process while listening to each person speak, then add visual imagery that represents the things each one says.

For example, suppose you're sitting at a meeting in which Mr. Espinosa is talking about selling your company's telecommunications products to foreign markets. "We have to find new markets for our products," he begins. "And one of the areas we're thinking about is India. We're also looking at China—a country with a huge population in which only a small percentage of people own telephones. In Mexico as well, a relatively small percentage of the population has phones, so the market potential in all the regions is fantastic."

You've already created a little story about Mr. Espinosa involving a hose that spins around his large, square jaw. Now, you focus on the key words from his contribution: *new markets, India, China, small percentage, Mexico, telephones, market potential.* You visualize the spinning hose making its way across a map of Asia, passing through the countries of India and China on its way to Mexico. The hose is sitting on top of a gradually expanding balloon, which makes you think of expanding markets. Suddenly, you have a memory of Mr. Espinosa's presentation—and whenever you recall it, you'll also remember that he's the one who made this particular contribution.

As you've seen, there is no single right way to create visual imagery from the words you hear. Although previously I've suggested that you try to develop weird, absurd, or humorous imagery, all that matters in this more content-rich situation is that your images should be interesting. If you can pump life into the images you choose and make a close connection between what you envision and the person who's speaking, your memory for spoken information will be greatly enhanced.

Practice #3:
Use Visualization Techniques

Practice the techniques I've just described as often as you can. Ideally, you should try out at least one each day over a two-week period. As with Practices #1 and #2, you can try them on the job or with your radio or TV.

Preparation. Identify a situation in which you listen to spoken information for 3 to 5 minutes.

Step 1: Identify your motivation. Determine a compelling reason why this information is important to you.

Tips for Reviewing Spoken Information

An important aspect of recall is *review*—the process of going over information at least once after first acquiring it. Review is especially important with spoken information, since your memory is your primary source, especially when there's no written text to back up the speech. Here are some tips for getting the most out of your review of spoken information.

If possible, review your memory of what you heard immediately after you hear it. At least, do it as soon as possible. If you wait until after lunch to go over the morning meeting, you're likely to confuse the first speaker's points with your lunchtime companion's conversation. Indeed, if you wait to mentally review the first speaker until after you've heard all three presenters, you're far less likely to remember key concepts—much less to attribute them correctly. Try to go over every unit of spoken information immediately—or as soon thereafter as you can. Use the time when, say, the first speaker is being applauded to quickly review her remarks so that by the time the next presenter begins, the words of the first are firmly cemented in your mind.

Visualize what you heard. Don't just remember words; *see* what you heard. Picture the frowning faces of those St. Petersburg salespeople or see the tense body language of the anxious speaker. The more visual your memories, the better you'll retain them.

Step 2: Instruct your brain. As always, give yourself a clear, focused, positive instruction.

Step 3: Use a technique from the "Converting Verbal to Visual Information" section (page 184). Pick one of the two techniques and focus on that. Try that technique for five working days or until you start to feel proficient with it. Then begin to work with the other technique. Keep going until you've used each technique at least five days a week. The more often you use these techniques, the more natural they'll start to feel, so don't let any initial discomfort get in your way. Soon, this approach will begin to seem automatic.

Use all of your senses. The more you draw on all five senses, the more complete your memories will be. Review what you saw, heard, smelled, tasted, and felt as you were listening to the speaker. Such recall will automatically enhance your memories of the spoken information.

Associate. Attach as many emotional responses, judgments, and associations to the spoken information as you can. If the story about the St. Petersburg sales force brings to mind a similar problem you heard about last year in Miami, let the Miami story into your consciousness. If the speaker reminds you of your sixth-grade gym teacher, give your memories of Ms. Wallaby or Mr. Jerome free rein. The more associations you have with the information you hear, the more chances you give yourself to retrieve it.

If the information is really important, review it again—and then again. A quick brushup after you've heard a talk, a conversation, or a videotape may be all you need—but if the information is really crucial, don't rely on a single review. Note in your date book or palm pilot that you have an appointment to review the material the following day, again two days later, and then a few days after that. You'll be surprised at what a huge difference it makes.

If you didn't use active listening strategies when you first heard the information, be sure to use them when you review. Ask questions, recall body language, and bring in all the other techniques that you may have forgotten or decided not to use at the time. You'll have the experience of hearing the information all over again—and your memory will improve accordingly.

Practice #4:
Review What You've Heard

Ideally, you should now be reviewing information any time you hear something you'd like to remember. At the very least, commit to spending 1 or 2 minutes reviewing some spoken information each day for five consecutive days. As with Practices #1, #2, and #3, you can review information you've heard on the job or on the radio or TV.

Preparation. Identify a situation in which you've heard something you want to remember.

Step 1: Identify your motivation. Find a strong reason why this information matters to you and why it would be useful for you to be able to recall it whenever you like.

Step 2: Review your memories. Spend 1 or 2 minutes going over the information you recall, using the approach described above. If the information is particularly important to you, review it again two days later. Review it a third time one week from the date of your first review.

Step 3: Evaluate your progress. After five consecutive days of reviewing spoken information, try to recall what you reviewed each day. What is your sense of your progress? To what is extent does reviewing spoken information help you recall it?

MORE WAYS TO REMEMBER
SPOKEN INFORMATION

Here's another set of suggestions for retaining the things you hear. Feel free to pick and choose among these ideas, using them separately or in various combinations. You may find yourself relying on all of them equally or on one or two favorites; there may even be some suggestions here that you never use. If you can, I advise you to give each one a try just to find out how it works for you. In the end, though, you're the best authority on yourself. Choose what you think will work.

Focus on the sequence of events. For some types of spoken information, it's helpful to think about how a situation has evolved or to try to determine a sequence. You can visualize the progression or evolution that's being described or identify and number individual steps. As an active listener, you may want to intervene with questions that help you and the speaker clarify the sequence or that allow you to summarize or repeat your understanding of the sequence. Alternatively, you might take notes that focus on identifying a set of numbered or lettered steps. (You might also make use of the techniques in chapter 9 to help you associate numbers with other information.) This type of sequential focus is especially appropriate in negotiations, as you try to keep track of how discussions have developed, and in presentations that concern the history or development of a situation.

Synthesize ideas as you hear them. Sometimes you'll be involved in a conversation, presentation, or conference in which one or more speakers are presenting a number of different ideas. The temptation is to wait until all the presenters are done or the conversation is finished before you begin to link those ideas together—but don't give in to that temptation! If you wait until the last point is made, you'll find that the last point or two are all you remember. Instead, begin developing visual images or focused memories of each point as you hear it, then find ways to synthesize either the images or the ideas as you listen.

For example, suppose you're in a fast-moving conversation with three out-of-town clients about problems with your company's customer service policy. Each client is free associating about his or her experiences.

Ms. Jenkins: . . . And sometimes, when I call your office, it takes several minutes before I'm put through to the right person. I find it extremely frustrating, as though nobody has even bothered to set up good channels of communication.

Mr. Kim: Yes, and I've had trouble, even when I do get put through, with being made to wait on hold for quite a long time, which frankly is rather annoying . . .

Mr. Marquez: Excuse me, but I'd like to say something about the invoicing format. I've been quite confused by the itemizing system you're using . . .

Ms. Jenkins: Oh, yes, me, too!

Mr. Kim: Well, frankly, that doesn't bother me, but I have had problems with relating the invoice numbers with the catalog listings . . .

As you can see, the concerns are coming thick and fast. If this were a formal meeting, you might be taking notes, but suppose this conversation erupts at a company luncheon in honor of your out-of-town visitors. You can't whip out a tape recorder or even make a few discreet notes, but you do want to recall these very specific concerns.

The solution? Zero in on either key concepts or key images and find ways to link them. If you've created visual images for each customer, you can start adding images that relate to each one's complaints. Alternatively, you can create a numbered list that you repeat to yourself as the conversation continues.

Concerns	Option #1: Realistic Image	Option #2: More Visual Image
Jenkins can't get through	Ms. Jenkins, frustrated, is unable to speak to the person she wants.	Ms. Jenkins is unable to "get through" a tiny door.
Kim on hold	Next to Ms. Jenkins stands Mr. Kim, waiting impatiently with a phone in his hand.	As Ms. Jenkins looks through the door, she sees Mr. Kim being "held" in midair by a giant hand.
Marquez: itemized invoices	Beside the other two, Mr. Marquez is studying an itemized invoice.	Mr. Marquez is beside the other two, buried under a confusing pile of numbers.

And so on. The main thing is not to wait until the conversation is over to start thinking about—and remembering—the key ideas.

Slow things down if you're on information overload. No one—not even the world's greatest memory expert—can function at top speed for hours without a break. When there's too much information, everyone has trouble absorbing it all, let alone thinking clearly about it. If you can, find a way to "slow the flow" by asking a question, repeating a summary, or suggesting an actual break. Or ask the speaker or the participants to focus for a moment on a single aspect of the problem so you have a chance to really grasp one concept before going on to the next.

Break down complicated messages or instructions into many different parts. Again, no one can absorb everything at once. You'll remember from chapter 2 that scientists have named seven to nine as the maximum number of information bits that any person can memorize at one time. You can cheat the system a bit by "chunking," that is, putting many different types of information into a single chunk and then memorizing seven to nine big chunks. But you still may need to break down complicated messages, instructions, or other information into pieces that you memorize one at a time.

Exercise #2: Recalling Travel Directions

How many times have you had trouble keeping someone's spoken travel directions in your mind long enough to arrive at your destination? This useful exercise may help you negotiate the open road—and it will certainly sharpen your listening skills in many business situations.

Step 1. Write a set of complicated travel directions and ask a friend or colleague to read them to you, or ask a friend, colleague, or neighbor to give you actual directions to a place you've never been.

Step 2. As you hear the travel directions, picture exactly what you would do if you followed them. See yourself turning left at the white church. Visualize yourself looking at the odometer and noting that 0.9 mile has gone by. Imagine yourself scanning the highway for the "Millerville" sign.

Step 3. After you've heard and visualized the travel directions, repeat them to your friend or colleague. As you say the directions, visualize once again what you would do if you followed them.

Step 4. Ask your friend or colleague to help you evaluate your performance. How much did you remember? What in particular did you forget? Do you know why you forgot the items you did? What would you do next time to remember them?

Note: Feel free to employ active listening techniques, too—interrupting to ask a clarifying question, summarize, or repeat the speaker's exact words. Experiment until you've discovered which techniques help you retain the information you hear.

Exercise #3: Using Music to Help You Visualize

Music can be a powerful aid to your visual abilities because it leaves you alone to create your own mental pictures. Many people find music very evocative, inspiring them to visualize all sorts of scenes, whether real-life memories, fantasies, or simply daydreams. See how music can help you develop your memory.

Step 1. Set aside 15 to 20 minutes to listen to the radio one day. Choose your favorite station so you're listening to music you enjoy. Record the radio broadcast as you listen to it.

Step 2. As the DJ announces the title of each selection, invoke your active listening techniques. Create a visual image in your mind of each title, just as you did in chapter 7 to recall various names. Then, when you hear the music, allow its sounds to create additional visual information that you integrate with the title. For example, if the DJ announces a song called "Prisoner of My Heart," you might visualize a heart with a little set of prison bars in the center, from which the desolate songwriter looks out. Then, when you hear the actual song, either the music or the lyrics may make you think of birds flying out from the prison bars, winging their way to freedom.

Step 3. After you've heard a number of songs, use your recall of the visual images to write down each title. How many can you remember?

Step 4. If possible, listen to the songs without the DJ's announcements. How many titles can you recall?

Step 5. Alternatively, you can do this exercise with a CD. Listen to the CD all the way through, reading each title aloud off the jacket as the corresponding song begins. Then replay the beginning of each song, perhaps using the reshuffling feature to scramble the order, and see how many you can identify by name.

Note: This technique works just as well for classical and instrumental music and even for music with titles such as "Opus #3" or "Köchel Number 4." ("Köchel" is the designation given to each work by Mozart.) You just have to get creative with your visualizations for both the abstract titles and the wordless music.

REMEMBERING SPOKEN INFORMATION IN BUSINESS SITUATIONS

Finally, I'd like to share some specific suggestions for remembering spoken information in the 10 situations I identified at the beginning of the chapter. As you become familiar with the techniques in this chapter, you'll go on to develop your own strategies for responding to each of these situations, but here are some ideas to get you started.

One-on-One Discussions

This exercise may help you with recalling one-on-one conversations.

Exercise #4: Conversational Recall

Step 1. Find a quiet, comfortable place to sit and allow yourself 5 to 10 minutes to complete this exercise. Begin by recalling three to six conversations that you've had in the past week. Play each one back in your mind, trying to remember as much as possible of each one.

Step 2. Write down all the details of what you remember. You may find yourself recording only the essence of each conversation, a number of supporting details, or key words and phrases. Just let the conversations return to you in whatever form seems most natural and record what you can. You may even find yourself reconstructing entire conversations word for word.

Step 3. Look at what you've recorded about the first conversation you've chosen. Ask yourself, "Why was I able to remember these facts about this conversation?" Here are some possibilities.

- It was highly visual.

- It involved a lot of energy.

- The person to whom you were speaking was very important to you.

- The subject about which you were speaking was very important to you.

- The conversation was related to other issues that you were dealing with at the time.

- Your job prospects or some other vital issue in your life depended on your remembering the conversation.

- You had an important action to take as a result of the conversation.

Perhaps one or more of these reasons were why you remembered the first conversation, or perhaps you had quite another reason. Just note whatever reasons seem correct to you.

Step 4. Repeat the process with each of the other conversations you recorded.

Step 5. Look at all the conversations you've recorded and all the reasons you've identified. These are reasons that "just happened," but you can choose to make them work for you deliberately. Think about ways that you can bring the most useful reasons to bear on future conversations.

Social Situations

You can use a similar process to find ways of improving your memory for social situations with colleagues, clients, or potential business connections.

Exercise #5: Social Recall

Step 1. Again, find a comfortable place where you can take 5 to 10 minutes to complete this exercise. Begin by recalling a party or gathering that you attended at least two years ago—an event that has really made its way into your long-term memory. Play back the event in your mind, trying to remember as much as possible about it.

Step 2. Write down all the details of what you remember. Feel free to free associate, jotting down visual memories, words, people, thoughts, impressions, and other kinds of responses. You may find yourself focusing on conversations, clothing, emotions, music, actions, or some other aspect of the gathering. Or you may discover that you remember either a bit of everything or some other aspect of the party entirely. As you've learned by now, don't force any memories; just let them emerge and write them down.

Step 3. Look at what you've recorded about the party you attended. Ask yourself, "Why was I able to remember these ideas, images, or conversations?" Here are some possibilities.

- You had strong feelings about the event itself.
- You had strong feelings about a person or people at the event.
- Something important to you happened at the party or as a result of the party.
- Something funny happened at the party.
- You interacted with an unusual number of people.
- You interacted with particular intensity with one or more people.

Step 4. Look at all the information you've recorded and the reasons you've identified for remembering it. Again, ask yourself how you can draw on your "natural" reasons for recalling information, deliberately creating circumstances in which these reasons will apply.

Exercise #6: Remembering a Joke

Step 1. Write down or retell aloud a joke or anecdote that you've heard in the past five years.

Step 2. Ask yourself why you were able to remember this joke.

Note: This exercise is particularly useful if you're the kind of person who doesn't easily remember jokes or anecdotes. In that case, analyzing why you recall the ones that do stick with you can provide valuable information about how to improve your memory for spoken information.

Meetings

I've already made several suggestions that should improve your memory for "meeting information." Here are a few more.

Make predictions about what might happen during the meeting. Then pay attention to see if your predictions were correct. Whether you guessed right or not, you're far more likely to pay attention and remember what you hear if you're listening with the intention of checking out your predictions.

Pay special attention to statements that summarize points. Listen extra hard for such phrases as *in other words, in conclusion, to summarize, to sum up, as I've explained,* and *as we've seen.*

Pay special attention to phrases that emphasize important points. Listen carefully for such expressions as *most important, central, crucial, key,* and *finally.*

If you're taking notes, take just enough. Again, the Mind-Mapping technique in chapter 6 will help here. Avoid the temptation to bury yourself in note taking, which can actually interfere with both your concentration and your memory. Instead, use your notes to punctuate your memory of key items so that choosing exactly what to record becomes part of the process of paying attention.

Negotiations

You can draw on the techniques you've already read about to help you stay on top of what's said during negotiations. Here are a few more tips.

Be aware of each negotiator as an individual. Often, a group of negotiators does not operate as a united front. The more aware you are of each individual member of the opposition's team, the more flexible and effective you can be. Make a point of remembering each person's name, title, and place in the company. Perhaps you'll realize that you need to play to Ms. King, the executive VP in charge of sales, rather than to Mr. Wallace, a mere marketing rep. Likewise, keep track of personal remarks, interests expressed, and other individual data. Even if it leads only to more amicable and chatty coffee breaks, remembering the information will serve you well. Also, knowing which team member asked which question can be invaluable—if you remember enough to keep them all straight.

Focus on the key elements of every discussion and review them afterward. Sometimes a negotiation over many different issues can jump back and forth from point to point. Some clever negotiators even employ this tendency as a deliberate tactic to cause confusion. Instruct your mind to help you select the key points in every session and to dismiss the trivial issues or the remarks made in passing. Support your focus by reviewing what you've heard after each session or at strategically timed breaks during a session.

Speak to your opponents by name. It's not only courteous to use people's names, it will also help you remember who is who. A side benefit is that using each negotiator's name will often help you remember what you said to them.

Phone Calls

These days you can't even go to lunch without answering your cell phone. Here are some tips to help you remember everything you hear.

Don't write (except to take notes). And don't check your e-mail or engage in any other activity while you're on the phone—at least, not if you want to remember what's been said. Remember how in chapter 2, you learned that multitasking is the enemy of memory? Use an active listening technique to help you stay focused, make a Mind Map of the conversation, and/or allow your eyes to move about the room.

Interact with the other person or people. It's very difficult to listen for long periods of time without doing something active—so become interactive. At the very least, respond with "Yeah," "How interesting!" or "I didn't realize that." At the very most, ask provocative questions, summarize what you've heard, and/or offer heartfelt responses. Just do *something*!

Analyze what's important to remember and focus on that. Unless the conversation is very unusual, you're unlikely to need to recall every single word. All you need is the key elements, so figure out what they are and zero in on them.

Use visualization and association to connect each idea to the next. This is an especially useful approach when you're engaged in a long phone call about a wide variety of subjects—talking to your absent boss, for example, and getting instructions on how to handle many different situations back in the office, or meeting a new client by phone and getting a wide-ranging sense of his concerns. Identify each key idea, visualize it, and then find a way to associate it with the idea that came just before. When you get off the phone, you should have one long story made up of a sequence of images. Review it once or twice, and you'll be able to recall the entire conversation.

Make a few key notes to record the call. If you get up to 30 or 40 calls a day, you may find that they all blend together. Find a distinctive way to notate every call. If you've zeroed in on the main idea of each one, you'll need only a few words or phrases to evoke everything that was said.

Practice #5: Notate Your Phone Calls

If phone calls are a significant part of your job, try this practice 1 or 2 minutes a day for five consecutive days.

Preparation. Complete a phone call. Have a writing instrument and paper ready.

Step 1: Create an "abbreviation" for the call. Jot down a few words or perhaps a visual symbol that captures the essence of the call. Don't use more than one or at most two lines of a ruled notebook or legal pad. The more concentrated and concise your notation, the better.

Step 2: Review your notes. At the end of the day, look at the notations you've made. How much can you recall of each phone call you recorded?

Presentations or Conferences

If you're listening to a presentation or lecture:

Step 1. Use the speaker's name and face—and the visual images you develop for them—to connect the information to the speaker.

Step 2. Employ Mind Mapping to help you follow and recall a long presentation.

Visualizing a Voice

One way of focusing on phone calls is to give free rein to your associations with the speaker's voice, especially if you've never seen her face. Converting the sound of a voice into a visual image will help support your efforts to visualize and recall the words you've heard as well as the tone of voice, implied meanings, and general attitude. Here are some possible visual associations—or feel free to develop your own.

- Syrupy voice: Maple syrup
- High-pitched voice: A balloon floating high in the air
- Squeaky voice: A mouse
- Rough voice: Sandpaper
- Gravelly voice: Gravel
- Foreign accent: A visual image that you associate with that country
- Husky voice: A rough blanket
- Voice that frequently changes pitch: A musical instrument
- Hoarse voice: A frog (in the person's throat) or perhaps a horse
- Commanding voice: A military officer
- Weak voice: A child
- Slow voice: A dunce cap
- Loud voice: A megaphone
- Monotone: A steamroller going over asphalt or concrete

Demonstrations or Instructions

In these cases, you want to remember a series of steps in the order they were presented. I recommend making a numbered list, then using the techniques explained in chapter 9 for recalling numerical information to help you associate a number with each step.

Videotapes

A videotape is easier to recall than an audiotape because you're able to use your eyes and ears at the same time. When everything is presented to you, though—both aural and visual information—you tend to get lazy and let your imagination slide. Try to find ways of becoming an active viewer, just as you've learned to become an active listener.

- If you can, pause the tape at key intervals and ask yourself what was the most important information you just learned.

- Ask questions about what you're viewing and then watch closely to see if you can learn the answers.

- Summarize what you're learning as you absorb it.

Ideally, you would watch a particular videotape several times. First, view it without interruption, simply absorbing what you can. Then formulate your questions and intentions—What do you want most to know? Why is this information important to you?—and watch the tape again in a slower, more focused manner, zeroing in on what you specifically need to recall. This process is analogous to first scanning a book and then focusing on the aspects you care about most.

If you get only one viewing, instruct your mind to identify the essential aspects as you watch. If appropriate, mentally assign a number to each key point and then use the technique explained in chapter 9 to relate each number to its concept.

Audiotapes

When you're given only audio information, you have to listen more intently, converting verbal concepts into visual images. Moreover, if you listen to something in your car, you have to be able to balance the whole process with safety. (The best memory in the world won't keep you from running into a tree—so pay attention!)

As with videotapes, it's ideal if you can stop an audiotape at key points. This is especially important if you're listening to a recording by a non-professional speaker. Most speakers tend to drone on. If their voices aren't interesting, it will be hard for you to focus on their words—so take frequent breaks if you can and try to stay an active listener if you can't.

Exercise #7:
Remembering the Radio News

Step 1. Listen to a news program on a public radio or all-news station.

Step 2. Use your favorite strategy to focus on first 3, then 5, and finally 10 minutes' worth of audio information. Keep trying this exercise until you can recall all the key points from a 10-minute news broadcast. Again, consider making a numbered mental list of each news story or memorable item, then use the technique in chapter 9 (on numerical information) to remember each item on your list.

Note: You may want to record the news program so you can check your memory.

Elevator Talk

Conversations conducted in an elevator are the essence of spoken information captured under pressure. You may have only 10 or 20 seconds to grasp and retain what someone is saying to you. Yet people often do share crucial information in elevators, and you may well want to be "quick on your mind" to recall what you've heard.

Again, the key is to identify the main elements of what you're hearing and concentrate on remembering them. Instruct your mind to stay open and attentive, and listen as closely as you can. Then, as soon as possible, find a private place where you can recall, review, and perhaps write down what you heard. At the very least, stand in the hall as you exit and think for a moment about what you just heard. You'll be more likely to remember spoken information if you go over it in your mind immediately after you've heard it.

LISTENING HARDER *AND* SMARTER

Ironically, the key to recalling spoken information is to not worry too much about forgetting it. Nothing saps your concentration like anxiety. Every second you spend worrying about forgetting something is a second in which you haven't really listened to anything—except your own nervous thoughts.

In this chapter, I've described several techniques that you can use to your advantage. For any of them to work, though, you'll need to give yourself a break and simply focus, without worry or expectation. Knowing why you want to listen and trusting that you can remember what's important to you will take you a very long way in improving your memory for spoken information.

CHAPTER 9

MASTERING NUMERICAL
INFORMATION

few years ago, in an analysis of the back-room operations
at a major New York City brokerage firm, executives discovered just how costly poor numerical memory could be.
A study of the multi-million-dollar firm turned up a higher-than-expected
error rate that was costing them far too much. When a client called to
order, say, 5,000 shares of stock, the order might be incorrectly entered
into the corporate computer as 500 shares. If the stock price went up, the
company was liable for the difference.

That's where I came in. The partners asked me to give their brokers
an extensive series of workshops on memory training, focusing on observation, concentration, and short-term memory. My techniques helped
the firm reduce its error rate, saving the partners huge sums—and reducing tension among the employees.

Afterward, I spoke with Leslie, one of the brokers who'd taken my
course. "I know I make fewer mistakes," she told me. "But what's almost
more important is the sense that I can trust myself. It's easy to confuse
numbers when you work with them all day—after a while, they all start
to look alike. With your system, every number is part of a unique story,
and I couldn't get them mixed up if I wanted to!"

THE BENEFITS OF REMEMBERING NUMERICAL INFORMATION

In my experience, there are two types of people—the ones who think they're good at math, and the ones who know they're not. Both types can benefit enormously from my memory techniques. If you're an accountant, an engineer, or another type of math whiz, your memory for specific numbers will only get better if you use my system. If, on the other hand, you're the type who has to check a phone number six times before dialing it, your numerical memory will improve even more dramatically. My system will help you master phone numbers, prices, statistics, tables—anything involving figures.

Certainly, that's what the people at Hazeltine discovered. Hazeltine was a major U.S. defense company where I taught my techniques to engineers, technicians, physicists, and systems analysts. As a result of employees' improved memory for numerical data and because of their newly enhanced ability to recall previous solutions to technical and manufacturing problems, the company was able to reduce errors that occurred in its manufacture of defense systems and equipment.

Understandably, the folks at Hazeltine were already fairly confident of their numerical memory when I began working with them. After all, they knew technical data about engineering, physics, and computer technology that I could barely follow. To show them how much further their numerical memories could expand, I started the workshop by circulating copies of a letter-size sheet of paper that was filled with a solid grid of numbers, organized by column and row. There's nothing quite as scary—even to a roomful of math whizzes—as a paper filled with numbers.

"Ask me to tell you any number on that page," I invited them. "Just call it out by column and row."

Slowly, the participants called out places in the grid—and were amazed to find that I could supply them with the correct number every single time.

"Now it's your turn," I told them. "I'm going to teach you how to do the exact same thing." Some were skeptical, others were intrigued, and many more were simply dumbfounded, but they learned how to memorize that and even more demanding numerical information—and you can, too. All it takes is the same three techniques we've been learning all along: paying attention, visualizing, and associating.

> *Numbers are intellectual witnesses that belong only to mankind.*
> —Aristotle, *Metaphysica*

LIVING IN A DIGITAL WORLD

When I was growing up—not *that* long ago!—people had addresses, seven-digit phone numbers, and Social Security numbers that were hardly ever used. No area codes, cell phone numbers, access codes, or pager numbers. No credit cards, computer passwords, online account numbers, or confirmation numbers for financial business conducted by phone. Not being a numbers person, I hesitate to estimate, but it seems to me that there were about 10 percent as many numbers in my daily life when I was in my early twenties as there are today.

If, like me, you tend to be a word person, you too may find yourself somewhat overwhelmed by the growing number of occasions in which numbers are vital to our daily life. Even if you are a numbers person, you may occasionally feel a bit deluged by all the digits. Also, of course, once you leave home and check in at the office, you're likely to come upon even more situations in which numbers are necessary.

- Phone calls to clients—area codes, phone/pager numbers, extensions
- Your own telephone work—calling-card numbers, voicemail access codes
- Access codes for computers and online accounts

- Confirmation numbers for business conducted by phone or online

- Addresses

- Profit-loss statements

- Significant dates

- Printouts of statistics

- Charts from banks and investment companies showing interest rates, earnings, and rates of return

- Flight numbers and schedules

- Location codes for various branches of your business

- Numbers of locations in which a product can be bought or sold

- Inventory numbers for stock

- Sales and marketing figures

- Product knowledge in which numbers are used to describe benefits or features

- Stock prices and mutual funds, past and current performance

Each of these situations presents a similar challenge: How do you keep the numbers from getting mixed up? Words, by their very nature, tend to evoke unique images. Moreover, the order of words is inextricably bound up with the images they create. To paraphrase the old joke, it's pretty easy to distinguish the mundane headline "Dog Bites Man" from the startling news item "Man Bites Dog."

Numbers, however, are more difficult. At a glance, 859 looks pretty similar to 958, and even the most numerically literate among us may need a few moments to distinguish 3750954 from 4590573. Yet, as my students at the brokerage house discovered, mixing up similar digits can have costly—even catastrophic—results.

The solution? Observe the digits closely (pay attention), convert them into images (visualize), and weave the images into a story (associate). Once I show you how to use the Numerical Memory Matrix System, you'll never have to struggle with digits again. Plus, you'll expand your memory power to such an extraordinary extent that you'll begin to amaze friends, colleagues—and yourself.

> *"Can you do addition?" the White Queen asked. "What's one and one and one and one and one and one and one and one and one and one?"*
>
> *"I don't know," said Alice. "I lost count."*
>
> —Lewis Carroll, *Through the Looking Glass*

MAKING NUMBERS EASIER TO DIGEST

When you have to recall a number, do you feel as bewildered as Alice facing the White Queen? Well, take heart—you're not alone. Fortunately, there are several things you can do to make numbers easier to work with. Most of this chapter is devoted to the Numerical Memory Matrix System, in which you'll learn to translate even the longest and most complex sets of digits into easy-to-remember images. First, though, let's look at two simple things you can do to boost your numerical memory.

Chunking

Remember back in chapter 2, when you learned that even memory experts have a built-in limit on how many items they can remember? For most mere mortals, that limit kicks in at seven items, although some of you manage to push your memories as far as nine.

There's a nifty solution to this memory problem, however, which has come to be known as chunking. Even though you may be able to remember only seven items at a time, there's no built-in limit on how large each "item" may eventually be. When you remember a phone number, for example, you've learned to chunk it automatically into smaller bits.

202-	555-	4598
area code	first three digits	last four digits

If you've memorized your Social Security number, you probably chunk that as well.

401-	87-	2834
first three digits	middle two digits	last four digits

Think about how you chunk other long numbers you've memorized: caller access codes, for example, or the numbers of your credit cards or checking account. Chances are, you've developed a kind of rhythm in which you break long sequences down into several smaller chunks. You probably can't recall the number digit by digit (especially if it has more than nine digits)—but you can easily remember two, three, or even more "chunks" of numbers.

Although many of us inadvertently memorize often-used series of digits, I don't really recommend chunking as a long-term memory solution. The Numerical Memory Matrix System works much better. I do recommend chunking for short-term memory, however; it's perfect for recalling a number just long enough to write it down or to use it once, such as when you're getting a phone number from directory assistance or when you're copying an account number from a printout. We won't spend much time on chunking in this chapter, but here's a brief exercise that will help you take advantage of this short-term memory skill.

Exercise #1: Number Chunking

Step 1. Make a list of all the long numbers you've memorized: phone numbers, account numbers, and the like. Just jot them down quickly on a blank piece of paper—but notice how you recall them. Become aware of the chunking techniques you've already mastered and see if

you can notice anything specific that may help you in other situations. Do you prefer the rhythm of a phone number, for example, or
do you automatically chunk your numbers in groups of four, five, or
six? Do you look for some kind of pattern within the number to help
you or simply break it down the same way each time? See if you can
figure out your own personal "chunking style."

Step 2. Next, look at the following list of numbers. Don't even try to
memorize them; just copy them from the book onto a blank piece of
paper. What do you notice about this process?

4153306709
601405567
482178439698667
32347795863409
12192006

Step 3. Here are the same numbers, chunked. Try copying these.
What do you notice now?

415-330-6709
601-40-5567
4821-784396-98667
323-477-9586-3409
12-19-2006

Step 4. You've probably already figured out that the numbers have
common patterns.

415-330-6709: Telephone number, including area code
601-40-5567: Social Security number
4821-784396-98667: Credit card number
323-477-9586-3409: Calling card number (phone number plus
four-digit access code)
12-19-2006: Date

Step 5. Next, practice copying the following numbers. See how quickly and yet accurately you can copy the digits. Use chunking to help you.

549356809853449: Credit card number

21529865867: Phone number

90483956091298: Calling card number (phone number plus four-digit access code)

01051985: Date

608458956: Social Security number

Step 6. Copy the following random numbers, chunking them in whatever pattern works for you. Don't even try to keep them in your long-term memory—you'll soon learn a system that works far better than chunking—but do use chunking to keep these numbers in your short-term memory long enough to copy them accurately.

Hint: Although these numbers don't necessarily correspond to the patterns we've reviewed—Social Security numbers, phone numbers, and the like—you may want to take advantage of those familiar rhythms as you chunk these unfamiliar numbers.

1250395686

920948674

340928323

453623409586249

494502348234

Using Preexisting Associations

Although most numbers tend to be abstract, some do have preexisting associations. "Lucky 7," "sweet 16," and "Heinz 57" are only some of the numbers we routinely associate with words, images, and events. Moreover, because the human brain tends to seek patterns and invoke associations whenever it can, we all tend to have strong associations with the most commonly used digits. Here are some examples.

1: You're number one; first base; being all alone; the one and only

2: Twins; two hearts that beat as one; double your money; second base

3: Triplets; third base; the Holy Trinity; third time's the charm

4: Four corners; four directions; four-wheel drive

Exercise #2: Identify Your Associations

Step 1. What associations do you have with numbers that may help you remember particular digits, numerals, and figures? Start by filling in your automatic associations for each of the following numbers. Don't worry if you don't have any associations with a number that's listed; just leave the space blank. The goal is not to create associations but simply to become aware of the ones you already have.

1: _____

2: _____

3: _____

4: _____

5: _____

6: _____

7: _____

8: _____

9: _____

10: _____

11: _____

12: _____

13: _____

16: _____

18: _____
21: _____
39: _____
50: _____
57: _____
75: _____
100: _____

Step 2. Now, what about the numbers I haven't asked you about? Fill in the following numbers. Ask yourself whether these combinations of digits tend to leap out at you when you encounter them elsewhere.

Your birthday: _____
Spouse/partner/significant other's birthday: _____
Mother's birthday: _____
Father's birthday: _____
Sibling's birthday: _____
Sibling's birthday: _____
Friend's birthday: _____
Friend's birthday: _____
Other important dates: _____ _____ _____
Significant area codes: _____ _____ _____ _____
Numbers in addresses: _____ _____ _____ _____

Step 3. Finally, take a few moments to cast your mind over any other numbers that have powerful associations for you. They may have specific meaning in your life; remind you of a song, movie, TV show, sports hero, or historical date; or simply be numbers that you've always liked. For example, one of my friends is fond of the number 98, and she tends to remember anything with a 98 in it just because she enjoys that figure. Retrieve as many significant numbers as you can and note them here.

Number	Why I Remember It
_____	_____
_____	_____
_____	_____
_____	_____
_____	_____

Now that you've identified your associations, I hope you remember how to use them! (If not, flip back to chapter 6 for a quick review.) Simply intertwine the image that comes automatically to mind with other significant information.

Suppose, for example, that you have a meeting with a client on the 16th floor. Picture your client at a *Sweet 16* party, and you won't have to keep checking the address as you stand in the elevator. Or say you're joining a friend in a restaurant at the corner of 39th and Main streets. Tell yourself that the *main* thing about this friend is that, like all famous movie stars, he never goes past his *39th* birthday. Visualizing your friend in sunglasses, being interviewed by a gossip columnist who wants to know his true age, may help you retrieve the address when you need it.

Since you are now studying geometry and trigonometry, I will give you a problem. A ship sails the ocean. It left Boston with a cargo of wool. It grosses 200 tons. It is bound for Le Havre. The mainmast is broken, the cabin boy is on deck, there are 12 passengers aboard, the wind is blowing East-North-East, the clock points to a quarter past three in the afternoon. It is the month of May. How old is the captain?

—Gustave Flaubert

THE NUMERICAL MEMORY MATRIX SYSTEM: HOW TO INSTALL NUMBERS IN YOUR LONG-TERM MEMORY

I like the quotation from Flaubert because it works on the same principle as the Numerical Memory Matrix System. Instead of being concerned with the actual math, Flaubert's playful, nonsensical word problem focuses on a little story full of images—the broken mainmast, the 12 passengers, the windy deck. None of these details will help you solve the numerical "problem" of the captain's age, but they will help you recall the scene with surprising vividness.

In the same way, the Numerical Memory Matrix System won't necessarily improve your math skills, but it will help you remember any number or series of numbers that you choose. With this system, you will greatly astound your friends and impress your colleagues—and unless they've also taken my workshop or read this book, they won't have a clue as to how you've done it!

The system actually goes back to the ancient Greeks, although it was popularized in the 17th century and has been in use ever since. It's based on translating abstract numbers into concrete visual images and then associating the images into a story. The process involves several steps, so be patient. Although it can take you some time to understand and then a bit more time to master, I assure you that the results will be worth it in the end.

Step 1: Translate Digits into Sounds and Letters

Luckily, our numerical system includes only 10 digits: 0 through 9. Every number in the system is a combination of those basic 10 figures, so we'll start by associating each digit with a specific letter or letters as well as a sound or a set of sounds.

Numerical Memory Matrix Alphabet

1	2	3	4	5	6	7	8	9	0
t	n	m	r	L	J	K	f	p	z
d					g*	C**	v	b	s
th					dg	G**	ph		c*
					sh	Q			
					ch	ng			
					tch				

* Soft sounds (*g* as in *gel*; *c* as in *cereal*)

** Hard sounds (*C* as in *casino*; *G* as in *go*)

Notes: Any double letter—the double *r* in *hurry*, for example, or the double *z* in *jazz*, counts as only one number.

Silent letters—like the *g* in *design* or the *gh* in *bright*—don't count.

Vowels have no numerical value in this system, nor do the letters *w*, *h*, and *y*, since those consonants have soft sounds, like vowels.

Numerical Alphabet Sounds

1 = Dental sound (t, d, and th)

2 = Nasal sound (n)

3 = Humming sound (m)

4 = Rolling sound (r)

5 = Liquid sound (l)

6 = Soft sound (j, soft g, dg, sh, ch, and tch)

7 = Hard sound (k, hard c, hard g, q, and ng)

8 = One of the fricative sounds (f, v, and ph)

9 = One of the plosive sounds (p, b)

0 = Sawing or sibilant sound (z, s, and soft c)

Step 2: Create Interactive Images

In Step 1, we learned how to replace each digit with a consonant sound. In Step 2, we'll use those consonant sounds to form words—words that we can visualize. In fact, because the visual aspect of this process is so important, I don't even like to call them words. I prefer the term *interactive images*.

To form your word—or image—start with the sound or letter associated with each digit, then create a visual word containing that sound. Here are some examples of how a number might become an image.

1 = *t*oy
2 = i*nn*
3 = *m*ow
4 = *r*ye
5 = *L*aw
6 = *J*aw
7 = *K*iwi
8 = *f*oe
9 = *p*ie
0 = *z*oo

Note that each word contains only one consonant sound. That's because when we get into double digits, we'll need to include two consonant sounds, and for triple digits, we'll be looking for three.

Double Digits	Triple Digits
10 = *t*oe*s*	100 = *d*i*s*ea*s*e
11 = *t*ee*th*	101 = *d*u*st*
12 = *t*u*n*a	102 = *d*e*sign*
13 = tea*m*	103 = a*th*ei*sm*
14 = *t*owe*r*	104 = *d*ow*s*e*r*
15 = *t*owe*l*	105 = *t*a*ss*e*l*

Note, too, that each word can easily be translated into a visual image. The number 1, for example, can be any word that includes the single consonant sound *t*, *d*, or *th*. *To*, *doe*, *tee*, *tea*, or *dew* would also work fine. *Day* is harder to visualize, and *too*, *do*, and *the* are darn near impossible, so although those are words that fit the sounds we want, they aren't really images. And images are what we need to complete our next step.

Questions and Answers about the Numerical Alphabet

Q: Why do some numbers have more than one letter?

A: Some sounds can be grouped together, such as *f* and *v* or *t* and *d*. Although we're used to thinking of these sounds as different, they actually belong in the same sound family. Also, some sounds are represented by the same letter. *S* and soft *c* for example, make exactly the same sound.

Q: Why are some letters capitals and others lowercase?

A: Some letters were chosen for the ways that they visually resemble the digits.

   1 = t because they are each made with one basic downstroke. (Also, if you print a capital *T* and then take off part of the crossbar at the top, it looks like a *1*.)

   2 = n because a lowercase *n* has two strokes. (Also, if you print a capital *N* and turn it on its side, you can see a *2*.)

   3 = m because a lowercase *m* has three strokes. (Also, if you turn an *m* on its side, you'll see a *3*.)

   6 = J because a reversed capital *J* looks like a *6*.

   7 = K because a cursive *K* (as on a Kellogg's cereal box) begins with a stroke that looks like a *7*. You can also find two *7*s—one in the top and one in the bottom part of the *K*.

Step 3: Associate the Images to Create a Story

Once you have an image for each digit, string those images together to make a memorable story. If you're trying to remember the numeral 349, for example, and you've translated each of the three digits into an image—*mow*, *rye*, and *pie*—you might visualize a gardener working hard to *mow* the lawn so he can take a break and eat a ham on *rye* sandwich and a nice big piece of *pie*.

---

8 = f because a cursive *f* has two small loops that resemble an *8*.

9 = P because a reversed capital *P* looks like a *9*.

Q: Okay, what about the rest of the numbers?

A: The others depend more on sounds or other associations.

4 = r because of the r sound in the word four and because the fourth letter in four is *r*.

5 = L because in the Roman numeral system, L is 50, and because Lincoln is on a five-dollar bill. (Also, if you hold up your left hand with the fingers together and the thumb extended at a right angle, the *five* fingers form the letter *L*).

0= z because the word *zero* starts with *z* and ends with *o*.

Q: Are any digits associated with vowels?

A: In this system, the vowels have no numerical value, and neither do the letters *w h*, and *y*. Why is this? Because if we restrict the code to hard sounds, we can use vowels (and *w*, *h*, and *y*) to add some flexibility as we create a wide variety of numerical "words."

At this point in the workshop, I usually have one or more students who simply explode in frustration. "Learning this system is going to be *much* harder than memorizing the numbers themselves!" someone is sure to say.

"I don't understand how it works!" another student may add.

I know it can seem confusing at first, but bear with me. Soon it will become clear—and much easier to use than any other way of remembering numbers.

Or suppose you're trying to remember the four-digit number 5218. First, you'd translate the digits into images.

5 = *Law*
2 = *inn*
1 = *toy*
8 = *foe*

Then you'd visualize the images and associate them to create a story.

A bunch of *Law*makers were meeting at an *inn*, where they planned to send a trick *toy*—maybe an exploding cigar—to their worst *foe*.

Step 4: Associate the Number with the Situation in Which You'll Use It

Suppose 349 is the extension of your colleague in accounting. Picture your coworker *mow*ing the lawn and enjoying his ham on *rye* and his *pie*, and his extension will work its way into your long-term memory bank.

Or say that 5218 is the number of your new suite, and you keep forgetting it, so you look for a way to associate the little story you created with your own offices. Perhaps the lawmakers met at your office before they went to the inn. Or maybe your suite is the home of their foe. Visualizing a connection between your suite and the story means that you'll always be able to retrieve the numerical sequence.

Exercise #3: Translate Digits into Words

Step 1. Here are some numbers. Use the technique you've just learned to translate each numeral into a word. Don't rely on the words you've been given; start practicing the process of creating your own.

45
5
8
7
20
49
120
314
4952

Step 2. Next, for each number, create a little story linking the words you've created for each digit. Your story can make sense or be completely absurd—just be sure it's something you can visualize.

Step 3. Finally, incorporate into your story the following information about each number.

45: Your locker number at your new health club
5-8-7: The combination of the lock on that locker
2049: The suite where your favorite colleague works in her office across town
120: The telephone extension of your tech-support person
314: Your computer access code
4952: Your boss's birthday (April 9, 1952)

I believe there are
15,747,724,136,275,002,577,605,653,961,181,555,468,044,717,914,
527,116,709,366,231,425,076,185,631,031,296 *protons in the universe and the same number of electrons.*

—Sir Arthur Eddington, *The Philosophy of Physical Science*

GETTING INTO DOUBLE DIGITS

By now, you may not be surprised to learn that you can easily use the Numerical Memory Matrix System to memorize even those numbers that are as long and complicated as Sir Arthur Eddington's estimate (although you probably wouldn't want to waste your memory on such an outdated concept of physics).

However, creating a story that incorporates one digit at a time could take you quite a while, so once again we come back to chunking—breaking up long numbers into multidigit groups.

Let's start small. Here are some two-digit images to get you started. The process will work best for you, though, if you create your own images. As you read each item on my list, try to create your own "two-digit" word, translating each digit into the letters and sounds that you then combine.

11 = *teeth*	29 = *nape*	47 = *rock*	65 = *jewel*	83 = *foam*
12 = *tuna*	30 = *maze*	48 = *roof*	66 = *Jewish*	84 = *furry*
13 = *team*	31 = *mouth*	49 = *rope*	67 = *Jockey*	85 = *fuel*
14 = *tower*	32 = *moon*	50 = *lasso*	68 = *Chevy*	86 = *fish*
15 = *towel*	33 = *Miami*	51 = *light*	69 = *Jeep*	87 = *fog*
16 = *teach*	34 = *mayor*	52 = *lion*	70 = *Kiss*	88 = *fife*
17 = *tag*	35 = *mail*	53 = *loom*	71 = *coat*	89 = *VIP*
18 = *TV*	36 = *match*	54 = *lawyer*	72 = *coin*	90 = *Pizza*
19 = *tub*	37 = *mug*	55 = *lily*	73 = *coma*	91 = *Pet*
20 = *noose*	38 = *Mafia*	56 = *leash*	74 = *crow*	92 = *Pen*
21 = *nude*	39 = *mop*	57 = *leg*	75 = *Keyhole*	93 = *Puma*
22 = *neon*	40 = *rose*	58 = *love*	76 = *cage*	94 = *Pier*
23 = *name*	41 = *radio*	59 = *lobby*	77 = *CoKe*	95 = *Pool*
24 = *Nero*	42 = *rhino*	60 = *chess*	78 = *coffee*	96 = *Peach*
25 = *Nile*	43 = *Rome*	61 = *jet*	79 = *cop*	97 = *Pig*
26 = *notch*	44 = *roar*	62 = *china*	80 = *fuse*	98 = *Puff*
27 = *neck*	45 = *royal*	63 = *Jam*	81 = *fat*	99 = *PoPe*
28 = *navy*	46 = *rich*	64 = *Jar*	82 = *fan*	100 = *disease*

Exercise #4: Using Double Digits

Step 1. Here are some multidigit numbers. Chunk each number into two-digit units, then translate each numeral into a series of words.

45433210
66849382
93847596

Step 2. String the words together into a story for each numeral. Have fun; be creative! The more you enjoy this process, the more quickly and easily you'll be able to use it.

Step 3. Finally, incorporate into your story the key information about each digit.

45433210: Credit card for a major department store
66849382: Access code for a company computer
93847596: Departmental number that you frequently enter on invoices

Do not worry about your difficulties in mathematics;
I assure you that mine are greater.
—Albert Einstein

Practice #1: Memorizing Numbers That You Often Use

Step 1. Read through the following lists of numbers and situations. Complete the lists by noting some figures that you'd like to memorize.

Area Codes
305: Miami
212: New York City (Manhattan)
702: Las Vegas
617: Boston

Area code you'd like to memorize: _____

Area code you'd like to memorize: _____

Area code you'd like to memorize: _____

Social Security Numbers

123-92-4570

Your Social Security number: _____

Credit Card Numbers

6751-1000-3948-9460

Your credit card number: _____

Your credit card number: _____

Your credit card number: _____

Lock Combinations

Right 25; left 18; right twice to 10

Your lock combination: _____

Checking Account Numbers

3694625

Your checking account number: _____

Phone Numbers

212-801-4261

Phone number you'd like to memorize: _____

Phone number you'd like to memorize: _____

Phone number you'd like to memorize: _____

Phone number you'd like to memorize: _____

Addresses

215 East 41st Street

3857 North Winston Street

Address you'd like to memorize: _____

Address you'd like to memorize: _____

Address you'd like to memorize: _____

Travel Itineraries

Leaving JFK on American Airlines flight 800, connecting to flight 341

Your flight information: _____

License Plate Numbers

757W812

Your license plate number: _____

Step 2. Go through the following series of steps, working first on area codes, then Social Security numbers, and so on down the list.

1. Convert each set of digits into a word or words.

2. Link the words in a story.

3. Associate the story with the appropriate situation.

You can decide whether you want to translate the numbers in units of single, double, or triple digits. Experiment to find out what works best for you.

Step 3. If you like, compare the words you create with some of my examples.

Area Codes

305: Miami—*missile*
"During the Cuban *Missile* Crisis, people in Miami were worried."

212: New York City (Manhattan)— I*ndian*
"The *Indians* sold us Manhattan."

702: Las Vegas—*Casino*
"You'll always find a *casino* in Las Vegas!"

617: Boston—wa*tchdog*
"A Boston terrier makes a good *watchdog*."

Social Security Numbers

123-92-4570—*denim*-*piano*-*reLiCs*

"She wore *denim* as she sat playing the *piano* in a parlor full of old *relics*—and then I asked her to put her Social Security number on our invoice, so she could buy a new piano-playing outfit!"

Credit Card Numbers

6751-1000-3948-9460—*JuGGLed*-*dioceses*-*improve*-*preaches*
"The priest *juggled* trips to different *dioceses* along with all his other duties. He was traveling around, checking out other priests' sermons, seeking to *improve* the way he *preaches*."

Lock Combinations

Right 25; left 18; right twice to 10—R-*InhaLe*/L-*dive*/RR-*dizzy*

"The swimmer wore a bright magenta bathing suit [I put that in to make the whole image more memorable for myself.]. She looked to the *right* as she began to *inhale* deeply. Then she looked to the *left* as she took her *dive* into the pool. She made *two* laps around the pool, turning *right* each time, as she began to get *dizzy* from all that deep breathing."

Checking Account Number

3694625—*matchup*; *originaL*
"I'll *match up* my *original* checking account from when I was a kid with this one."

Phone Numbers

212-801-4261—*Indian*-*feast*-*rain*-*chat*
"The *Indian* is having a *feast* in the *rain* as I *chat* with this person on the phone."

Addresses

215 E. 41st Street—*NoodLe* E. Hea*rt*
"The woman who lives there made a giant *noodle* for her boyfriend, *Everett*, and won his *heart*."

3857 North Winston Street—Hemophi*Lia*C N. Churchill
"The *hemophiliac* prince rode *north* on his huge white steed. . .
hoping to visit the *church* on the *hill* so he could pray for his disease to be cured." [or . . . "hoping to visit *Winston Churchill*, who
had access to a new cure for the disease."]

Travel Itineraries

Leaving JFK on American Airlines flight 800, connecting to flight
341—President Kennedy-American-*faces-married*
"*President Kennedy*, a great *American*, looked at the *faces* of his
children and the woman he had *married*, wondering how to tell
them goodbye."

License Plate Numbers

757W812—C*L*ock-Western-*Fade-in*

"As the *clock* started to tick, the *Western* began playing on the
movie screen, with a *fade-in* on the hands of the cowboy holding
the reins of his horse."
(By the way, my own license plate says, "Mr. Memory," which I
hope is easy to remember. At least I never have to worry about forgetting it!)

As you can see, I have fun coming up with "memory matrix images"
that inherently relate to the situations involved. I was particularly pleased
when I came up with *casino* to remember Las Vegas's 702 area code. I
don't always get that lucky, but when I do see such a great connection, I
try to take advantage of it.

Now, I know this process seems difficult and confusing at first, and
maybe even a bit intimidating. But think for a moment about a system
you've already memorized—the alphabet. Remember how long it took
you, way back when, to recall those 26 letters in "alphabetical order"
and how daunting that memory task seemed? But now you know
without even thinking about it that *a* comes before *b*, or that *t* comes
later in the alphabet than *d*.

How did you develop your facility with the alphabet? Through practice. Your facility with the Numerical Memory Matrix System is no different. The more you use the system, the easier it will become, until one day it will seem automatic, just as using the alphabet is now.

I can't give you any set time frame for mastering this system or any one way of approaching it, because different people have different capacities and learn in different ways. I can promise you, though, that *using* the system, a little bit at a time, will have great results—so don't worry. Just find a way to incorporate a little daily practice into your routine. Check back with yourself in a few weeks, and *voilà*! You'll discover that without your even realizing it, the system has become familiar to you.

I remember once going to see [the mathematician Ramanujan] when he was lying ill at Putney. I had ridden in taxi cab number 1729 and remarked that the number seemed to me rather a dull one, and that I hoped it was not an unfavorable omen. "No," he replied, "it is a very interesting number; it is the smallest number expressible as the sum of two cubes in two different ways."

—Geoffrey H. Hardy, *Ramanujan*

THE POWER OF NUMERICAL MEMORY

Very few of us look at the world the way Ramanujan did, with ordinary and apparently meaningless numbers like 1729 translating themselves into significant and fascinating images. By using the Numerical Memory Matrix System, any of us can begin to see numbers in a whole new way—as concrete visual images that can be incorporated into stories that aid our memories. With this system, you'll be able to remember a wide variety of useful information, including the following items.

- Numbered lists
- Sets of instructions
- Pages of books and magazines
- Charts of financial information

Everything should be made as simple as possible, but not simpler.
—Albert Einstein, *Reader's Digest*, October 1977

Numbered Lists

As you can see, most of the time you are creating unique images for each situation so that the stories you spin from those images are indelibly associated with the situation in question. But you can also choose a "standard" set of images for the numerals 1 through 10—familiar images that you can then use to make lists.

Suppose you decide that for list-making purposes, *1* is always *toy*. If you incorporate a toy into the first item on every one of your to-do lists, you'll always know it's the first item. By asking yourself where the toy is, you'll always be able to call up that item. Likewise, you can incorporate a *2*—*inn*—into every second item, a *3*—someone *mow*ing—into every third item, and so on.

Suppose, for example, that you've created the following list of things to do on Monday morning.

1. Call Jack Martin and ask him about the new marketing proposals.

2. Order flowers for your San Francisco colleague to congratulate her on her winning sales record.

3. Hire a temporary receptionist to fill in for the regular staff member, who's going on vacation next week.

4. Review the Seattle sales figures in preparation for a 2 P.M. meeting with your supervisor.

5. Ask a Portland, Oregon, colleague to fax you her sales figures so you can decide whether to introduce the idea of opening a Portland office.

Here's how you might apply the Numerical Memory Matrix to memorizing the to-do list.

Step 1. Translate digits into sounds and letters.

Step 2. Create interactive images. If you like, use the images I've already given you for numbers 1 to 100 as your "permanent" digits.

1= *t*oy

2 = i*nn*

3 = *m*ow

4 = *r*ye

5 = *L*aw

Step 3. Associate the images to create a story.

Step 4. Associate the number with the situation in which you'll use it. Here's how you might integrate "digital images" into the first three tasks on the list.

1. Call Jack Martin about marketing proposals.

See Jack Martin with the marketing proposals spread out over his desk as he answers the phone. Twined all around the phone cord and spread all over the proposals is a giant Slinky. (If Jack Martin is a name you have difficulty remembering, you might incorporate imagery relating to that name as well. For example, you could add a *Jack*-in-the-box and a *Martian* to the image.)

2. Order flowers for your San Francisco colleague to congratulate her on her winning sales record.

Envision a room at an inn, the Golden Gate Bridge shining in the background, with your colleague sitting in the room surrounded by flowers and holding a sales chart with an arrow extending upward.

3. Hire a temporary receptionist to fill in for the regular staff member, who is going on vacation next week.

Picture your receptionist's desk full of grass, which a temporary employee is mowing.

Exercise #5:
Recalling Numbered Lists

Step 1. Continue the process you started above by creating mini-movies for the last two items on the to-do list (4. Review Seattle sales figures . . . 5. Ask Portland colleague . . .).

Step 2. Create your own numbered to-do list. Try using this system to create visual imagery for each item on it.

Step 3. Use this system to recall each item that you have to do. Note that you can either remember each item in order or ask yourself specific questions about any item on the list. For example, if you're wondering about the fifth item on the list, just think of *law*, and you'll find that you remember the entire story you created incorporating that image. If you're wondering about item 7, visualizing a *kiwi* will trigger the whole story—and the whole memory.

Imagination is more important than knowledge.
—Albert Einstein, *On Science*

Sets of Instructions

You can use the same approach to memorize a set of instructions, as long as you number each step. For example, suppose you're trying to master the feature on Microsoft Word that allows you to edit documents with your edits remaining visible. A colleague is showing you how to use this feature, and you note the instructions in a series of numbered steps.

Step 1. In Microsoft Word, click on "Tools" on your toolbar.

Step 2. Select "Protect Document" from the dropdown menu.

Step 3. Click "OK" on the little box that pops up.

Step 4. Make any changes you like to the document. You'll notice that your additions appear in a different color, while your deletions show up either with a colored line through them or as a side note marked "Deletion."

Next, visualize each step, working in the images of *toy*, *inn*, *mow*, and *rye* (or whatever images you have chosen for your "standard" numerals).

Step 1. In Microsoft Word, click on "Tools" on your toolbar.

Picture the Tools feature on the toolbar—but see a little toy monkey reaching down to point to the feature. Instead of using a regular mouse, envision yourself using a toy mouse to make the click.

Step 2. Select "Protect Document" from the dropdown menu.

Visualize the menu in the window of a snowbound inn. Think of protecting the inn from the coming blizzard.

Exercise #6: Recalling Lists of Instructions

Step 1. Continue the process by creating mini-movies for the last two items on the list of instructions (3. Click "OK" . . . 4. Make any changes you like . . .).

Step 2. Create your own list of instructions. Use this approach to create visual imagery for each item.

We think in generalities, but we live in details.
—Alfred North Whitehead

Pages of Books and Magazines

Here is where I really wow my workshop participants. I get out several issues of *BusinessWeek* and invite my students to leaf through them. One of them calls out a page number from an issue, and I rattle off a brief description of every article, advertisement, and cartoon on the page. Another student calls out a different page number from another issue, and I repeat the performance. When they are suitably impressed, I present them with the real kicker: They, too, can learn to assimilate written information in this way. In fact, now that they understand the Numerical Memory Matrix, it won't take them much more than 1 minute per page to work their way through a standard magazine.

My clients who work in advertising, publishing, and graphic design are thrilled by the possibility of being able to assimilate printed material in this way. My clients in other fields are eager to apply this technique to instruction manuals, reports, contracts, and other written information. Here's how it's done.

Step 1. Turn to the first page you wish to memorize. Suppose it's page 5. If you're using the images I've provided, you'll reach for *law* as your standard image for 5. This tells you that you'll begin your set of associations with an image of the law.

Step 2. Choose the first item on the page you want to assimilate and begin a story that incorporates both this first headline and the page number's image.

Let's say it's an article entitled, "Executive Salaries Rising Swiftly." You might visualize a group of executives who have just heard about a new law that requires their salaries to increase. To reinforce the idea of "rising swiftly," perhaps you'll even picture this group of executives getting on a swiftly rising elevator, copies of the new law clutched in their hands.

Step 3. Choose another item on the page and incorporate it into your story. Suppose the next article is about falling stock prices at Blue Sky Airlines. You might envision the executives taking the elevator up to the roof of the building, where they board a private jet labeled "Blue Sky Airlines" and take off into the blue sky. Suddenly, the airplane takes a dangerous nosedive as the executives inside worry about their falling stock prices.

Step 4. Continue with your story until you've incorporated every item on the page that you wish to memorize.

Exercise #7: Recalling Written Information by Page Number

Step 1. Find a magazine, newspaper, book, report, or other form of written information. Apply this approach to 5 to 10 pages.

Step 2. Ask a friend, colleague, or family member to test you on the pages you've memorized—or test yourself. If your recall is less complete than you'd like, evaluate which aspect of the process you might improve. Are you not paying close enough attention to the stories you're creating or to the information you're assimilating? Are you visualizing uninteresting or vague images rather than compelling, concrete mental pictures? Are you having difficulty associating the images into a coherent story? Identify your problem areas so you can work on them specifically.

Step 3. Continue to repeat this process until you feel you've mastered it. Make a special effort to apply it to material that you will actually find useful to recall.

There are three kinds of lies: lies, damned lies, and statistics.
—Mark Twain, *Autobiography*

Charts of Financial Information

Mark Twain to the contrary, there are definitely times when statistics come in handy. If you work with financial information, for example, you may find it extremely useful to be able to memorize charts, tables, and other figures. Whether you want to impress a client or negotiating partner or simply have complex information at your fingertips, you can use the Numerical Memory Matrix System to help you recall statistics and financial information.

Amount Invested at 10 Percent	5 Years	10 Years	20 Years	30 Years
$150,000	$37,956	$23,628	$17,268	$16,272

Let's suppose you have occasion to work with clients who want to know how much their investments will yield over time. You want to explain, using the chart above, that if they invest $150,000 at a rate of 10 percent, they can withdraw $37,956 per year over 5 years, $23,628 over 10 years, and so on.

Of course, you can always simply consult a chart, but if you'd like to memorize the information, begin by converting the numbers to images.

	law	*toes*	*noose*	*maze*
Amount Invested at 10 Percent	5 Years	10 Years	20 Years	30 Years
$150,000	$37,956	$23,628	$17,268	$16,272
*toLL*s (plus 000)	*mu*G, *po*Lis*h*	*enemy*, *geneva*	*du*Ck, *anchovy*	*dish*, *no*GG*in*

Next, create a story that begins with *tolls*; links *law*, *mug*, and *polish*; proceeds to an incident involving *toes*, *enemy*, and *geneva*; and so on. Here's an example.

I was driving along, worried about my retirement, because I like to travel and I wanted to be able to pay my *tolls*. I was so worried, I forgot to obey the *law*, and I was stopped by a police officer. She pointed to the coffee *mug* in the cup holder of my car. "That coffee looks like shoe *polish*," she commented.

My *toes* curled. Clearly, she was being sarcastic, treating me like some kind of *enemy*. "Is it against the *Geneva* accords to drive around with bad coffee?" I asked with equal sarcasm.

"You'd better be careful, or you'll end up with your head in a *noose*," she said angrily. "And they don't give you *duck* with *anchovy* sauce in traffic school, either!"

I could see we had gotten into a *maze* of confusion, and I wanted to get home and enjoy a tasty *dish* I was planning to prepare. "I'm sorry," I said, scratching my *noggin*. "Let's start again. What have I done wrong?" But the only thing I had done wrong, I thought, was not saving enough money to invest in my retirement!

Exercise #8: Recalling Charts and Financial Information (Part 1)

Step 1. Create new words for the figures in the chart on page 235, then create your own story to enable you to remember it.

Step 2. Apply this approach to a chart or table that you have occasion to use in your work. Memorize all or part of the chart.

Step 3. Ask a friend, colleague, or family member to test you on the numbers you've committed to memory—or test yourself. Identify any areas where your approach needs work.

Step 4. Focusing on the trouble areas you've identified, continue to use this process until you feel you've mastered it.

Exercise #9: Recalling Charts and Financial Information (Part 2)

Step 1. Memorize the following table.

Stock	Closing Price	P/E Ratio
Cisco	24.50	37
Wal-mart	58¼	28
Marriott	41.06	20
Pfizer	34.12	53

Step 2. Apply this approach to a chart or table that you have occasion to use in your work. Memorize all or part of the chart.

Step 3. Ask a friend, colleague, or family member to test you on the numbers you've committed to memory—or test yourself. Identify any areas where your approach needs work.

Step 4. Focusing on the trouble areas you've identified, continue to use this process until you feel you've mastered it.

Remembering a Schedule

Finally, you can use the Numerical Memory Matrix System to help you remember your schedule. Most people have trouble remembering schedules based on numbers alone—2:30, 4 P.M., and so on. That's because numbers are abstract, and those times might mean anything. You might even remember "2:30"—but what exactly did you have to do at that time today? How do you keep from getting it mixed up with what you have to do at 4 P.M. or what you have to do at 2:30 tomorrow?

If you use images, however, you have something to "hang your hat on." Here's an approach that you might try.

Step 1. Assign each day a number, starting with Monday as 1 and ending with Sunday as 7.

Step 2. Convert both the day number and the time of day into an image.

For example, suppose you have an appointment Tuesday at 3 P.M. *Tuesday* becomes 2, and *3 P.M.* is, of course, 3. In the Numerical Memory Matrix System, 2 + 3 = n + m, from which you might create the word *enemy*. You'd combine the image of an enemy with other images relating to your appointment to develop a mini-movie that contains all the information you needed.

Or suppose you had a meeting Friday at 10 A.M. Friday is 5, so you have the three-digit number 510 to work with. Perhaps you'd convert the L (5), *t* (1), and *s* (0) into *Lotus*. A meeting Wednesday at 9:30 A.M. gives you 3-9-3, or *m-p-m*, from which you might make *wampum*.

Step 3. Add images that evoke information about your appointment: whom you're meeting, where, and about what.

Suppose that you're meeting your client Catherine Chenoweth on Monday at 1:30 P.M. in Room 201 of the Plaza Hotel. You've had a lot of practice by now, so I'll talk you through the process—you supply the images.

1. Create an image to help you remember the name *Catherine Chenoweth*.

2. Create images for Monday (1), 1:30, and 201.

3. Create an image for the Plaza Hotel, either by visualizing the hotel (if you know it well) or by creating an image for the word *plaza*.

4. Tie all these images together into a story, and *voilà*! If you add some imagery to tell you what the meeting is about or remind you of specific points you'd like to bring up, you're all set.

Exercise #10: Memorizing Items on Your Schedule

Step 1. Read through the following schedule.

Monday

9:00 A.M.: Breakfast meeting with Will Friedle at the Oak Room
1:00 P.M.: Lunch with Tanya Hodge, new client, at the Mojito Palace

Tuesday

10:30 A.M.: Meet my boss in her office to discuss sales figures for last three quarters (remind her that the sales staff is still pretty new!)
Noon: Call Jenny in San Francisco; get the projections for the next quarter

Wednesday

3:00 P.M.: Present plan for improving the training of new sales staff in Conference Room 4523
5:00 P.M.: Drinks with Abdullah Mahmoud—discuss the new Egyptian strategy

Step 2. Create a story for each item based on images you've created for the names, numbers, and concepts. Use the stories to memorize the schedule.

Step 3. Evaluate yourself. How much of the schedule can you remember? If your memory isn't at the level you would like, ask yourself which aspects of the process gave you problems. Translating numbers into images? Incorporating lots of detail into your stories? Making more memorable stories? Remember, practice makes perfect—so keep practicing. You'll get there in the end!

For More Practice

An excellent way to practice the Numerical Memory Matrix System is to use a deck of cards. Even if you're not a fan of card games, you might try this approach to sharpen your numerical memory skills.

Step 1. Assign each suit a number.

Clubs: 1
Diamonds: 2
Hearts: 3
Spades: 4

Step 2. Combine each suit number with the number on the card (the ace is 1).

Card	Clubs (1)	Diamonds (2)	Hearts (3)	Spades (4)
1	11	21	31	41
2	12	22	32	42
3	13	23	33	43
4	14	24	34	44
5	15	25	35	45
6	16	26	36	46
7	17	27	37	47
8	18	28	38	48
9	19	29	39	49

Step 3. For the "10" cards—10 of hearts, 10 of clubs, and so on—multiply the number of the suit by 10.

Clubs (1)	Diamonds (2)	Hearts (3)	Spades (4)
10	20	30	40

Step 4. For the picture cards, you should also multiply each suit by 10. Then add 50 across the board and set the other values as jack = 2, queen = 3, and king = 4.

a. Multiply each suit by 10.

Clubs	Diamonds	Hearts	Spades
(1 x 10 = 10)	(2 x 10 = 20)	(3 x 10 = 30)	(4 x 10 = 40)

b. Add 50 across the board.

10 + 50 = 60	20 + 50 = 70	30 + 50 = 80	40 + 50 = 90

c. Set the other values.

Card	Clubs	Diamonds	Hearts	Spades
Jack (2)	62	72	82	92
Queen (3)	63	73	83	93
King (4)	64	74	84	94

Step 5. Remember the image for each number. You can use the lists of images from 1 to 100 that I provide on pages 217 and 222 or create another list of your own. Either way, you should use a standard set of images each time you make a list—and that set of images is the one you should use to remember cards.

Exercise #11: Memorize a Deck of Cards

Step 1. Deal yourself five cards, noting each one. Tell yourself a story, incorporating each new image as you turn up the card. Then test yourself: See if you can remember all five cards in the order you dealt them.

Step 2. Repeat the previous step, using 10 cards. Continue up to 25, then 40, and finally 52.

COUNTING ON YOURSELF

Now that you know the basics of the Numerical Memory Matrix System, the sky's the limit. You can commit any series of numbers to memory for use in just about any situation. Although this system can seem a bit intimidating at first, I urge you not to give up. Just 5 minutes of practice a day—translating the license numbers of cars on your morning commute, for example, or running through the floor numbers on your elevator ride—can make a huge difference in making you comfortable with this approach. Once you're ready to use it, you'll start discovering all sorts of new situations where it will come in handy. Good luck—and keep practicing!

CHAPTER 10

MASTERING WRITTEN INFORMATION

My client Malcolm is a successful corporate lawyer. He called me last year for advice on how to handle a major trade negotiation. First, we discussed the system he would use to remember salient points in the contract. Then we reviewed the strategy he would use to win the negotiation—and it worked. By focusing on key elements of the contract, knowing that he had memorized the most important details, he was able to take complete control of the room whenever it mattered most. His opponents assumed that he knew the rest of the document as intimately as the four pages he had actually committed to memory—and they caved. His firm's fee on that $10 million contract more than covered my own.

Could Malcolm have swung the deal using notes instead of his own brainpower? Perhaps. Certainly, he had been a success even before he hired me, but his ability to manipulate facts, figures, and information grew as his memory grew. Also, his decision to memorize key points forced him to become even more specific than he usually was about his negotiating strategy.

WORDS, WORDS, WORDS

Do you ever have the feeling that you're drowning in a sea of written information? One of the most common complaints I hear during my workshops is from students who feel overwhelmed by the sheer number of printed pages that cross their desks in an average week. It sometimes seems that written information comes to us constantly in the form of:

- Articles, lists, or brief news items in general business publications (the *Wall Street Journal*, *Business Week*, and others), industry magazines and newsletters, and in-house corporate publications

- Reports, which, depending on your industry, may be anything from scientific studies useful in a medical equipment or pharmaceutical company to marketing reports or industry analyses

- Lists, such as a customers' bill of rights or a list of policies and procedures

- Instructions and manuals

- Transcripts or manuscripts of speeches by others

- Stories and jokes

- Your notes from a lecture, conference, or other event

- Your notes for a speech, presentation, or other type of oral report

- To-do lists

- Lists of foreign words and phrases

If you're like most of my clients, you look at the enormous amount of material that crosses your desk every week and simply despair. There's barely time to look at it all, let alone read it carefully. And there's certainly no way you're ever going to hold that much information in your memory. Right?

Well, yes and no. If I were to leave you with only one word of advice about remembering and retrieving written information, it would be *strategize*. No one can memorize thousands of pages of data—not even after they've taken my course! But all of us can read thousands of pages and then recall the key points that we've decided are most important.

In other words, memory and strategy go hand in hand. Once we grasp that simple fact, our effectiveness in the workplace skyrockets.

MAKING THE MOST OF OUR READING

Spoken information is temporary; it lasts only as long as it takes to say it, so the need for memory is obvious. If you don't pay attention to what's being said and find a way to capture it, the elusive speech will be lost.

Written information, obviously, is permanent. The book, report, memo, contract, or article exists; you can always go back to it—or at least you have the illusion that you can. In fact, there is so much written information in the world, and we're all so busy, that we tend to look at the pages coming in each week and say, "That's important—I'll read it later." Weeks later, you find yourself restacking or perhaps throwing out huge piles of information that you never read.

What's even worse, though, is that in most cases, the time we do spend reading is lost because most of us remember very little of what we read. In my experience, we all tend to get a bit lazy with written information, secure in the illusion that we can always refer back to it. But how often have you tried in vain to remember just which of the many reports or journals that cross your desk contains the information you're missing? Worse, we often don't even remember that the missing information exists. How many times have you cleaned out your office, only to discover a report that you had read but forgotten? "Wow," you say to yourself, "I wish I'd remembered I had this during the Buxley negotiations. . . or when I had to write that quarterly report. . . or the day Cipriano came into the office. It would really have come in handy then."

Once, when I got to this point in my workshop, a student objected strenuously. "Maybe other people don't take reading seriously," he said vehemently, "but I sure do. Whenever I read a report or a contract or even a memo, I do just what I did in college. I underline key words, highlight things I think will be important, and sometimes I even take notes."

"That's great," I replied. "So then you have no problems remembering what you read?"

The student looked abashed. "Well, no, I do," he admitted. "But it's not because I don't put the effort into it. I just have a terrible memory."

As I hope you've seen throughout the previous chapters, I don't buy that for a second. None of us has a memory so terrible that it can't be trained to remember what we've read. We just have to learn how to "work smarter, not harder." For most of us, when we read, the words stay on the page. By paying attention, visualizing, and associating, however, we can lift the words off the page and incorporate them into our minds—where they'll stay for as long as we need them.

THE POWER OF GETTING INVOLVED

In the rest of this chapter, I'll show you how to apply this truth to your business reading. First, though, here's a little exercise to remind you of what it's like when you *do* remember what you've read. Before we get started with a new arsenal of techniques, take a moment to think about reading that you have found memorable.

Exercise #1: Remembering Stories

Step 1. Think of a favorite book. It can be one you read recently, a long time ago, or even as a kid. You might choose a gripping novel of some kind, a thriller, detective story, romance, or even a "great work." You can also choose a nonfiction book that, for whatever reason, you still remember.

Step 2. Without thinking about it too much, fill in the following questionnaire. Don't stop to ponder the answers—if they don't come easily to mind within a few seconds, leave the space blank and move on.

Memorable Reading Questionnaire

Name of book: _____

Author: _____

What the book is about: _____

_____

_____

_____

_____

Particular scenes, images, or details that spring to mind:

1. _____

2. _____

3. _____

4. _____

(If you can easily think of more, grab a blank page and keep listing them.)

Times you have found yourself thinking or talking about this book:

1. _____

2. _____

3. _____

4. _____

(If you can easily think of more, grab a blank page and keep listing them.)

Step 3. Next, take a moment to visualize one of your favorite parts of the book. If the book tells a story—either true or imaginary—let your mind play over a particular scene, character, or setting that you particularly enjoyed. If it's a book that offers advice or explanations, spend a moment savoring a portion of the book that you found especially useful, insightful, amusing, or intriguing, perhaps thinking about times when that part of the book has come in handy or remembering how you felt when you first encountered it. For 2 or 3 minutes, allow yourself to daydream your way into the world of the book. Then get a blank piece of paper and jot down what you remember.

How did you do? If you drew a complete blank, don't worry. That simply means that very little you've read up to now has captured your imagination. In the rest of this chapter, I'll show you how to bring to life the words you read—even the dry-as-dust paragraphs in a contract or quarterly report.

On the other hand, if you found yourself flooded with images and memories, you already have an idea of what this chapter will entail. Once you attach images, memories, and personal responses to the words you read—no matter what they are—you'll always be able to remember them. Your job is to identify what's most important to you (that's where strategy comes in) and then to create images and stories out of those key points.

Remember, memory is not something that happens to you. It's something that you do, an active process that you consciously choose to undertake. Once you've actively engaged that process—paying attention to what you read, visualizing it, and creating associations with it—your memory for the written word will begin to amaze your friends, your colleagues, and even yourself.

REVISITING THE MEMORY PALACE

Remember back in chapter 6, when you saw how a Memory Palace could help cement your memories? The Memory Palace technique—also known as the Roman Room in honor of its Roman antecedents—draws on the power of associating images, facts, and ideas with specific places. Although most of us don't live in palaces, we can take advantage of this technique in any room or environment that we know well. This technique is especially useful for to-do lists and lists of relatively simple objects or concepts.

Step 1: Identify the first "object of memory." If you have a to-do list, start with the first item on the list. Or perhaps you're reading a memo and you want to make sure you can speak about it fluently at the meeting you're attending later that day. Boil the memo down to however many key points you want to recall. Likewise, if you're about to give a speech or a brief talk to a group of colleagues, you could make a list of points you want to cover.

Step 2: Associate the object with an item in the room. If you're sitting in your office, perhaps the first object that comes into view is your desk. Find a way to associate the first item on your list with the desk. If you're using a to-do list, perhaps your first item is stopping at the store to buy a quart of milk. You might visualize a quart of milk sitting on your desk—or better yet, see it spilling all over the desk and running onto the floor. Now that's a vivid image you're likely to remember!

Perhaps you want to remember a concept from the memo you're reading: "It has come to our attention that the sales figures for the previous quarter have dropped to an unacceptable level." Using the visualization techniques we've already discussed, come up with a clear mental picture of "dropping sales figures" and associate them with your desk. You might visualize a bunch of little numbers dropping from the ceiling onto your desktop, then bouncing on the hard wood and saying, "Ouch! Sales are down! That really hurts!" Or you might see the products you sell falling through your desktop and landing in a heap on the floor below. You're simply looking for any image that associates "dropping sales figures" and your desk.

Step 3: Continue this process around the room. Continue identifying items on your list and associating them with items in your office—perhaps your clock, your filing cabinet, or the bulletin board on the far wall. Your goal is always the same: to create a memorable visual image for the concept, task, or fact you're trying to remember and then to associate it strongly with a familiar item in the room.

Step 4: When you wish to recall your list, revisit your room. You can do this either literally or in your mind's eye. If you're sitting in the room where you created the images, simply look around. If you're somewhere else, bring the familiar room into your mind's eye. Either way, each familiar ob-

Strategies for Effective Reading

Often, when we read, we're thinking of other things, letting our minds wander to seemingly more important matters. It's similar to what frequently happens when we listen: Our minds decide, apparently on their own, to become involved with something else, and off they go. Then suddenly, you realize you've been staring at the same page for 15 minutes, and you still don't know what it says.

Just as with spoken information, the key is to get your eyes and your mind working together. Once they are operating as a team, they're unstoppable. Here are some suggestions for creating better teamwork.

Listen to relaxing instrumental music as you read. Some people find music of any kind distracting while they're focusing on written information, so if you're one of those people, ignore this advice. For many of us, though, there's something very helpful about having a quiet, soothing sound in the background. It's as though we're setting a boundary for our minds, saying, "If you want to pay attention to something else, check out this music." The musical background prevents your mind from going even farther afield.

Studies have shown that the form and structure of some kinds of music also help organize your mind, bringing it into coherent pathways that are conducive to study and memory. Classical and New Age music seem to be most helpful, but trust your own instincts. You may also find it helpful to alternate between different types of music or between music and silence. Asking your mind to adapt to different situations may use up some of the excess energy that would otherwise go toward daydreaming. If you're concerned about the effects of the background music on your family or officemates, use earphones, which tend to isolate you even further.

Try a background-noise machine. If your reading environment is full of distracting sounds, and you don't like reading to music, consider investing in a background-noise machine that plays sounds such as falling rain, ocean surf, and even city traffic. This noise is regular and

ject will be inextricably linked to the memory object you've chosen, and you'll easily retrieve all the written information you've stored.

---

predictable, which may be less distracting than the sounds of your home or office. Again, earphones will prevent the background noise from bothering those around you.

Take frequent breaks. If you don't give yourself a break, your mind is likely to take one for you. And if you don't realize you need a break, it will seem that your mind is being disobedient and incapable rather than simply asking for the time off that it needs. Some people can read for 90 minutes at a time with full concentration, but most of us need to stop and clear our minds every 15, 20, or 30 minutes. Your need for breaks may also vary depending on what you're reading, how long you've been working, and how hungry or tired you are. Whatever the situation, pay attention to your body's rhythms and work with them, not against them. You'll be surprised at how much more efficient you are in the long run.

Take *real* breaks. When you do take a break, make it the real thing. Don't read something else—such as your e-mail—and don't stay in the same physical position. Get up, do a simple stretching exercise, go to the bathroom, or get a glass of water. Then, when you sit down in your reading chair again, your mind will be put on notice that it's time to get back to work.

Don't try to "work through" hunger. If hunger is making it difficult for you to concentrate, try a high-protein snack, such as yogurt, or one that features complex carbohydrates, such as hummus or carrot sticks. Avoid sweet, starchy snacks, which tend to cause a sugar rush and then a crash. If you're having trouble sitting still, try substituting a non-caffeinated drink for your usual coffee or tea.

Give yourself a pleasant environment. If you're the type who can lose yourself in the printed page no matter where you are, you don't have to worry about this suggestion. If you find it hard to concentrate on your business reading, though, consider making a few simple changes to the environment in which you read. Eliminate clutter, which invites your mind to wonder about what all those intriguing or anxiety-provoking papers might be. Place something you like to look at within easy view so that when your eyes want a break, they don't have to wander all over the room—taking your mind with them. Do what you can to create an atmosphere of clarity and calm. You may be surprised at how much difference it makes!

Variation #1: The Journey

Some people like to use this technique in a more dynamic way. Instead of incorporating the objects in a familiar room, they use the elements they pass on a familiar journey. Is there a 15- to 20-minute walking route that you might use for your "memory journey"? A tree, a traffic light, a store, or a newsstand may all help trigger items on the written list you're trying to memorize. Perhaps that quart of milk is spilling over the traffic light or growing on the tree. Maybe those dropping sales figures are bouncing off the store's awning or falling through the roof of the corner newsstand. Just be sure that the journey is a familiar one. The goal is to associate something you already know well—a room, an area where you walk, or some other physical space—with something you're trying to learn.

Variation #2: The People You Know

If you're a "people person," you might adapt this technique to use with colleagues, family members, friends, or some other set of individuals. The principle is the same: Associate each item on your list with a familiar person by linking the two in a visual way. Perhaps that quart of milk is spilling over your officemate's head, or maybe you see your father holding it in his hand. Perhaps those dropping sales figures are swarming around your Aunt Lillian like pesky flies, or maybe they're spilling out of your best friend's purse. Your goal is to translate the information into a striking visual image and then link it to someone familiar.

Variation #3: People and Actions

As moviemakers know, the most memorable images usually involve action and motion. Someone standing still is harder to remember than a person who is actually doing something. If you're using people to trigger your memories, you might choose famous people who are strongly associated with famous actions. See Elvis playing his guitar, with the milk spilling over his blue suede shoes. Visualize Lauren Bacall puckering up her lips to whistle, with the low sales figures dropping out of her mouth. Again, the trick is to find images that will be memorable to you, so create mental pictures that you'll enjoy remembering. The more fun you have with these visualizations, the more easily you'll be able to bring them to mind when you need them.

Variation #4: The Body

This variation also goes back to ancient times. It involves using the parts of your own body as your basic "list." You can then associate each object on your new list with a body part. Most people find it useful to start with the head and work down and to choose a side—left or right—that will always come first. With this technique, your to-do list might look like this.

- Head: Buy a quart of milk (see a quart of milk balanced perfectly on your head).
- Right shoulder: Make a deposit at the bank (see a huge pile of money riding on your shoulder).
- Left shoulder: Call my computer guy and make an appointment (see the telephone sitting on top of the computer, with both objects resting on your left shoulder).
- Chest: Write my boss a memo about next week's vacation schedule (see a sheet of paper with a palm tree and an airplane on it pinned to your chest).

Keep going until your list is finished. If you need more items, move down the body more slowly. For example, on your head, use your left eyebrow, right eyebrow, left eye, right eye, nose, left cheek, right cheek, and so on.

By the way, this is one way you can beat the "seven- to nine-item limit" I've mentioned in previous chapters. As you've seen, your mind can usually hold only seven to nine items at a time, but if you use your body as a mnemonic device, you can remember as many items as your body has parts. If you wanted to impress clients by reeling off several key points in a contract negotiation or refer effortlessly at a meeting to each point in this morning's memo, using the parts of your body might be an ideal way to retain the information.

Practice #1:
Using the Memory Palace

Try this technique three times a week for one or two weeks, giving yourself 5 minutes each time. Don't worry if you can't remember all the items on your list so quickly. Practice makes perfect, and it will be more productive for you to work in short spurts than to drag the exercise on. If you stick with the practice, you'll find your memory getting more efficient, until you can eventually master a list of five or six items in the given time.

Preparation. Identify a written document that you'd like to recall. Choose one that can easily be turned into a list—a to-do list, a memo, a contract with a few clear points, or the items you'd like to bring up in a speech.

Step 1: Follow the Memory Palace technique. Use the steps I've explained to commit your list to memory.

1. Identify the first object on your list.

2. Associate it with an item in a familiar room.

3. Continue associating objects of memory with items in the room.

Limit yourself to 5 minutes to commit your list to memory. See how far you get in that time.

Step 2: Test yourself. Next, try to recall the items on your list by either looking at the objects in your room or visualizing your room in your mind's eye. How many did you remember?

Step 3: Evaluate yourself. If you remembered all the items, good for you! Next time, try to commit an even longer list to memory.

If you weren't as successful as you would have liked, ask yourself what you can do next time to improve the process. Remember, it always goes back to the three basic components of memory: *paying attention*, *visualizing*, and *associating*. Perhaps you weren't concentrating fully enough on the items you wanted to memorize. Maybe you didn't come up with vivid visual images, or possibly you didn't link the visual images closely enough with the familiar objects in your room. Give yourself an "A" for effort and try again later in the week. Keep practicing until you've mastered the technique.

Step 4: Try out the variations. Whether or not you're happy with your first try at the Memory Palace, check out each of the variations at least once. Be sure to test and evaluate yourself on each one. Each of us is different, and you may find that using objects seen on a journey, people, movie stars, or body parts just "clicks" with you in a way that objects in a room don't. Or you may discover that you like different variations for different memory tasks, preferring to use the journey approach with office memos and relying on the body parts technique for giving a speech, for example. You may even create your own variation, finding another type of "constant" to which you can associate the new list items that you're trying to memorize.

Talking without Notes

If you're giving a speech, and you don't want to look at your notes while you talk, try this useful technique. Arrive 30 to 45 minutes early to the room where you'll be speaking. Look at the various items you can see from the podium and connect each one to a different point in your speech. I work from ceiling to floor and from left to right, so I might begin with the picture on the wall to my left, move down to the table beneath the picture, proceed rightward to the drapes on the back window, go on to the windowsill below the drapes, and so on. Whichever order you decide to use, make sure you associate each item in your speech with an item in the room. Only you will know about the memory technique you employed; your audience will simply see you as extremely prepared and knowledgeable.

THE NUMERICAL MEMORY MATRIX

Another way of remembering lists is to use the Numerical Memory Matrix that you mastered in the previous chapter. This is a useful approach for any written information that's in some kind of ordered form: a list, a set of instructions, a chronology, or any other information in some kind of sequence. If the steps you want to remember aren't numbered already, add the numbers yourself. Then, as you did in the previous chapter, integrate the image for your number—*toy* for *1*, for example, or *law* for *5*—with an image for the item on the list.

The advantage of this approach is that you can remember exactly where each item comes in the process. With the Memory Palace, you work in sequence, traveling around the room in a particular order, but there's no easy way to recall whether the filing cabinet is 5, 6, or 7— although you may well remember that it comes "somewhere in the middle." With the Numerical Memory Matrix, you can choose to call upon any number you want, always knowing exactly where it falls in the sequence.

This approach is also especially useful when you want to link a number to a piece of written information. For example, suppose you're memorizing a list of safety regulations, as my students at Con Edison often have to do. It may be useful to associate the regulation's number— Reg. 601-2.5—with its content—"No valve is to remain uninspected for a period of more than 30 days." In such a case, you would translate the figure 601-2.5 into a verbal/visual image (perhaps a *gas toy* hanging from a *nail*) and then integrate that image with a mental picture of an uninspected valve. In this case, you'd also want to incorporate an image of 30, perhaps a *maze*. You'd see a sputtering valve at the center of a maze, with a little gas-powered automobile hanging from a nail above. Then, whenever you wanted to cite the regulation, you'd simply recall the image and translate it back into numerical data.

If you're computer literate, you can see that this process is analogous to random access memory (RAM). Just like a computer, you can pinpoint where a piece of information is located without necessarily following a prescribed sequence. Just thinking 5 (or the image you've created for that number) will access the information linked to that number. Then you can access 8 or 2 or any number you like. Without a memory system like this one, most people tend to remember in sequence. If they want to get to the fifth item on the list, they tend to have to go through the first four. With this system, though, you can send yourself right to page 8 or section 217, giving yourself extraordinary control over your own memory.

Practice #2: Apply the Numerical Memory Matrix to Written Information

Alternate this technique with the Memory Palace three times a week for one or two weeks, giving yourself 5 minutes each time. As before, try to remember several items within that time, but don't extend it; simply get as far as you can. The more often you practice this approach, the more quickly you'll find yourself using it.

Preparation. Identify a written document that you'd like to recall. Choose one that can easily be turned into a numbered list—a list of regulations, a set of instructions, or any of the types of written information you used in the previous practice: a to-do list, memo, contract, or speech.

Step 1: Follow the Numerical Memory Matrix technique. Use the steps I explained to commit your list to memory.

1. Translate each number on your list into an image.

2. Associate that image with another image that represents the item you want to memorize.

3. Continue associating items on the list with numbers until you've memorized the entire list or until 5 minutes is up, whichever comes first.

Step 2: Test yourself. Next, try to recall the items on your list. Start by remembering them in numerical order. If that goes well, try to remember items out of order, asking yourself to identify Number 7 or Number 4. How many did you remember?

Step 3: Evaluate yourself. If you remembered all the items, good for you! Next time, you can add some more items to your list. If you found yourself struggling, don't worry; analyze the problem. Did you fail to pay attention, visualize, or associate? Come up with a strategy and try again.

> *My name is Sherlock Holmes. It's my business to know what other people don't know.*
>
> —Sir Arthur Conan Doyle, *The Adventure of the Blue Carbuncle*

THE SHERLOCK HOLMES TECHNIQUE

So far, we've been concentrating on written information that falls easily into list form. But what about information that's more conceptual, such as you might find in an article, report, or book?

For that type of written information, I recommend the Sherlock Holmes technique. Put on your deerstalker hat, grab your magnifying glass, and let's begin!

Step 1: Boil each paragraph down to its essence. This approach is based on the awareness that books and reports are made up of pages, and pages are made up of paragraphs. Generally, each paragraph represents an idea, so when you go over written material, start by seeing yourself as Sherlock Holmes, an investigator who is looking for a new clue in each paragraph. Pluck out one or two words—no more—to represent each paragraph's main idea, or create a symbol that stands for the paragraph. Write the word or symbol beside the paragraph and number it "1."

Continue on to the next paragraph, numbering its clue "2." Usually, you'll have five paragraphs per page, for a total of five key words on the page.

Step 2: Create a story for each page. Next, take those five words and create a mini-story from them that represents the whole page. For example, in a page on offshore oil drilling, the five key clues might be:

1. Oil
2. Expenses
3. Regulations
4. Clogged pipes
5. Labor costs

The story you create from those words might involve oil workers trying to unclog pipes bubbling over with oil. Then a supervisor comes along with a huge sheaf of regulations in his hand. He hands each worker a $10 bill as an incentive to work faster.

The story will trigger the five words, which in turn will trigger the information on the page. If you read a 100-page document, you have 100 little stories to remember—but 100 stories are much easier to remember than a huge assortment of unrelated facts. If you want, you can use the Numerical Memory Matrix to work the page number into each story so you remember not only the information but also what page it's on.

I like associating page numbers with specific information because I know that location is a very powerful memory aid. Knowing where something is can be a fantastic way of remembering *what* it is. Just going to the page number can bring back the sentence that summarizes that page. If you've memorized, say, 100 page numbers, you've given yourself many more access points for the information you've stored.

Once you start using the Sherlock Holmes approach, you may notice a striking collateral benefit. The mere act of choosing one or two key words for each paragraph means that you're reading more closely, with more concentration, than you might usually do. You're also reading more actively, deciding what's important and how it relates to other key information. This kind of active reading is wonderful for improving your concentration because it gives you a specific goal. If you simply tell yourself "read more closely" or "concentrate harder," you may feel frustrated, exhausted, or simply resentful of having to work so hard. If you have a specific task to complete—selecting key words—your concentration and focus will automatically improve.

When I think of the Sherlock Holmes approach, I often recall the old joke about the student who wanted to cheat on a test. He copied all the key points from the textbook onto a sheet of paper, but the page was too large to be carefully concealed. He recopied the information onto a smaller sheet, concentrating only on the main points so that the information would fit. Nevertheless, the page was still too unwieldy, so he found a third way to boil down the material, until key words that would trigger each major concept were carefully printed on a tiny square that fit easily into the palm of his hand.

Not having taken my memory course, the student forgot the paper—but when he looked at the test questions, he discovered to his surprise that he knew every single answer. The process of copying and recopying the information, getting more and more focused each time, had actually enabled him to memorize it. In effect, he had used the Sherlock Holmes technique—and you can, too. What's more, when you do it, it won't even be considered cheating!

Step 3: Create a story for individual sections or the entire document. This last step isn't absolutely necessary, but it can be useful for longer documents because it forces you to identify the main point of the work. Here's another case where strategy comes in. Knowing why you're reading something and in what situations it may come in handy is always helpful. Creating an "overview story" forces you to look at the big picture and ask yourself why you need this information. Besides being good for your memory, "big picture" thinking is also good for your work.

Suppose you're trying to memorize a long, complex contract. Like my lawyer friend in the Introduction, you may determine that only one portion of the contract is really important, so right off the bat, choosing to focus on that one section sharpens your negotiating strategy as well as your memory.

Then you decide to come up with a "memory story" that encapsulates the entire contract. You realize that what your negotiating partner is really concerned about is protecting her intellectual property rights to the new training method she's devised, so you see her standing in front of a door, with the name of her method emblazoned on it in big block letters. She's standing with her back against the door, defending the contents in the next room from the hordes of thieves and pirates trying to rob her. Since it's intellectual property that's at issue, perhaps they're "intellectual pirates," wearing graduation robes and horn-rimmed glasses as they wave their sabers and cutlasses. Besides being an amusing image, this visualization may give you new insight into the issues that most concern your negotiating partner. You'll remember more of the written information you need—and you'll be clearer about your business strategy as well.

When I recently taught this technique to a group of Pfizer employees, a young woman in the workshop seemed a bit frustrated. "I'm a slow reader," she confessed, "and it already takes me a long time to go through all the material that crosses my desk. Won't your technique take even more time?"

I agreed that of course it would. This is a much slower process than a quick read, let alone the brief skim that most of us give the reading material we see each day. But how important is it to remember what you read? Sometimes we just need to know that we don't have to be concerned—reading a memo to find out whether it affects our department, for example, or skimming a report to be sure it contains nothing new. But if you're reading something that you'd prefer to recall, that upfront investment of extra time will pay off a hundred times over. The extra minutes you invest now mean you'll save hours by not having to go back and review your notes later on. Allocating more time earlier in the process may be the most efficient choice you could make.

Practice #3: Becoming Sherlock Holmes

This is such a useful technique that if you need to recall a lot of written information, I suggest you practice it every chance you get. At the very least, try to spend 20 minutes on it twice a week.

Preparation. Identify a written document that you'd like to recall. Choose one that's more about ideas and concepts than about discrete pieces of information: an article, report, contract, or book.

Step 1: Follow the Sherlock Holmes technique. Use the steps I explained above to memorize the written information.

1. Boil each paragraph down to its essence of one or two key words. If possible, write those key words in the margin beside the paragraph.

2. When you finish reading a page, create a story from the four or five key words in the margin.

3. Continue creating stories for every page you wish to memorize.

4. If you like, create "big-picture" stories for sections or for the work as a whole.

Step 2: Test yourself. A few hours later or the next day, try to recall the stories you've created. How much do you recall of the document you read?

Step 3: Evaluate yourself. If you remembered the entire document, good for you! Keep practicing, and you'll discover that the process goes even more quickly. If you found yourself forgetting more than you'd hoped, don't be concerned. Ask yourself which steps could use more work: paying attention, visualizing, or associating.

THE PYRAMID POINT STRATEGY

What if the information you're trying to remember is your own material, the data and concepts for a presentation you want to make or a point you want to argue? In that case, you might try the pyramid point strategy, which helps you boil your ideas down to simple, memorable concepts and then draw on your powers of visualization to recall them.

Let's say you're planning a new marketing strategy. Instead of just writing out your ideas in linear fashion, draw a pyramid. At each point of the triangle, write three of the key aspects of this strategy. Now you have nine key points, which, because of their visual layout, will be much easier to recall than nine items in a list. Moreover, your ideas are already organized— grouped into threes, which can in turn be broken down further if you need to go into more detail about each one. You might create triangles for each aspect of your strategy—long-term consequences, advertising, personnel— with the pyramid form helping you to visualize and recall each one.

The advantage of this approach, of course, is that it's visual. It not only helps you remember key points, it also helps you organize your thoughts in the first place. The extra effort you put into the organization will also make the material more memorable for you. As you've seen, memory is an active process, so the more energy you put into the material, the more likely you are to remember it.

Practice #4:
Using the Pyramid Point Strategy

You're already using a lot of new techniques, so save this one for your second week of working on written information. Try it out three times a week for about 5 minutes each time. Since you're applying this approach to your own concepts, feel free to take as long as you need. The time you spend trying to organize your ideas into this format will pay off not only in improved memory but also in greater clarity.

Preparation. Identify a type of written document that you want to create. Choose one that's more about ideas and concepts than discrete pieces of information: a speech, presentation, article, or report. And don't assume that because you have written an article or report, you will automatically remember it. You'd be surprised at how easy it is to forget even material that you've created. This approach ensures that you will hold on to the key points you've identified long after you've made your speech or filed your report.

Step 1: Follow the pyramid point strategy. Use the steps I explained above to organize and remember the written information you're creating.

1. Draw a pyramid.

2. Write three key aspects of your material at each point of the pyramid.

3. If appropriate, create additional triangles and incorporate more detail into your presentation.

Step 2: Test yourself. A few hours later or the next day, try to recall the pyramid(s) that represents your ideas. How much do you remember?

Step 3: Evaluate yourself. If you remembered all the key points, bravo! Keep practicing, and you'll expand your memory's capacity even further. If you found yourself forgetting more than you wished, don't dwell on the negative. Figure out a new way to pay attention, visualize, or associate, and try again.

WORD ENCODING

Use this approach when you're trying to remember a particular word or words within a text, such as the name of a company, a new term, or a foreign word. For example, suppose you're reading an article describing how the anti-cholesterol drug Lipitor, manufactured by Pfizer, is outselling a similar medication, Pravachol, made by Bristol-Myers Squibb.

Lipitor, according to the article, is doing 25 percent better than its rival, a significant advantage in sales. You want to remember not only the gist of the report but all the details. Where do you begin?

If I were trying to remember such an article, I might start with Lipitor, which to me sounds like "lip torn." Pravachol makes me think of "provocative." Pfizer makes me think of "fizzes," while Bristol-Myers makes me think of "my bristles" (on a brush). For 25 percent, I might visualize either a quarter with a big "25" emblazoned on it or, using the Numerical Memory Matrix, the letters *nL*—perhaps *Noel*, or Christmas.

Now, how would I put all these elements together? I might visualize someone with a *torn lip* that's *fizzing* where it's torn, so it needs to have medication—such as Lipitor—put on it. A *provocative* woman is trying to convince the person with the torn lip to kiss her, and she's offering him *25 cents* (or perhaps standing under a *Christmas* tree or under some letters that spell *N-O-E-L*). She's using *my bristly* brush on her hair, making her even more provocative. But the man with the torn lip isn't interested in the woman because he's so rich. In fact, he's *25 percent* richer than she is!

As you can see, this is a nonsensical story. That doesn't matter if it helps me remember the basic information: Pfizer's Lipitor is outselling Bristol-Myers's Pravachol by 25 percent. Of course, if you're familiar with drug companies and their medications, you won't need an elaborate visualization to remember the information because it already means something to you. Ideas that matter to us are always easy to remember. (Quick: What's your favorite food? Now, where's a good place to buy or eat it? You care about this information, so it's not something you're likely to forget.) If you're feeling deluged by strange names and terms, though, you need a way to make them stick in your memory. Our old standbys, visualization and association, will get the job done.

Practice #5: Encoding Words

Save this technique for the second week as well; try it out three times a week for about 5 minutes each time, alternating with Practice #4.

Preparation. Find a business article or a report in a field that interests you but that you don't know much about. Identify the key information in the written information that you'd like to remember.

Step 1: Follow the word-encoding strategy. Use the steps I explained to create images and associations for the written information you'd like to remember.

1. Boil the material down to a key sentence or two.

2. Create visual images for each unfamiliar term you'd like to remember.

3. Find a way to associate these images into a story.

Step 2: Test yourself. The next day, try to recall the article or report. Do you remember the key idea? How many of the key terms do you recall? Now, go back to the written information and see how you did.

Step 3: Evaluate yourself. If you remembered all the key terms and their relationship to one another, bravo! Now you see how useful this technique can be. If you felt it didn't work so well for you, try to figure out why. Was the fault in your summary, your images, or your story? Keep experimenting until you find a way of using this technique that works for you.

THE "CHOO-CHOO TRAIN" TECHNIQUE

I must have invented the name for this technique when my children were small! Nonetheless, I like using a simple name for this approach because it's such a simple—and useful—way to remember ideas that you need to keep connected. Just think of a children's choo-choo train, with each car strung behind the previous one, to understand that this technique is good for situations in which you want each idea to trigger the next.

Remembering a Speech

Suppose you're giving a speech on the economy, and you'd like to speak without notes. You're very familiar with the ideas—after all, it's your speech—but you want to be sure that each idea flows smoothly into the next. Here's what you might do.

Step 1: Identify each key point in the speech. Suppose your speech is about the future of the economy. You identify 10 major points you want to make, beginning with the introduction, "The future isn't what it used to be!" Although this sounds like a joke, you're actually quite serious as you explain that these days, the economy is so volatile that it's very difficult to predict.

This leads logically into your second point: "In the past, the economy was more stable, and so the future was much easier to predict than it is today." Proceed through your speech (or any other written information that you'd like to memorize), identifying each thought.

Step 2: Visualize the first image. Thinking about predicting the future makes me think of a fortune-teller, so I might imagine her squinting into her crystal ball, frustrated because she can no longer see the future.

Step 3: Visualize the second image in a way that connects it to the first. For my first point, I've already got the fortune-teller and the future-revealing crystal ball. Perhaps for my second point, I'll add a second crystal ball, labeled "the past." Although the "future" ball is cloudy (making it hard to predict), the "past" ball is clear.

Step 4: Visualize the third image in a way that connects it to the second one. Suppose my third point is that the bull market of the 1990s is at the root of the problem because, although it stimulated the economy, it also made the future harder to predict. Now I envision a bull with "1990s" emblazoned on its side. The bull smashes the crystal ball and runs off.

Step 5: Visualize the fourth image in a way that connects it to the third image. The bull has run out of the fortune-teller's shop and is free to run anywhere he likes to find my next image. We've left the first image—the fortune-teller with the crystal ball—far behind, creating a chain of mental pictures in which each idea leads to the next.

Remembering Words on a Page

I've also used this technique to recall the diverse articles on the printed page of a magazine. In my workshops, for example, I often pull out several old editions of *Business Week*, every page of which I've memorized. I invite my students to pick a page from any of the magazines and call it out. Then I amaze them by describing each article, advertisement, and cartoon that appears on the page. They're even more amazed when I show them how to perform such feats for themselves. Here's how it works, using the August 23, 1993, issue of *Business Week* (no. 3333).

Step 1: Use the Numerical Memory Matrix to recall the page number. Suppose we turn to page 34, which translates to the letters *m* and *r*. I picture a mare to get the story started.

Step 2: Integrate the page number image into the first article you want to recall. The first story on that page is about how the firing of CEOs and company presidents has affected company stock prices. Consequently, I envision all those fired CEOs riding out of town on their mare.

Note that the article as a whole included other information. As it happens, although stock prices tend to drop the day after a CEO is fired, they tend to be back where they were within a month after the dismissal. This new information isn't included in my image, but it doesn't matter. As soon as I visualize those CEOs riding out of town on their mare, that's enough to trigger my memory of the whole article.

Step 3: Connect each image with the next one. The second article concerns a lawsuit against American Airlines, which has been accused of driving rivals out of business through an illegal pricing scheme. American Airlines was able to convince a grand jury that their actions were blameless, but that's more detail than I need for my image. I simply imagine those poor, fired CEOs getting off their mare and onto an American Airlines flight. (Again, just the association with "American Airlines" is enough to trigger the content of the whole story.) Maybe the unemployed execs are flying to a new city, where they hope to find new jobs.

The third article describes the recall of several Saturn automobiles, so when my CEOs' flight touches down at their new destination, they go to the auto rental counter—and you guessed it: Only Saturns are available.

The fourth article concerns the Westinghouse company, which is cutting its costs and "reducing fat" in an effort to become more profitable. I envision my CEOs driving up to a building in search of new jobs and taking a Westinghouse elevator up to the top floor. There, they apply for work at the Dart Corporation, which the fifth article explains is in the midst of a family feud over who owns the company. Clearly, my CEOs aren't going to be hired today, so they take the elevator down and, seeking relaxation, pull out their Supersonic Mario Brothers Nintendo games, which of course is the topic of the sixth article.

Finally, they reach the street and begin walking along the sidewalk, and there is an image from the cartoon that's the final item on the page, a beggar in a fancy suit with a sign that says "Do you have any Grey Poupon?" The caption of the cartoon is, "The rich sure are hamming it up since the Clinton budget plan!" Again, that information isn't incorporated into my image, but it doesn't matter. As soon as I visualize the cartoon, the image will trigger the punch line.

You can see how well the choo-choo train technique would work to help you recall pages of text that include a wide variety of ideas. Of course, my clients in publishing and advertising often find it useful to memorize entire magazines, but even if you're in another field, you may find it useful to assimilate key information this way.

Although the page I chose from *Business Week* happened to be ad-free. you can easily incorporate an advertisement into your approach. If it's a small ad, zero in on the main image, just as you would focus on an article's headline. If it's a full-page ad, you can go into more detail if you like. Start with the name of the product or service but go on to add details about who uses the product, who's selling it, and what claims are being made. In fact, you can incorporate any information that you decide is useful. Again, strategy will tell you *what* to memorize—but I can show you how.

Practice #6: Creating a Memory Train

During your third week of practice, try this technique three times a week. Take as much time as you need to memorize a page. If you like, limit your practice to 5 minutes and see how much more you can remember each time you repeat the exercise. Eventually, you should be able to memorize an entire page in that time.

Preparation. Find a magazine or newspaper and choose a page to memorize. Read each element on the page—articles, ads, cartoons, graphs, charts, and so on—and identify the key point of each.

Step 1: Follow the choo-choo train technique. Use the steps I explained to create images and associations for the written information you'd like to remember.

1. Using the Numerical Memory Matrix, create an image for the page number.

2. Begin a story incorporating that image and an image for the first item on the page that you wish to memorize.

3. Link the first item to the second, the second to the third, and so on. Continue linking items until you've created and linked images for the entire page.

Step 2: Test yourself. Later that day, try to recall the page you memorized. How many items can you recall? Can you remember them at the level of detail you would like?

Step 3: Evaluate yourself. If you remembered everything you wished, good for you! You can continue using this technique, getting better and faster at it all the time. If your effort wasn't so successful, think about what you might do to make it work better. Make sure your summaries of each element are on target, your images are memorable and clear, and the links you create between images make sense to you. (They don't need to make sense to anybody else.) Sooner or later, you'll figure out how to make this technique work for you.

WORKING WITH FOREIGN WORDS AND PHRASES

If you have to memorize a few foreign words for dealing with overseas clients, my system can help you as well. All you have to do is create an English "sound-alike" for the foreign word and link it to the English definition of the foreign word. Here are some examples.

Foreign Word	English Sound-Alike	English Meaning	Image
cheval (French)	shovel	horse	Use a *shovel* to clean up after the *horse*!
couteau (French)	cut toe	knife	I *cut* my *toe* with that *knife*!
spiegel (German)	spy-gal	mirror	The *spy-gal* looked in the *mirror* and saw her enemy approaching.
cielo (Spanish)	ceiling	sky	The *sky* is like the *ceiling* for the Earth.
mundo (Spanish)	moon	world	The *moon* is like a whole *world* of its own.
chanoot (Hebrew)	cheroot	store	Go buy a *cheroot* in that Israeli cigar *store*.
mayim (Hebrew)	my hymn	water	*My hymn* is to water, because I'm always thirsty.

As you can see, the images are personal, idiosyncratic, and sometimes downright silly. But if they're enough to link a sound and a meaning, they'll help you remember a few key words.

READING AND REMEMBERING

One of my favorite "written memory" success stories took place at Condé Nast, the publishing company where I taught workshops to the senior staff. Editors, advertising directors, and other publishing staff soon learned about the awesome results they could achieve with their new powers of memory as they used my techniques to memorize every one of the previous year's issues, page by page, ad by ad. Armed with this impressive data, they were able to approach their advertisers with suggestions for how these companies might make the best use of their advertising dollars—suggestions that paid off handsomely for the company.

Condé Nast is, of course, a publishing company, but whether your business creates words, goods, or services, you'll find it useful to remember what you've read. Not only will your recall of specific documents impress your clients, colleagues, and supervisors, but you'll also find that as you practice this system, your ability to focus, concentrate, and apply information to new situations will vastly improve.

CHAPTER 11

HOW MUCH
HAVE YOU IMPROVED?
A SELF-EVALUATION

N ow that you've spent some time improving your memory, let's look at the results. Here's a test that will let you compare your performance with what you were able to do when you took the pretest in chapter 3.

If you do well, that's terrific! You've obviously learned your lessons well. Keep practicing—and watch your memory continue to improve.

If you still have trouble with one or more areas, though, I urge you not to despair. After each question, I've provided suggestions for what you might do to improve your performance in whatever aspect of memory is giving you trouble.

POSTTEST: MEASURING YOUR IMPROVEMENT

Paying Attention

Choose a room you know well, but a different one than you chose for the pretest. Set a timer for 5 minutes and, as quickly as you can, begin to jot down everything you recall about that room: colors, objects, furniture, and every detail you've ever noticed about it.

When the timer goes off, rate yourself. What percentage of the room do you believe you "covered"? What percentage did you simply not have time to write about?

Next, evaluate yourself by checking the actual room. What percentage were you able to cover? Was it the same amount you thought you'd recalled? Note the relationship between what you thought you remembered and what was actually there. Use this scale to rate yourself.

Everything or nearly everything—10 points
Most of the information—8 points
Half of the information—6 points
One third or less—4 points
Hardly anything—2 points

Your *old* score for paying attention: _____

Your *new* score for paying attention: _____

If you're not satisfied with your results, go back and reread chapter 4. Review the exercises and practices in that chapter and choose one or two that you think would be particularly helpful to you. Before you can remember something, you have to notice it—so paying attention is an important starting point for improving your memory. Once you've mastered the art of paying attention, huge improvements should follow in every other aspect of your memory.

Observing

Choose another unfamiliar environment, different from the one you chose for the pretest. Again, you might select a new coffee shop, a part of your office building you don't usually visit, or a block in your neighborhood where you rarely walk. Give yourself 5 minutes to observe this environment closely, noticing every detail you can.

When the 5 minutes is up, find a place to sit and make notes on what you saw. Jot down every detail you recall.

Next, evaluate yourself. Return to the new place and compare it with your notes. How much of the new environment did you notice and recall? Use this scale to rate yourself.

Everything or nearly everything—10 points
Most of the information—8 points
Half of the information—6 points
One third or less—4 points
Hardly anything—2 points

Your *old* score for observing: _____

Your *new* score for observing: _____

If you're not happy with your results for this question, ask yourself why you failed to observe as much as you might have. Did you let yourself be distracted? Were you thinking of other things? Did embarrassment or self-consciousness play a role? Can you identify the reason for your less-than-stellar performance?

Once you've figured out where you might have gone wrong, review chapter 4, paying particular attention to the sections on observation. Complete any practices and exercises in that chapter that you think might be helpful.

Concentrating

Once again, go to a drawer with a number of objects in it, remove 20, and place them on your desk or table. Set your timer, giving yourself 3 minutes to remember as many items as you can.

When the timer goes off, turn away and write down as many objects as you can remember without looking at them. Then turn back and evaluate yourself. Give yourself ½ point for each item you recalled.

Your *old* score for concentrating: _____

Your *new* score for concentrating: _____

If you're not happy with your ability to concentrate, review some of the concentration exercises in chapter 4, particularly the sections on instructing your mind and using a mandala. See if you perform better on this particular activity if you begin with 2 minutes of deep breathing, mental instruction, and gazing at a mandala.

You might also take advantage of some of the other techniques you've learned. Perhaps you could create a story that links the various objects on the table, or you could visualize each one in an unusual way. You might number each object and create a new image integrating the number image and the object image. Or you might chunk the objects by classifying them: red objects, writing implements, things you eat, wooden objects, and so on.

Visualizing

Set a timer for 5 minutes, then look at the following list of names and come up with a visual image for each one.

Name	Visual Image
Mr. Luke Johnson	_____
Dr. Miriam Corell	_____
Ms. Cynthia Schultz	_____
Dr. Haji Beridian	_____
Ambassador Marc Bonheur	_____
Mrs. Jobeth Crowe	_____
Mr. Jeremy Horowitz	_____
Pastor Leonard Ingram	_____
Ms. Aisha Ndaye	_____
Mr. Rogelio Vaccaro	_____

When the timer goes off, evaluate yourself. How many names could you visualize within 5 minutes? Give yourself 1 point for each name.

Your *old* score for visualizing: _____

Your *new* score for visualizing: _____

By now, creating visual images should be second nature to you. If you're having trouble coming up with images on the spot, however, review the material in chapter 5 and do each practice at least once more. You might also glance at chapter 7 and review the various categories of names—occupations, locations, animals, minerals, adjectives, and names with preexisting associations.

Associating

Again, set the timer for 5 minutes. Use the time to create a story that incorporates as many of the visual images possible from the previous list of names. When the timer goes off, give yourself 1 point for each image.

Your *old* score for associating: _____
Your *new* score for associating: _____

If you had trouble creating a story at this point, try to figure out where the problem lies. Is it that you aren't visualizing the images clearly, you can't get interested in your own story, or you simply feel overwhelmed by the number of images you have to link? Perhaps you need to make your story simpler, or maybe it needs to be wilder and more outrageous. It may help to review the principles of storytelling in chapters 5 and 6. Find the storytelling exercises in those chapters and review them as well.

Recalling People Information

Set the timer for 10 minutes. Look at the following pictures and see how many of these people's names, faces, and identifying details you can memorize in that time.

Carl Metzger
Plays golf, lives in Oklahoma City, works in advertising

Andrew Houlihan
Has a new blue bike, collects stamps, is energetic

Kim Chang
Friendly, plays piano, designs Web sites

Marina Kurczak
Reserved, works as a translator for the United Nations, loves to bake

Derek Rogers
Shy, a carpenter, lead performer in a dance company

Rozsika Kodaly
Outgoing, loves cruises, is a fashion writer

Anthony Pelligrino
Sales rep for Mercedes Benz, vacationed in Anguila

Denise Clendenin
Warm-hearted, likes old movies, works in hotel marketing

John Campanius
Professor of archeology, loves a good cigar

Next, without looking back at the previous page, look at the photos below and see how many people you can identify and what you recall about each one. When you're finished, check back to see how many you got right. Give yourself 1 point for each time you correctly supplied a name and at least one detail.

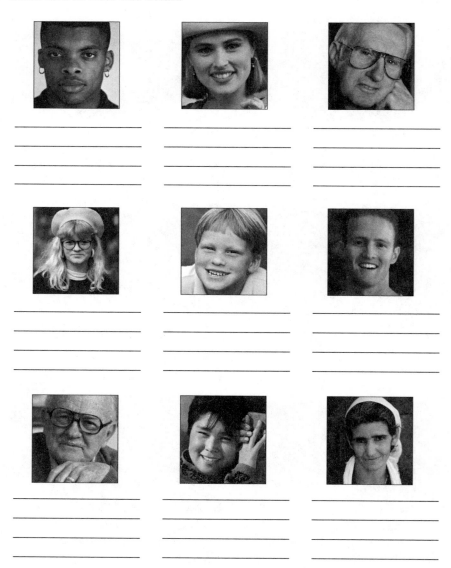

Your *old* score for recalling people information: _____

Your *new* score for recalling people information: _____

If you have trouble recalling people, take a moment to analyze the problem. Is it that you're not concentrating on the faces? Failing to select an outstanding feature? Not quickly creating a story that incorporates the name and information you've been given? Figure out where you're falling short, then read the corresponding section of chapter 7. Repeat the practices in that chapter as needed.

Recalling Spoken Information

Arrange to tape 5 minutes of TV or radio news. Set the timer for 5 minutes. Listen to the program carefully while you're taping it, without taking notes (and without looking at the television). Jot down as many of the main ideas as you can remember, then compare your notes with a second hearing of the broadcast. Use this scale to rate yourself.

Everything or nearly everything—10 points
Most of the information—8 points
Half of the information—6 points
One third or less—4 points
Hardly anything—2 points

Your *old* score for recalling spoken information: _____
Your *new* score for recalling spoken information: _____

If you're not remembering spoken information as readily as you'd like, review chapter 8 to see where the problem is. You might repeat some of the practices from that chapter and then try this question again.

Recalling Numerical Information

Set your timer for 5 minutes and use the time to memorize as many of these phone numbers as you can.

301-499-5576

702-398-3989

800-668-0900

732-322-0232

501-312-1646

212-477-9989

201-744-5767

973-880-3016

714-434-9878

323-615-4230

When the timer goes off, stop working. Then take a clean sheet of paper and, without looking at the numbers, write down as many as you can. Next, check your work. Give yourself 1 point for each phone number you recalled correctly.

Your *old* score for recalling numerical information: _____

Your *new* score for recalling numerical information: _____

If you had trouble with any aspect of this exercise, go back to chapter 9 and review the Numerical Memory Matrix System. Make sure you can rattle off the letter equivalents for each digit, practice turning those letters into words, and review the process of using the words to create stories.

Recalling Written Information #1

Choose a 500-word article from your favorite business magazine or newspaper and memorize as many key points of the article as you can in 5 minutes.

When your 5 minutes is up, take a blank piece of paper and, without looking at the article or any notes you may have made, jot down the main ideas and key details that you remember from the article. Then evaluate yourself using this scale.

Everything or nearly everything—10 points
Most of the information—8 points
Half of the information—6 points
One third or less—4 points
Hardly anything—2 points

Your *old* score for recalling written information #1: _____

Your *new* score for recalling written information #1: _____

If you weren't happy with your score for this exercise, return to chapter 10 and review the various strategies for remembering written information: the Sherlock Holmes technique, the pyramid point strategy, and so on. Did you choose the appropriate technique for the task? Do you need to review the technique and the practice associated with it?

Recalling Written Information #2

Choose a business document from your job and identify a 500-word section that you'd like to memorize. Give yourself 5 minutes to memorize the document's key ideas.

When your time is up, jot down those ideas and key supporting details without referring to the document or any notes you may have made. Then evaluate yourself using this scale.

Everything or nearly everything—10 points
Most of the information—8 points
Half of the information—6 points
One third or less—4 points
Hardly anything—2 points

Your *old* score for recalling written information #2: _____

Your *new* score for recalling written information #2: _____

Again, return to chapter 10 if you weren't happy with your score for this exercise. Make sure you understand the range of techniques available to you and how to use each one. Do you need to choose a different strategy or simply to practice a little more?

Evaluation

Add up your scores. In theory, the highest you could get is 99 points (because there's room for only nine photos on a page), although I'll confess that I've made this test fairly difficult. How did you do?

Your *old* score: _____

Your *new* score: _____

In my view, anyone who scores 75 or higher has passed my course with flying colors. If you scored between 50 and 75, you should congratulate yourself—and keep practicing. If you scored less than 50, or if your new score wasn't much of an improvement over your old one, try to analyze what went wrong. Did you fail to understand a technique, not give yourself time and space to concentrate, or simply not practice enough as you read the book? Once you've analyzed the problem, come up with a strategy to address it. Remember, memory is an *active* process. What you get out of it is directly proportional to what you put into it.

CONCLUSION

As we come to the end of our time together, so to speak, I'd like to share a more personal story.

Many years ago, my parents celebrated their 25th wedding anniversary. As you can imagine, my older brother, Harvey, and I were relatively young at the time, and we were certainly the youngest people at the dinner that was held in their honor at a local restaurant. Most of the people attending were friends and relatives of my parents and were members of their generation, people who had grown up in the United States or Europe during the early part of the 20th century.

At the dinner, a photograph was taken of the people at the anniversary table, including my parents, my brother, myself, and the people to whom my parents were closest. There must have been three dozen people in that picture, all smiling joyfully into the camera.

Recently, I had occasion to look at the photo again (it hangs in the hallway of my house), and I realized with a shock that every single person in the picture, with the exception of my brother and me, had died. As I looked at those smiling faces, a host of memories came flooding back. I began to recall the names, histories, habits, and attitudes of people I hadn't thought about in years. They represented a whole generation—an entire world—that had now passed on. Staring into one face after another, I felt myself return for a moment to my youth, when these had been the people I looked up to, depended upon, and admired.

Now, I'm not only a father but also a grandfather—in fact, I'm even older than some of those people were when that picture was taken. The only life they have is now what we give them with our memories.

I can't tell you how grateful I am to have that photograph! More important, though, I can't begin to express how glad I am that I've had the chance to develop not only my memory but also those of thousands of other people during my 30 years in the business world. Throughout this book, we've seen how memory can make you more effective, more efficient, and more powerful on your job. Now that you've learned some of what your memory can do, take a moment to be grateful, too, for how it enriches your life.

Looking at that photograph, I was reminded again of what I so often tell my students: Memory isn't only about the past, it's also about the present and the future. Although the people in that photograph are now gone, they live on through what I've learned from them, how I use their lessons, and the lessons I teach my own children. Likewise, your use of your past, your memory and experience, is the most valuable gift you have to give your company, your colleagues—and yourself. Hopefully, your memory is an even more precious possession now that you see how much you can accomplish with it. Use it—and enjoy it—well!

REFERENCES

Introduction

Abrahamson, Eric. "Change without Pain." *Harvard Business Review.* July/August 2000:78.

Chapter 2

Gordon, Barry, and Lisa Berger. *Intelligent Memory: Improve the Memory That Makes You Smarter.* New York: Viking, 2003.

Rupp, Rebecca. *Committed to Memory.* New York: Crown Publishers, 1998.

Chapter 4

Gordon, Barry, and Lisa Berger. *Intelligent Memory: Improve the Memory That Makes You Smarter.* New York: Viking, 2003.

Chapter 6

Buzan, Tony, with Barry Buzan. *The Mind Map Book.* New York: Dutton, 1993, 1994.

Mason, Douglas, and Michael Kohn. *The Memory Workbook.* Oakland, CA: New Harbinger Publications, 2001.

Chapter 7

Fulfer, Mac, J.D. *Amazing Face Reading: An Illustrated Encyclopedia for Reading Faces.* Self-published, 1996.

Herold, Mort. *You'll Never Forget a Name Again!* Chicago: Contemporary Books, 1992.

McCarthy, Michael J. *Mastering the Information Age: A Course in Working Better, Thinking Harder, and Learning Faster.* Los Angeles: Jeremy P. Tarcher, 1991.

Young, Lailan. *The Naked Face: The Essential Guide to Reading Faces.* New York: St. Martin's Press, 1994.

Chapter 10

Donovan, Priscilla, and Jacquelyn Wonder. *The Forever Mind: Eight Ways to Unleash the Powers of Your Mature Mind.* New York: William Morrow, 1994.

SUGGESTED READING

Abrahamson, Eric. "Change without Pain." *Harvard Business Review.* July/August 2000:78.

Bolles, Edmund Blair. *Remembering and Forgetting.* New York: Walker, 1988.

Bradford, Shannon. *Brain Power.* New York: John Wiley & Sons, 2002.

Burley-Allen, Madelyn. *Listening: The Forgotten Skill.* New York: John Wiley & Sons, 1982.

Buzan, Tony, with Barry Buzan. *The Mind Map Book.* New York: Dutton, 1993, 1994.

Donovan, Priscilla, and Jacquelyn Wonder. *The Forever Mind: Eight Ways to Unleash the Powers of Your Mature Mind.* New York: William Morrow, 1994.

Fulfer, Mac, J.D. *Amazing Face Reading: An Illustrated Encyclopedia for Reading Faces.* Self-published, 1996.

Furst, Bruno. *Stop Forgetting.* Garden City, NY: Garden City Books, 1948, 1949.

Gordon, Barry, and Lisa Berger. *Intelligent Memory: Improve the Memory That Makes You Smarter.* New York: Viking, 2003.

Herold, Mort. *You'll Never Forget a Name Again!* Chicago: Contemporary Books, 1992.

Hersey, William D. *Blueprints for Memory.* New York: Amacom, 1990.

Lorayne, Harry, and Jerry Lucas. *The Memory Book.* New York: Stein & Day, 1974.

McCarthy, Michael J. *Mastering the Information Age.* Los Angeles: Jeremy P. Tarcher, 1991.

McKim, Robert H. *Thinking Visually.* New York: Dale Seymour Publications, 1980.

Mason, Douglas, and Michael Kohn. *The Memory Workbook.* Oakland, CA: New Harbinger Publications, 2001.

Minsky, Marvin. *The Society of Mind.* New York: Simon & Schuster, 1985.

Rupp, Rebecca. *Committed to Memory.* New York: Crown Publishers, 1998.

Schank, Roger C. *The Connoisseur's Guide to the Mind.* New York: Summit Books, 1991.

Wurman, Richard Saul. *Information Anxiety.* New York: Bantam Books, 1989, 1990.

Young, Lailan. *The Naked Face: The Essential Guide to Reading Faces.* New York: St. Martin's Press, 1994.

———. *Secrets of the Face.* Boston: Little, Brown, 1984.

ABOUT THE AUTHORS

For more than 30 years, **Frank Felberbaum** has been president of Memory Training Systems, a global memory development and consulting corporation based in New York City, with more than 175 major corporate clients, including Pfizer, Con Edison, Marriott, Turner Corporation, Kraft, Citicorp, G.E. Capital, IBM, Revlon, Bergdorf-Goodman, and Condé Nast. He was the founder and director of the Memory Training Institute in Geneva, Switzerland, has established the first memory-training program in a U.S. public high school, and helped set up a memory-training club at Brandeis University in Waltham, Massachusetts.

In 1991, Felberbaum was a keynote speaker at the first World Memory Olympics in London. In 1995, he represented the United States at this annual international event. From 1997 to the present, he has trained and coached many of the mental athletes at the U.S. Memory Championships held in New York City.

Felberbaum appeared twice with Alan Alda on the PBS series *Scientific American Frontiers*. He has also appeared on ABC's *20/20 Downtown* and on "A Smarter You," hosted on ABC by Iyanla Van Zant. Other TV appearances include features on the Learning Channel, C-Span's *Close Up,* and NBC's *Nightly News*. Felberbaum has been featured in a number of magazines and newspapers, including the *New Yorker, Fortune, Self, Restaurant Business, Meetings, USA Today, Newark Star-Ledger, Newsday,* and the publication of the American Society for Training & Development. Felberbaum lives in New York City.

Rachel Kranz is currently at work on *Healing Hands,* a novel about memory and history, the sequel to her novel *Leaps of Faith.* She has collaborated on numerous books on science and medicine, including *Everything You Need to Know to Have a Healthy Twin Pregnancy,* with Gila Leiter, M.D., and numerous young adult books on topics such as eating disorders, anxiety and depression, child abuse, and prejudice, leading her to win two awards from the New York Public Library for best teenage books. She is the author of the young-adult book *Straight Talk about Smoking,* and numerous reference works, including *Library in a Book: Affirmative Action,* winner of the Choice 2003 award for best academic title, and *African-American Business Leaders and Entrepreneurs.* Her documentary videotapes have been widely distributed, viewed on public television, featured at the prestigious Global Village Festival, and awarded the Hometown, USA, award two years running. Her radio journalism has been broadcast on National Public Radio's *All Things Considered* and on Minnesota Public Radio, where she received the Clarion Award of Women in Communications, Inc., and a regional award from United Press International. Her articles and reviews have appeared in the *Nation, Newsday, New York Daily News, The Women's Review of Books,* and *Utne Reader,* and included in the anthology, *The Good Life: The Best of Utne Reader.* Kranz lives in New York City.

For more information on the Business of Memory Training Systems, contact:

Frank Felberbaum, President
Memory Training Systems
718-884-0305
mrmemory@optonline.net

INDEX

Underscored references indicate boxed text.

Written information (*cont.*)
  pages of books and magazines,
    233–34, 268–69
  pyramid point strategy, 263–64
  remembering stories, 246–48
  Sherlock Holmes technique,
    258–62
  strategies for reading, 250–51
  strategizing needed for, 244–45
  talking without notes, 255, 267
  train technique, 266–70
  using the pyramid point strategy,
    263–64

  volume of, 244–45
  word encoding, 264–66
  as zone of information, 11

Y
Young, Lailan, 140

Z
Zones of information, 10–11